HOLDING THE LINE

HOLDING THE LINE

*Inside the Nation's Preeminent
US Attorney's Office and Its Battle
with the Trump Justice Department*

GEOFFREY BERMAN

Former US Attorney for the
Southern District of New York

PENGUIN PRESS | NEW YORK | 2022

PENGUIN PRESS
An imprint of Penguin Random House LLC
penguinrandomhouse.com

Copyright © 2022 by Geoffrey Berman
Penguin Random House supports copyright. Copyright fuels
creativity, encourages diverse voices, promotes free speech,
and creates a vibrant culture. Thank you for buying an
authorized edition of this book and for complying with
copyright laws by not reproducing, scanning, or distributing
any part of it in any form without permission. You are
supporting writers and allowing Penguin Random House to
continue to publish books for every reader.

ISBN 9780593300299 (hardcover)
ISBN 9780593300305 (ebook)

Printed in the United States of America
1   3   5   7   9   10   8   6   4   2

Designed by Amanda Dewey

For Joanne, Jeremy, Matthew, and Elisabeth,
and the men and women of the Southern District,
past, present, and future

CONTENTS

Part Three. PRIORITIES

Part Four. NEAR AND FAR

Part Five. THE FINAL DAYS

PREFACE

My lead deputy, Robert Khuzami, received an urgent phone call from a top official at the US Department of Justice.

The midterm elections were less than two months away. The results would determine not just which party controlled the House and Senate but also if the next two years of the Trump presidency would be dogged by congressional investigations.

Khuzami spoke with Edward O'Callaghan, the principal associate deputy attorney general. Despite the convoluted title, O'Callaghan held a powerful position within DOJ. His message to Khuzami was unambiguous: it was time for me, Geoffrey Berman, the US Attorney for the Southern District of New York and lifelong Republican, to take one for the home team.

I had been close to Khuzami since we worked together as young prosecutors in the Southern District in the early 1990s, and when I came back to take the top job, he agreed to join me. He came into my office and closed the door. "You're not going to believe the conversation I had with O'Callaghan," he said before sharing the details.

The top leadership at DOJ wanted me to bring criminal charges against Gregory Craig, a private attorney who had once been President Barack Obama's White House counsel. And they wanted me to do so before Election Day.

Khuzami related that O'Callaghan told him, bluntly, "It's time for you guys to even things out."

"You've got to be fucking kidding me," I said.

"I wish," he said, "but no."

The charges I was told to bring against Craig involved allegations that he had violated the Foreign Agents Registration Act, or FARA, while representing Ukraine's former prime minister. Our office had been investigating the potential FARA violation for months. But DOJ's rationale had nothing to do with evidence or law.

O'Callaghan kept reminding Khuzami that our office had just prosecuted two high-profile Trump loyalists—Congressman Chris Collins, a Republican from New York, and Trump's private attorney, Michael Cohen.

We both understood that O'Callaghan was only the messenger. He was himself an alumnus of the Southern District with a solid reputation. Still, it was galling for those in our office who knew him to learn that he was the one delivering that message.

I ignored the edict. We investigated—thoroughly—but there was, at best, a marginal case to be made. Even if we were foolish enough to go forward, I doubted the charges would ever stand up in front of a jury.

This episode was not a one-off. It was part of a pattern. Throughout my tenure as US attorney, Trump's Justice Department kept demanding that I use my office to aid them politically, and I kept declining—in ways just tactful enough to keep me from being fired.

I walked this tightrope for two and a half years.

Eventually, the rope snapped.

PREFACE

The Southern District of New York, known as SDNY, or simply the Southern District, is not just one among ninety-three US attorney's offices across the United States and its territories. George Washington appointed the district's first prosecutor in 1789. The SDNY predates the Department of Justice by eighty years.

It is sometimes referred to as the Sovereign District of New York, which, as backhanded compliments go, is pretty much a classic of the form. What the moniker signifies is that the office is both admired and envied. Among the criminal class, it is feared. Its stubborn independence is sometimes read as arrogance.

But my resistance to Trump's chosen leaders of DOJ was never a matter of pride or turf. It was about protecting a bulwark of the rule of law, a monument to our nation's highest values.

Part of what gives SDNY its unique status is geography. The Southern District encompasses all of Manhattan along with the Bronx and six counties to the north of the city. Its headquarters, an unremarkable nine-story building at 1 St. Andrew's Plaza in lower Manhattan, sits on the doorstep of Wall Street. Very little of any import or scale takes place in the world without some of the money behind it moving through New York's financial institutions. That has long given SDNY not just a national but a global reach.

The office is a magnet for elite legal talent. There were 220 prosecutors who worked under me, including 15 in an office in White Plains. Commonly called AUSAs (the full title is assistant United States attorney), they were generally young, many of them in their late twenties or their thirties. But it was nobody's first job. They came from top law firms, in many cases after first serving in prestigious judicial clerkships after law school.

All of them started out in our version of boot camp, a year in the general crimes unit. Everyone in the office worked long hours, including nights and weekends, for a fraction of the salaries they could earn in the private sector. It was collaborative work; the office functioned as one team.

We partnered on cases with agents from the FBI's New York field office, which has its own legendary reputation, along with highly trained agents and officers from the Drug Enforcement Administration, New York City Police Department, Department of Homeland Security, Postal Inspection Service, and Bureau of Alcohol, Tobacco, Firearms, and Explosives.

The combination of these potent resources, both human and structural, sets the Southern District apart. It was the SDNY that won convictions against the financial fraudsters Bernard Madoff, Ivan Boesky, and Michael Milken. It prosecuted terrorism cases tied to the 1993 World Trade Center bombing and the 1998 US embassy bombings in East Africa. It put Francis Livoti, the New York Police Department cop who choked and killed Anthony Baez, behind bars. Seventy years ago, SDNY prosecuted the spying cases against Alger Hiss and Ethel and Julius Rosenberg.

I did my best to carry on this tradition during my tenure as US attorney. We pursued some of the nation's most important and high-profile prosecutions: against Chris Collins, the congressman, who pleaded guilty to a brazen insider-trading scheme (and was later pardoned by Trump); Michael Cohen, the president's former lawyer and fixer, who was convicted on campaign finance and tax charges; and Jeffrey Epstein, the notorious sex trafficker of girls and young women who committed suicide in prison before we could bring him to trial. (The office later indicted and convicted at trial his close associate and accomplice, Ghislaine Maxwell.)

A case we brought against the Turkey-based Halkbank, for conspiring to violate US sanctions against Iran, demonstrated our ability to take on highly complex investigations that sprawl across national borders. I believe we improved life in New York, by convicting members of a brutal drug gang, known as Nine Trey, with the rapper 6ix9ine as our star witness, and by forcing the New York City Housing Authority to address horribly inadequate conditions endured by hundreds of thousands of its tenants. Our ability to use the power of the law to return paintings stolen by Nazis to the heirs of the families that once owned them was a source of deep satisfaction to me and many others within SDNY.

At all times, we strove to do our jobs without fear or favor. We prosecuted friends of the president. And we prosecuted one of his most persistent antagonists: Michael Avenatti, the lawyer who represented Stormy Daniels. A core objective in the preamble of the Constitution is to "establish Justice." Inherent in that mission is that partisan political concerns do not enter into any decision making. That was our North Star.

IN THE PAGES THAT FOLLOW, I write about some cases in which we were allowed to do our jobs without interference from Main Justice, meaning the attorney general and those who work under him in Washington. I've done so because I think it's important to show how things are *supposed* to work.

But from start to finish, over the whole course of my tenure at SDNY, there were too many times when it did not work that way and obstacles were put in our path. These were not bureaucratic snafus. They were attempts to aid the president's friends and punish his enemies.

Some, though not all, of those roadblocks were put up by William P. Barr, who became attorney general on February 14, 2019, Valentine's Day.

There's an image of Barr that will follow him for the rest of his days. It is from June 1, 2020. He is shoulder to shoulder with Donald Trump in front of St. John's Episcopal Church after a throng of mostly peaceful protesters have been forcibly cleared from nearby Lafayette Square. Trump is carrying a Bible, which he holds up for the cameras.

The president's walk from the White House with Mark A. Milley, chairman of the Joint Chiefs of Staff, and Barr, the nation's top law enforcement official, was a grotesque stunt on many levels. And it was something all Americans could see.

But there was much hidden from view about Barr and the Department of Justice during the Trump administration, and I believe it is essential to lay it bare. I do so not to settle scores but in the hope that daylight and transparency might prevent it from happening again.

Over the course of my tenure, demands came down from Main Justice that were overtly political—among the most outrageous of them, pressure to pursue baseless criminal charges against John Kerry, who had served in the Obama administration as secretary of state.

We were badgered, without success, to remove all references to "Individual-1"—President Trump—from the charging document against Michael Cohen.

In a case involving what questions could properly be asked as part of the US census, we were pressured not to reveal evidence indicating that a member of the president's cabinet had omitted relevant information in testimony to Congress.

We did finally indict Halkbank, but it happened only after needless and improper delays and after a nose-to-nose confrontation I had with Barr.

My last interaction with Barr took place during a tense meeting inside his suite at the Pierre hotel in New York. His goal was to edge me out of my job, which he attempted to do by dangling a position he imagined I might like better. I made it clear I wasn't interested. If I was replaced by his handpicked successor, an outsider to SDNY—which was his plan—it would have impeded, delayed, or possibly shut down any of a number of politically sensitive investigations.

Several hours after Barr and I met, on a Friday night, he issued a press release saying that I was stepping down. That was a lie.

A lie told by the nation's top law enforcement officer.

I had certainly not stepped down and had no intention to do so; he had fired me, via press release. The first I learned about it was when people started calling and texting me.

I never granted an interview as US attorney. The testimony that I gave to Congress in July 2020 covered only the two days leading up to my departure from the job. No one from SDNY with knowledge of these matters has been interviewed or written about them. Until now, there has not been a firsthand account of what occurred in the Southern District of New York during the two and a half years I was its leader.

HOLDING THE LINE

Part One

MAKE IT
A RENTAL

1

Of Course
I'm Interested

You may already have some questions.

What made me a candidate for this job? Why did I take it? And, more pointedly, what the hell was I thinking?

I'll do my best to explain.

I was born in Trenton, New Jersey, and raised first in that capital city before we moved to a suburb just beyond the city limits. My father was a lawyer and then a real estate developer; my mother, before having children, was a teacher in the Trenton public schools. They were Democrats.

I became a Republican after college. It might have been a little bit of a rebellion, but mostly you pick a side, right? And I had come to believe that many of the programs that Democrats were initiating came with unintended consequences.

I was fiscally conservative and socially liberal, a Rockefeller Republican, which I know sounds quaint now, maybe even ridiculous— as if I were identifying with some kind of lost tribe. But I'll hold fast to it. In New Jersey, being a Republican meant supporting people like the former governors Christine Todd Whitman and Tom Kean, who was chairman of the 9/11 Commission. They are admirable public servants and fully reasonable human beings.

After graduating from Stanford Law School, I clerked for a federal judge, then moved on to a private law firm where I was fortunate to work under Robert Fiske Jr., who was US attorney for SDNY for four years in the late 1970s. I then became an associate counsel to the independent counsel Lawrence Walsh, who led the Iran-Contra investigation.

I was hired as an AUSA at SDNY in 1990 and worked there through my early thirties. It was a formative experience, as it is for almost everyone who passes through that office. I served under the US attorneys at the time, Otto Obermaier and then Mary Jo White, a trailblazer as the first female to lead the office. She would become a mentor and friend.

Over the next twenty-five years, I would return to private practice, then step away to work in my father's business, which had grown to include the development of an arena in Trenton and ownership of a minor-league hockey team. I went back to the law as a managing partner in the New Jersey office of Greenberg Traurig. All the while, I contributed money to Republican presidential candidates and to Republicans running in statewide and local races.

I also worked on campaigns, not at a particularly high level—I didn't have the time or inclination for that—but as a sort of dependable unpaid legal soldier. On Election Days, I answered phones when problems or challenges came up at polling places.

You don't get certain kinds of appointments if you are invisible to people in politics, but that was not the primary reason for my involvement. I wasn't looking for a job. I was a political junkie. I enjoyed being a small part of that scene, and philosophically I leaned Republican.

I sometimes dreamed of coming back to SDNY, maybe as part of the executive staff or something like that. But the top job? That's a lightning strike. You'd be better off aiming to be a big-league baseball player, because there are hundreds of guys doing that at any given time. But there's only one US Attorney for the Southern District of New York.

MAY 30, 2017

I was driving home from work when my phone rang. It was a call from the White House. My heart started to race. I pulled in to an empty parking lot to take the call.

I had been anticipating this call for months, hoping it would bring news that I was being nominated as a US attorney—though not in the Southern District. That wasn't the one I was expecting. And it never occurred to me that I'd interview with the president himself.

"The president wants to meet you," I was told.

Before I go any further, let me get this out of the way: I was wrong about Donald Trump.

With the beginning of the 2016 presidential primary season, my involvement in Republican politics became less casual. I worked for his campaign and then in the presidential transition, in each case as a volunteer, but at a high enough level that I got to know Don McGahn, who would become Trump's first White House counsel. Don and I never had a truly close relationship, but he seemed to respect my experience and abilities, and I certainly respected his.

At that point, I still believed that Candidate Trump was an act, a smart guy playing a role. I thought he would be transactional, and I mean that in a positive sense. He was a Democrat turned Republican, and I figured he was not wedded to the hard edges of either ideology. I imagined that he would be able to make deals with both sides. He'd govern from the center and be great for the country.

I now know that to have been craziness. But I wasn't the only one who felt that way.

McGahn was my entry into what you might call the sweepstakes for top jobs in the Department of Justice. But the competition for those coveted roles in a new administration always involves some combination of politics, personal relationships, and dueling allies. McGahn was probably the lawyer closest to Trump, but he was not the only one.

Elsewhere in that orbit was Rudy Giuliani, the president's lawyer and longtime friend and himself a former US Attorney for the SDNY. He had a favored candidate for the SDNY job (not me) and possibly a voice in other law enforcement appointments in the New York region. As it happened, I had recently been witness to an unusual episode involving America's Mayor, which seems worthwhile to mention here.

When a high-profile attorney joins a new law firm, partners are encouraged to market the new lawyer to existing clients. It's known as cross-selling. I organized such a cross-selling dinner in May 2016, introducing a new partner to the lawyers at a large financial institution that was one of my top clients.

The new man was Rudy Giuliani. He had joined us with a couple of attorneys from his previous firm.

The dinner was an utter and complete train wreck. We mingled beforehand with drinks, and Rudy consumed a couple of glasses of wine. At first, he was quite personable and charming. Then dinner was served.

Rudy continued to drink. At one point he shifted the conversation from his time as mayor to his work for Trump on immigration. A few days earlier, Trump had suggested making Rudy the head of a commission on radical Islam.

Rudy proceeded to share with my clients a wholly inaccurate, alt-right history of the creation and development of Islam, stating that it was an inherently violent religion from its origins to today.

The people around the table seemed aghast at the nonsense he was spewing and the passion with which he was doing it. Worried about the bizarre turn the conversation had taken, Marc Mukasey, one of the lawyers who had come over with Rudy from their previous firm, leaned over to one of the bank's in-house lawyers and quietly asked how he thought the meeting was going.

"Well," the lawyer replied, "it couldn't get any worse."

But it did get worse. Rudy took out his phone and showed the group drawings of violent acts purportedly committed by Muslims. I don't know if he might have been drinking before he even arrived. He wasn't slurring his words or anything like that. But his impulses had control of him.

One of the executives I knew well—a Jew whose family had emigrated from Egypt—confronted Rudy directly, saying that he was familiar with Islam and that it was not a violent religion.

For some reason, Rudy thought this man was Muslim, even though he was wearing a yarmulke and had ordered a kosher meal. As a lifelong New Yorker who had been mayor for two terms, Rudy was clearly acquainted with Jews, but he somehow failed to pick up on these telltale signs. He kept going.

"I'm sorry to have to tell you this," he said, "but the founder of your religion is a murderer."

It was unbelievable. Rudy was unhinged. A pall fell over the room.

After several seconds, I broke the silence with a stab at humor. "Well, that's seven years of client development down the drain," I announced.

People laughed uncomfortably. The dinner soon ended. The story never made it into the press, but it did get around among a certain set.

A few weeks later, at the annual reunion of hundreds of former SDNY prosecutors who had worked for Mary Jo White, someone came up to me and said, "So, Geoff, I heard you had quite a dinner with Rudy."

"You heard about it?" I replied.

"Geoff," this person answered, "there is not a single former AUSA in this room who has not heard about that dinner."

TRUMP INITIALLY SAID that he intended to keep Preet Bharara, who served admirably through both terms of the Obama administration, as the US Attorney for the Southern District. When Trump changed his mind, that set off the jockeying for the position.

One possibility was my new law partner, Marc Mukasey, an excellent trial lawyer and SDNY alum. His dad, Michael Mukasey, is a former US attorney general and federal judge and a close friend of Rudy's. Marc was clearly Giuliani's preferred candidate.

Indeed, four days after Trump's election, there was a story in the *New York Post*, with a large picture of Marc, saying that he was on a short list for the Southern District and "a favorite of Donald Trump's."

No other names were mentioned, implying that it was a very short list. It didn't take a genius to figure out who was behind the story.

THROUGH THE FIRST MONTHS of the Trump presidency, I awaited word of my rumored nomination for a different post—US Attorney for New Jersey. I was interviewed for the position by Attorney General Jeff Sessions and Deputy Attorney General Rod Rosenstein in late April 2017. They were both polite, though a little stiff, and I couldn't blame them. I was probably their tenth interview of the day.

I earlier met with the two Democratic senators from New Jersey, Robert Menendez and Cory Booker. I got along with them both. Booker was charming and charismatic. We talked a lot about his interest in federal programs designed to help inmates leaving prison to find jobs and to help nonviolent offenders avoid conviction altogether. Everything seemed to be falling into place.

But then the momentum behind my nomination hit a huge wall—a wall named Chris Christie.

Christie was the former governor of New Jersey and a 2016 presidential candidate. He'd also been US Attorney for New Jersey prior to running for governor. Christie was said to be in frequent contact with President Trump, and he was promoting his preferred candidate for US Attorney for New Jersey: Craig Carpenito.

Carpenito was a former AUSA in New Jersey, and as a defense attorney he had represented Christie in the "Bridgegate" scandal. (Christie's allies were reported to have closed local on-ramps to the George Washington Bridge in order to punish political opponents whose constituents would be most affected by the ramp closures.)

All kinds of stuff flies around in the media before these positions are filled. A story said that my name was originally floated for the

New Jersey job by Jared Kushner, based on a business relationship between my father and the Kushner family. But my family had no business dealings with the Kushners, and the extent of my relationship with Jared was that I'd been introduced once and shook his hand.

It's possible, however, that Jared might have supported my nomination over Carpenito, just based on the Kushners' contentious history with Chris Christie, who as a prosecutor had put Jared's father in jail for tax evasion and other charges. Jared was rumored to be against anything Christie was for, so for all I know, that could have included opposing my perceived rival for the job I thought was coming my way.

MY MEETING WITH THE PRESIDENT happened just three days after I got that phone call from the White House.

On Friday, June 2, 2017, I arrived early at the Eisenhower Executive Office Building, which housed most of the attorneys working at the White House Counsel's Office. After saying hello to some friendly faces I knew from the transition, I prepared for the meeting the way I usually prepare for big events: I paced.

I walked up and down the wide hallways, focusing on all the reasons why the president should nominate me for US Attorney for New Jersey. Down the hall, I recognized Craig Carpenito talking on his cell phone. He would meet with President Trump after me.

A few minutes before 4:00 p.m., I walked over to the West Wing of the White House, where Don McGahn was waiting for me. McGahn said there had been a change in plans. I was no longer being considered for New Jersey. That position was going to Carpenito.

I was crestfallen.

"Instead of New Jersey," McGahn continued, "you'll be meeting with the president for the position of US Attorney for the Southern District of New York . . . assuming, of course, you're interested."

Was I interested? Surely the question had to be rhetorical.

"Of course I'm interested," I said to McGahn.

McGahn walked me through a private hallway, past the desk of the president's assistant and several Secret Service agents, and into the Oval Office. The president was there waiting. The afternoon sun gently illuminated the gold-hued curtains behind the president. It was all surreal.

The president, who had opted for the same Resolute desk once used by President John F. Kennedy, rose to shake my hand. His handshake was firm but not too strong. The vibe in the room felt comfortable and surprisingly informal.

"Mr. President, this is Geoff Berman," said McGahn.

"Good to meet you, Geoff, please have a seat," the president said.

"Geoff, what you have to understand is that the Southern District is so much better than New Jersey," the president said, thinking perhaps that given the choice, I would have opted for New Jersey.

"I know, Mr. President, I know."

It was a short meeting, probably less than ten minutes. Trump did most of the talking. He went through my résumé and talked about the 2016 election, which at that point was seven months in the past. But he was still reveling in what an amazing upset it had been.

There was no request for a loyalty pledge, and none was given. Toward the end, he instructed McGahn to put my name in the slot for nomination for the Southern District.

"Thank you, Mr. President," I said.

In the final minutes of the meeting, the president and I discussed his favorite topic: real estate.

I had not lived in New York for fifteen years. I was living in Princeton, New Jersey, and in order to be US Attorney for the SDNY, I would need to move to the Southern District or within twenty miles of it. It wasn't as if I were a carpetbagger: I had lived in the city for many years, and all three of my kids were born there.

The president said to get a place right away in downtown Manhattan, close to the SDNY offices, where there were a number of nice buildings. His last words were a bit ominous regarding my chances of actually making it through the confirmation process.

"Make it a rental," he warned.

SENATORS HAVE TRADITIONALLY ENJOYED a "blue slip" privilege: a nominee for a judgeship or US attorney needs the consent of the senators in the state where he or she will serve before the Senate Judiciary Committee will consider them. The Republican senator Chuck Grassley, chairman of the Senate Judiciary Committee at the time, said that he would respect the blue slip privilege for US attorney nominees. To move forward, I needed the support of New York's two Democratic senators.

Chuck Schumer invited me to meet with him in early October 2017 after Trump chose me to lead the Southern District. The Senate minority leader's office at the Capitol was massive and spectacular, with beautiful, vaulted tiled ceilings. The meeting started out fine. We discussed my résumé. He then asked me to rank on a scale of one (most conservative) to one hundred (most liberal) several Democratic and Republican politicians, including himself.

That seemed like an unusual approach, but I think he was trying to get a sense of my center of gravity. These sessions are a bit of a dance. You hope not to say anything that disqualifies you, but you're there to be helpful, and you want to candidly answer the questions you can.

He asked me about Senators Ted Cruz and Bernie Sanders, and I think I ranked them at the poles of their respective parties. He asked me to rank himself on the scale, and I gave him a grade of sixty—moderately liberal—and he said he used to be that, "but I'm a seventy now" as the leader of the Democrats in the Senate.

He didn't ask me to give myself a number. He said, "Describe yourself. Where do you fit in?"

I said that I was previously known as a Rockefeller Republican.

As we said our goodbyes, I admired a portrait of Eleanor Roosevelt on Schumer's wall, and he gave me a brief tour of his artwork. When he came to a picture of the Brooklyn Bridge, he pointed and said, "This is Brooklyn. This is Manhattan. And you see this corner of land here? That's New Jersey. That's where you're from."

It was a funny line, delivered with excellent comedic timing. We both laughed. But it did not bode well for my nomination.

SENATOR KIRSTEN GILLIBRAND refused to meet with me at all, not because I was unqualified, but simply because I had met with President Trump. She would not deliver my blue slip. So that was that. There would be no Senate confirmation, and I was never formally nominated.

There was another option, apart from nomination and Senate confirmation, available to the White House. The attorney general has statutory authority to appoint an interim US attorney. The catch is that the appointment is only temporary; it lapses after four months. After that, the judges of the district are tasked with appointing a US attorney who will hold office until a successor is nominated and confirmed by the Senate. They have complete discretion; they can pick anyone.

When George "Jed" Doty III, an associate White House counsel, raised this option with me, I was not enthusiastic. I didn't want to run the risk of being in the position only four months. I wanted to be nominated and considered by the Senate in the normal way. Surely, I told Doty, the politics of the blue slip could be worked out with the senators from New York.

But they couldn't be. Doty ultimately told me that if I did not accept the interim appointment, the White House would have to select someone who would. After seeking the advice of Mary Jo White and Bob Fiske, I told Doty that I would take the appointment.

In January 2018, Attorney General Jeff Sessions appointed me interim US Attorney for the Southern District. On the day of my swearing in (I would start the job the next morning), a blizzard shut down most of New York, including federal and state offices and courthouses.

The SDNY chief judge, Colleen McMahon, opened her courtroom and administered my oath. On January 4, 2018, I raised my right hand and swore, as those in my position have done since 1789, to support the Constitution of the United States and to discharge to the best of my ability the duties of US Attorney for the Southern District of New York.

My family was all there. I felt neither joy nor accomplishment; I felt the weight of the oath.

Almost four months later, I was summoned to the chambers of Chief Judge McMahon. She got right to the point. They had unanimously reappointed me US attorney.

That was an honor, and it also might have provided an added layer of protection. I believed—and I think the courts would have backed me up—that the manner in which I came into the position meant that I could not be fired by an attorney general or even the president. Only the judges could remove me.

The longer I was in the job, the more important that felt.

2

WE ARE GOING TO LOSE COHEN

I visited the offices of the Southern District many times for meetings and witness interviews in the years after I served as a young AUSA. But coming back as its leader was not something I ever prepared for. The office's esteemed longtime administrator, Ed Tyrrell, greeted me in the lobby. As I walked the eighth-floor hallway to my new office, I was flooded by memories: of my swearing in as an AUSA on September 17, 1990; of long-ago cases; of my rookie colleagues from those early days and the bonds we formed.

I passed portraits of the office's former leaders: Elihu Root, Henry Stimson, J. Edward Lumbard, Bob Fiske, Mary Jo White. I just hoped that my tenure would honor their legacies.

My first duty was to introduce myself. I convened an all-hands meeting that first afternoon in the Pfeffer second-floor library. It's the biggest common space in the office, and everyone was able to crowd in.

Most had never been through a leadership transition. Preet Bharara was US attorney for almost eight years, and he had hired the majority of the attorneys who were gathered in the library. Both Preet and his deputy, Joon Kim, who was acting US attorney for about ten months prior to my arrival, were beloved. And rightly so. They did a fabulous job.

I knew people in the room were anxious, and many were downright skeptical. After all, I had met with Trump. They had no way of knowing that I had made no loyalty pledge to the president.

All I could do that afternoon was tell everyone of my devotion to the Southern District and its mission of pursuing justice without fear or favor. "I love the office," I said. "And I will work tirelessly to uphold its integrity, reputation, and independence. Politics will never enter into any decision. That is my commitment not only to you but to all those who have served here in the past, to all those who have occupied the position I was sworn in to, and to all who will come after us."

My brief speech seemed to hit the mark. Ideally, from there, I would have had a month or two to ease into my new job. I'd show everyone that I was up to it—that I was not some lackey or hack. But less than two weeks in, I was confronted with a crisis that put me at odds not only with one of the SDNY's most important units but also with my executive staff.

Late on a mid-January afternoon in 2018, the chief of the criminal division, Lisa Zornberg, and the counsel to the US attorney, Joan Loughnane, came into my office with important news. Both are talented and able. They'd been appointed by Bharara, but had agreed to stay on during the transition in the office.

At the time, I'm sure I trusted them more than they trusted me. I came into the job with an SDNY pedigree, a big deal inside the halls of 1 St. Andrew's Plaza, but it had been nearly a quarter century since I worked there. From the perspective of most of those in the building, I was an unknown dropped into the Southern District by Donald Trump.

They informed me that the chiefs of the office's public corruption unit, Tatiana Martins and Russell Capone, had just received a call from the former head of their unit, Andrew Goldstein. Months earlier, Goldstein had left SDNY to work for Special Counsel Robert Mueller on his investigation into Russian interference in the 2016 election.

Goldstein informed Martins and Capone that Mueller was investigating Michael Cohen, the president's personal lawyer, for bank fraud relating to his taxi medallion business. Mueller wanted to pursue the Cohen investigation—but in conjunction with a US attorney's office—because it fell outside his mandate. The idea was that we would be the partner to Mueller's team.

Although not emphasized by Goldstein, there were also reports in the press of other potentially problematic conduct by Cohen that was clearly not Russia related, and therefore beyond Mueller's scope. Prior to the 2016 election, Cohen paid hush money to two women alleged to have had affairs with Trump. The issue was whether those payments—to Stormy Daniels and Karen McDougal—amounted to illegal contributions from Cohen to the Trump campaign.

Of course, this was about more than just one or two illegal campaign contributions by a random New York real estate lawyer. Cohen was Trump's attorney and personal fixer, which meant any investigation into his dealings had the potential to implicate the president of the United States.

I KNEW THAT EVERYONE would expect me to jump at this proposition. Partner with Mueller? Why not? He had a gold-plated résumé. He was widely admired for his rectitude. Goldstein, who made the approach, was highly respected and trusted at SDNY. In addition, it's no secret that prosecutors like to be involved in big cases, and the Cohen prosecution had the potential to become the highest-profile criminal investigation on the planet.

The preliminary evidence was solid, and both Zornberg and Loughnane urged me to sign off. But I had doubts, and it had nothing to do with potential blowback from Main Justice.

From day one, my primary goal as US attorney was to protect the reputation and independence of SDNY. Any joint investigation with Mueller's team could undermine that—particularly if we were not the ones steering the ship. Under the terms outlined by Goldstein, the SDNY would have to agree with the Mueller team on all aspects of the investigation, including on the question of whether to indict.

I know what I'm describing here may sound like merely a turf battle—a skirmish involving egos and professional rivalries. But I could think of no other instance in SDNY history where our office ceded authority on a criminal case to another prosecutor.

There's an old expression that you finish the way you start. If I sacrificed our autonomy two weeks into the job, where would it end? If the next request came from Main Justice—for example, to call the shots on a case that would ordinarily be ours alone—what would be my rationale for saying no? They could easily say, you partnered with Mueller, but now you're rebuffing us?

A joint investigation meant that our office's reputation would be permanently linked to Mueller's. I had no control over him or his people. I did not want any missteps by the special counsel's office reflecting badly on SDNY.

In hindsight, I was right to be concerned. We later learned, through Bob Woodward's reporting, that Mueller had agreed—inexplicably—to biweekly supervisory meetings between his staff and Deputy Attorney General Rod Rosenstein's staff. Had SDNY agreed to Mueller's terms, as communicated through Goldstein, all of our investigative steps on Cohen—including our theories for prosecution—would have been subject to biweekly review by Rosenstein. Bottom line: giving Rosenstein or his underlings insights into our investigation could have severely undermined our work.

I asked Zornberg and Loughnane to get back to Goldstein and decline the offer. Tell him we would be happy to consult, but the Southern District would, in my words, "be the ones driving the bus."

Later that afternoon, they came back to my office, this time with Martins and Capone in tow. I had a seating area adjacent to my desk with a couch and a couple of chairs. It was meant to be informal—or, as much as it could be considering the kinds of things that got discussed inside our building.

This meeting was especially tense. They had delivered my message to Goldstein. It was not well received. In fact, they told me that he was pissed.

Our team was convinced that if our office did not agree to a joint investigation, Mueller would refer the case to the US Attorney's Office for the Eastern District of New York instead. This was no small concern. There is a healthy rivalry between the Southern and the Eastern Districts. Losing a case as big as Cohen would have been a blow to office morale.

I was up-front with everyone. I told them it worried me that they all disagreed with my judgment.

Two of Mueller's deputies were former supervisors in the Eastern District. My staff warned me that he could, and would, comfortably take the case to them. "If you reject a joint investigation," Martins said, "we are going to lose Cohen."

Everyone backed her up. It was an angry, sullen crew that turned and walked out of my office, and I had some moments afterward when I began to doubt my decision.

IT HELPS TO HAVE CLOSE, trusted advisers to lean on at moments like this. But I was alone, in several different ways. I have already mentioned Rob Khuzami, my longtime friend and colleague, whom I brought back as deputy US attorney. Our backgrounds were different. His father's side of the family traces back to Persia. He was raised in upstate New York by parents who were ballroom dance instructors. We had long counted on each other for guidance on just about anything that came up in our personal or professional lives. But in those early days, as we were debating how to handle the Cohen case, he had not yet received his security clearance.

My senior counsel was to be Audrey Strauss, an icon of the New York bar and, like Mary Jo White, a pioneering female prosecutor. I first met Audrey when I joined the staff of the Iran-Contra investigation and have considered her a mentor ever since. At barely five feet two inches tall, she is a dynamo, but of a particular kind. Audrey is known for her wisdom and judgment, and when I was US attorney, I counted on her to ask the incisive questions before we leaned too far forward. If there was a gap in our evidence or flaw in our thinking, she zeroed in on it. Like Rob, she agreed to return to SDNY, but she was also not yet on board.

I couldn't talk to either of them about the Cohen case and use them as sounding boards to test whether I was handling it correctly.

Confidentiality rules prohibited it, because they did not have their clearances.

The youngest of my three children was a senior in high school, so my wife, Joanne, was still living at our house in Princeton. I was working constantly—getting briefed on cases and meeting with law enforcement partners—and returning, long after dark, to an apartment I had rented. (It was downtown, just as the president suggested, about a five-minute walk from the office.) And then I stayed up very late, reading up on ongoing cases.

My big worry was that those working for me would misinterpret my insistence on maintaining independence as a smoke screen for an unwillingness to take on a politically sensitive case. If I lost Cohen, I'm not sure I could have recovered. They would have figured I got what I wanted.

As the US Attorney for the Southern District, you manage more than two hundred brilliant, high-powered, high-achieving, and, sometimes, high-strung human beings. There are high stakes to every case. Quite often—like in the Cohen prosecution—cases rise to the level of national import. It amounts to a lot of pressure. You can't let it paralyze you, but you certainly feel it.

In the midst of the struggle over Cohen, I made the short walk home from the office to my Tribeca apartment. I remember the night as especially cold. I don't drink alone as a rule, and I had never come home and had a drink before unless we were entertaining. But I quickly downed two vodkas on the rocks.

The next day Goldstein got back to us. He backed off the requirement of a joint investigation and agreed that the Southern District would conduct the investigation as we saw fit. He asked for just one thing: if SDNY and the FBI had discussions with Cohen or his lawyer about cooperation, we would inform Goldstein and allow someone from the Mueller team to be present. I did not believe that such an accommodation would impinge on our independence or link our reputation to Mueller's.

With that sole concession, the Cohen investigation was ours. As tense as the episode was, I did not fully understand the suspicion over my role until months later, when Capone told me that people in the office thought I was intentionally sabotaging our chance to run the case. If it had gone another way, my opportunity to be regarded as a credible leader of SDNY would have been lost.

ABOUT SEVEN MONTHS LATER, in August 2018, Michael Cohen stood up before Judge William H. Pauley III in a packed courtroom at 500 Pearl Street in Manhattan and pleaded guilty to eight criminal counts. He was fifty-one years old at the time and had been living the life of a wealthy man, with some of his riches coming from his association with Donald Trump and much of the rest of it through his ownership of New York City taxi medallions. Before the era of Uber and Lyft, these were worth a great deal of money, as much as $1.2 million each, but Cohen fell into debt as their value plunged.

The talented prosecution team, composed of Andrea Griswold, Thomas McKay, Nicolas Roos, and Rachel Maimin, had significantly expanded the investigation of Cohen beyond the Mueller referral. As they began drafting the indictment and preparing the evidence for the grand jury, Cohen surprised everyone by abruptly deciding not to fight the charges. His decision to plead all but assured he would be giving up his freedom for some stretch of time.

His offenses included tax evasion and making false statements to a financial institution, along with the crimes that, rightfully, garnered the most attention—two counts of making illegal campaign contributions. Cohen admitted that he paid $130,000 to Stephanie Clifford, known as Stormy Daniels, and arranged for $150,000 to be paid by the *National Enquirer* to Karen McDougal. Both claimed to have had affairs with Donald Trump, and the payments, made during the 2016 presidential campaign, were intended to buy their silence. (The *National Enquirer* paid Clifford for exclusive rights to her story but without any intention to actually publish it—a so-called catch-and-kill scheme meant to benefit the then candidate Trump.)

I did not supervise the Cohen investigation. I was concerned that some might perceive my prior volunteer work as a lawyer for the Trump campaign to be a conflict.

I raised the issue myself, and the ethics office of Main Justice concluded that the prudent thing for me was to be recused. In hindsight, I'm not sure that was necessary. My involvement in the campaign was marginal and I had no relationship with Cohen, but in a case with stakes that high I wanted to avoid even the whiff of a conflict.

Even though I was not overseeing the Cohen case, I still had to deal with other issues involving it, all of them deriving from the same source: Main Justice, and its attempts at interference.

THE FIRST TIME Main Justice interfered was when the information was being finalized. (After Cohen agreed to plead guilty, the charging instrument became an "information" rather than an indictment.) It was about forty pages long, and it referenced a person identified as "Individual-1" as having acted in concert with Cohen.

This language may seem unusual, but it's a convention and, in fact, a part of DOJ policy to identify people in this manner if they are part of the story you're trying to tell in an indictment but are not charged. Sometimes these unnamed people are victims; for example, in sex crimes, you preserve their anonymity by calling them Victim-1, Victim-2, and so forth.

Other times, it is not a mystery. There was zero doubt as to the identity of Individual-1: it was Donald J. Trump. (There's no exception that says, well, if everyone is going to be able to figure it out, you can name them.)

"On or about June 16, 2015, Individual-1 began his presidential campaign," read the criminal information eventually filed by SDNY. "While MICHAEL COHEN, the defendant, continued to work at the Company and did not have a formal title with the campaign, he had a campaign email address and, at various times, advised the campaign."

Elsewhere in the document: "In or about January 2017, COHEN left the Company and began holding himself out as the 'personal attorney' to Individual-1, who at that point had become the President of the United States."

Consistent with DOJ guidelines, we first submitted the information to the Public Integrity Section at Main Justice. They signed off.

We then sent a copy to Rod Rosenstein, informing him that a plea was imminent. The next day, Khuzami, who was overseeing the case, received a call from O'Callaghan, Rosenstein's principal deputy.

O'Callaghan was aggressive.

Why the length, he wanted to know. He argued that now that Cohen is pleading guilty we don't need all this description.

Khuzami responded, What exactly are you concerned about?

O'Callaghan proceeded to identify specific allegations that he wanted removed, almost all referencing Individual-1. It quickly became apparent to Khuzami that, contrary to what O'Callaghan professed, it wasn't the overall length or detail of the document that concerned him; it was any mention of Individual-1. Khuzami and O'Callaghan went through a handful of these allegations, some of which Khuzami agreed to strike; others, to ensure a coherent description of the crime, he did not.

At one point the exchange was heated. Khuzami said, What do you want here? Just a bare-bones information reciting the charging statutes?

In other words, it would say that Cohen violated various laws—and name the statutes that he ran afoul of—but would be nonspecific about what he actually did. And, most important, *whom* he did it with. It would be nothing more than a three-page information.

O'Callaghan responded, Why not?

Khuzami rejected the idea outright.

Sensing that this was going to be a long and adversarial process, Khuzami told O'Callaghan that he was now aware of O'Callaghan's concerns and the team would redraft the information and remove certain nonessential details.

The team was tasked with the rewrite and stayed up most of the night. The revised information, now twenty-one pages, kept all of the charges but removed certain allegations, including allegations that Individual-1 acted "in concert with" and "coordinated with" Cohen on the illegal campaign contributions. The information now alleged that Cohen acted in concert and coordinated with "one or more members of the campaign." But in the end, everything that truly needed to be in the information was still there.

This was part of an emerging pattern. If we held our ground with Main Justice, we could usually avert the worst consequences of their interference. But the game they played was nonetheless wrong and dangerous. The Department of Justice was not a private law firm dedicated to the president's personal interests, and it was shameful when they operated as if they were.

The most consequential details that O'Callaghan wanted removed still wound up in the public record, simply because Cohen acknowledged them in open court. He testified that Trump not only knew about the six-figure payoffs designed to keep Stormy Daniels and Karen McDougal from going public but had orchestrated them.

With regard to McDougal, Cohen said that he and "the candidate worked together to keep an individual with information that would be harmful to the candidate and to the campaign from publicly disclosing this information. After a number of discussions, we eventually accomplished the goal by the media company entering into a contract with the individual under which she received compensation of $150,000."

As for Stormy Daniels, Cohen admitted that he had, "in coordination with, and at the direction of, the same candidate, [arranged] to make a payment to a second individual with information that would be harmful to the candidate and to the campaign to keep the individual from disclosing the information. To accomplish this, I used a company that was under my control to make a payment in the sum of $130,000."

Our charging document, along with Cohen's testimony, made everything fully understandable to the public. A headline in *The Wall Street Journal* was typical of the way the media played it: "Michael Cohen Pleads Guilty, Says Trump Told Him to Pay Off Women."

COOPERATION IN THE Southern District means *full* cooperation—taking responsibility for all criminal actions, not just a select few. If any one area of a defendant's life is off limits, we do not recommend leniency in sentencing. (Some districts are more transactional: you give a little, you get a little.)

When defendants agree to this and become cooperating witnesses against others, their testimony is more credible. Our prosecutors can tell juries that if the cooperator is caught lying, the agreement can be revoked and he or she will be prosecuted not only for the crimes covered at trial but for a host of others that the cooperator copped to as part of his agreement.

The SDNY rules also serve as a powerful investigative tool, because when you acquire absolute cooperation, your avenues for making other cases expand dramatically. We often learn of additional criminal activity—whole new threads of wrongdoing that in some instances we knew nothing about.

Michael Cohen wasn't going for any of this. He eventually agreed to assist Mueller's office and said that he was willing to cooperate with us as well. But his promise came with an important caveat: he would not discuss his business activities outside his work for the Trump Organization.

Without a cooperation agreement in hand, Cohen's lawyer, Guy Petrillo, initially told our office that Cohen would take his chances in front of a jury. We were shocked when Petrillo called just a few days before the indictment was to have been filed with the news that Cohen had decided to plead guilty to the tax and campaign finance charges.

Three months later, Cohen pleaded guilty again, this time to lying to Congress about his involvement in a Trump Tower deal in Moscow. Those charges were brought by the Mueller team.

At his sentencing hearing in New York, in front of Judge Pauley, Cohen requested leniency because he had cooperated in his own way. Cohen and his lawyers thought that should be enough to keep him out of jail.

Petrillo, himself an SDNY alum, went so far as to mock the SDNY's stringent rules for cooperation agreements. "The rules of the Southern District of New York as to how every case of cooperation should proceed, of course, were given to us by the minor gods, and woe unto those who fail to follow their scriptures," Petrillo told Judge Pauley. (For the record, I thought Petrillo's reference to SDNY and the "minor gods" was pretty funny.)

We argued against leniency. "Mr. Cohen, he chose not to pursue the path of full cooperation," the SDNY prosecutor Nicolas Roos said at the sentencing hearing. "No one is attempting to penalize Mr. Cohen for not cooperating. Quite the opposite, there is no obligation to cooperate.

"But for all the hypothesizing that Mr. Petrillo has done, Mr. Cohen can't have it both ways. There is a standard way in which this office conducts cooperation. Your Honor is familiar with it. There is no reason, no matter the significance or the nature of the case, whether or not it receives public attention, for us to depart from that practice. We've treated Mr. Cohen just the way we treat every other defendant."

Pauley sentenced Cohen to three years in prison for tax evasion, bank fraud, and campaign finance violations. He was also forced to pay $1.5 million in fines and restitution.

"While Mr. Cohen has taken steps to mitigate his criminal conduct by pleading guilty and volunteering useful information to prosecutors," Pauley said, "that does not wipe the slate clean. Mr. Cohen selected the information he disclosed to the government. This Court cannot agree with the defendant's assertion that no jail time is warranted."

THERE WAS A POSTSCRIPT to the Cohen case, courtesy of William P. Barr, who did not become attorney general until six months after Cohen's guilty plea. (Jeff Sessions was the AG through the guilty plea.)

While Cohen had pleaded guilty, our office continued to pursue investigations related to other possible campaign finance violations. When Barr took over in February 2019, he not only tried to kill the ongoing investigations but—incredibly—suggested that Cohen's conviction on campaign finance charges be reversed.

Barr summoned Rob Khuzami in late February to challenge the basis of Cohen's plea as well as the reasoning behind pursuing similar campaign finance charges against other individuals. Khuzami was told to cease all investigative work on the campaign finance allegations until the Office of Legal Counsel, an important part of Main Justice, determined there was a legal basis for the campaign finance charges to which Cohen pleaded guilty—and until Barr determined there was a sufficient federal interest in pursuing charges against others.

Barr headed the Office of Legal Counsel in 1989 through the middle of 1990. He knew its powers, and as Trump's attorney general he knew how to use it as a cudgel to accomplish his goals.

The directive Barr gave Khuzami, which was amplified that same day by a follow-up call from O'Callaghan, was explicit: not a single investigative step could be taken, not a single document in our possession could be reviewed, until the issue was resolved.

And if Main Justice decided there was no legal basis for the charges? The attorney general of the United States would direct us to dismiss the campaign finance guilty pleas of Michael Cohen, the man who implicated the AG's boss, the president.

There are certainly times when prosecutors belatedly discover exculpatory evidence and then, properly, ask courts to vacate guilty verdicts or pleas. Or, occasionally, a defendant will plead guilty, but his co-defendants are later found not guilty at trial. In those cases, prosecutors sometimes conclude that they did not have as strong a case as they believed, and seek leniency, or a reversal of the conviction, for the defendant who pleaded guilty.

But to come in, six months after the fact, and suggest reversing a conviction because of some new legal theory? That is highly unusual, if not unprecedented.

About six weeks later, Khuzami returned to DC for another meeting about Cohen. He was accompanied by Audrey Strauss, Russ Capone, and Edward "Ted" Diskant, Capone's co-chief. Barr was in the room, along with Steven Engel, the head of the Office of Legal Counsel, and others from Main Justice.

A fifteen-page memo, drafted by Engel's office, had been provided to our team the day before, which they were still analyzing. I learned later that it was an intense meeting.

As they relate to the Cohen saga, and others I recount in this book, I've tried not to make assumptions about the motivations of Barr or anyone else. I'm a lawyer, trained to deal in fact.

But Barr's posture here raises obvious questions. Did he think dropping the campaign finance charges would bolster Trump's defense against impeachment charges? Was he trying to ensure that no other Trump associates or employees would be charged with making hush-money payments and perhaps flip on the president? Was the goal to ensure that the president could not be charged after leaving office? Or was it part of an effort to undo the entire series of investigations and prosecutions over the past two years of those in the president's orbit (Cohen, Roger Stone, and Michael Flynn)?

We could only guess. It certainly seemed clear that Barr did not want the Cohen case spiraling in new directions.

ONE WAY FOR BARR to accomplish that would have been to put the Cohen case in the hands of someone to whom he felt closer. About a week after our office tussled with Barr and Engel, Barr attempted to do just that. Word was passed to me from one of Barr's deputies that he wanted Richard Donoghue, the US Attorney for the Eastern District of New York (who would later transfer to Main Justice to work under Barr), to take over supervision of anything I was re-cused from.

They were not concerned about the routine recusals that inevita-bly arise—for example, cases in which my former law firm might have represented one of the parties. Their attention was focused on whatever investigations might be developed out of the Cohen case.

The call came from Seth DuCharme, senior counselor to the at-torney general for criminal, national security, and cyber matters. (DOJ has basically cornered the market on long-winded titles.) He spoke very formally, as if he were reading from a script.

"I am calling on behalf of the attorney general," he said. "He has decided that Rich Donoghue is going to be supervising all the cases that you are recused from. The attorney general has spoken to Rich, and he has agreed. Rich will be at the Southern District in two days, and the briefing will begin then."

I responded quickly, and without a preamble. "Seth," I said, "that's not going to happen."

"You don't understand," he countered. "This is not a request. This is a directive from the attorney general."

Those were the magic words, words that I would hear repeated in other confrontations with Barr's Main Justice. For me to oppose a directive from the attorney general or deputy attorney general would be perceived as insubordination. By doing so, I knew I was risking that Barr would seek to fire me.

There would be many times that I found work-arounds to Barr's worst ideas—ways in which I could delay them, or give him a little of what he wanted, without sacrificing our fundamental principles. But this was an imminent, direct attack. Donoghue was headed our way in two days.

I couldn't treat it incrementally. I had to punch back. I told DuCharme, "There is no way Donoghue is setting foot inside the Southern District."

Immediately afterward, I went into Audrey's office and recounted what had just happened. Her first response was what she always said after hearing some kind of crazy or disturbing news: "Oh my."

Audrey and I knew DuCharme. We both understood that he was just another of Barr's messengers.

The Donoghue directive was never revisited by Main Justice. I never got a callback on it. After DuCharme passed along my response to Barr, the attorney general apparently decided a fight over this would not be worth the fallout.

BARR HAD BEEN THE US attorney general once before, but it was long ago, in the early 1990s under President George H. W. Bush. After Trump put him back in the game, he seemed determined to be the administration's most valuable player.

Whatever his motivations, Barr's insertion of himself into the

Cohen case created a crisis. I was briefed on Main Justice's interference (after clearance from our ethics office), though I was still recused from any substantive decisions.

Barr had backed down on imposing Donoghue on the office, but he was still not done with his efforts to short-circuit the Cohen case. We submitted numerous memoranda to Main Justice, supporting the legal basis of the campaign finance charges against Cohen. Strauss took over negotiations in mid-April, but there was still no resolution. (After serving with distinction for a year, Khuzami had left the office to return home to DC, where his family was still living.)

We were effectively stalled. Audrey arranged to travel to DC, at the end of April for one final meeting with Barr—a last-ditch attempt to persuade him to let us go forward.

If Barr resisted, I was prepared to go nuclear. I would have unrecused myself from the case and directed the team to complete the investigation—in direct opposition to Barr's directive. I would have expected him to ask the president to fire me.

I had already spoken to private attorneys who would represent me should I be fired under these circumstances. (I did not share with my lawyers the conflict with Main Justice, just that I might be fired.) My defense: Because I was court appointed, the president could not fire me. I could be removed only by the judges of the Southern District or when a new nominee was confirmed by the Senate.

It did not get to that point. Audrey, prodigious talent that she is, convinced Barr that our investigations should be completed and that there was no basis to dismiss any of the charges against Cohen.

I told my lawyers to stand down. But I knew, even then, that it was only a matter of time before I would have to call on them again.

3

The Census Question

In early 2018, New York State and numerous other states and cities filed a lawsuit against the US Department of Commerce. It challenged the department's decision to include in the US census a question asking whether a respondent was "a citizen of the United States."

The once-a-decade count of the US population is mandated in the Constitution (Article I, Section 2) and enormously important. It determines how many congressional seats each state gets—and thus how many Electoral College votes they cast—and where hundreds of billions of dollars in federal funds are distributed.

The complainants argued that asking about citizenship would frighten households with noncitizens and discourage them from participating. As a result, New York and other states with large immigrant populations would lose out on their proper share of federal spending and political representation.

The Trump administration, however, insisted that the impetus for adding the immigration question had nothing to do with domestic politics or curbing illegal immigration. Rather, it was merely so the Department of Justice could use the responses to better enforce the Voting Rights Act provisions that protect racial minorities and non-English-speaking citizens from discrimination.

In other words, their argument was that this new census question was not intended to disadvantage anyone. It was just the opposite. They were seeking to *help* citizens born outside the United States cast votes without interference.

I think it's fair to say that this strained credulity. Anyone paying even a modicum of attention to the nation's politics knew that anti-immigration rhetoric was one of the animating forces of Trump's campaign.

Almost all US attorney's offices have a civil division that enforces civil statutes, just as their criminal divisions prosecute drug dealing, public corruption, organized crime, and so forth. US attorneys also have a duty to defend the US government against lawsuits brought in their districts, and that is how we came to be involved in the census case and how the Trump administration became, in essence, our client.

But attorneys in the Southern District, like lawyers everywhere, also have an obligation to the truth. And that became an issue in the matter of the *State of New York et al. vs. the United States Department of Commerce.* To put it bluntly, we could not become co-conspirators in an effort to whitewash what was really going on.

BEFORE I TOOK THE JOB, Bob Fiske and Mary Jo White, both former Southern District US attorneys, advised me that civil cases can be particular sources of friction. Even in relatively tranquil times, they can lead to rifts with Washington, especially when they involve accu-

sations of wrongdoing by federal officials or agencies. Fearful of providing fodder to political opponents or the press, presidents and their
attorneys general may prefer to hand off civil cases to Main Justice
attorneys in Washington who are supervised by political appointees
rather than to career attorneys in US attorney's offices.

Main Justice quickly informed the chief of our civil division, Jeffrey Oestericher, that they would solely handle the census litigation.
In retrospect, I guess you could argue that I should have let them. It
certainly would have saved us some headaches. I am glad, however,
that we were involved because it ultimately served the cause of
justice.

SDNY has typically sought a role in these kinds of civil suits,
even when cases have been filed (as this was) in multiple jurisdictions. We have a larger civil division than most other offices, staffed
by about sixty AUSAs, so we have the expertise and bandwidth. And
the judges in our district prefer that SDNY AUSAs, who know the
court's rules and practices, be the ones to appear before them in
complex civil matters. (Obviously, our personal political views on the
government's position do not enter into this, nor do any opinions on
whether we think they ultimately have a winning argument.)

On an early trip to Washington as US attorney, I met with James
Burnham, a political appointee in DOJ's Civil Division, and made
the case for our involvement. I told him that among other issues, the
optics would be terrible if Main Justice took such a high-profile case
away. People would wonder why the Justice Department would so
publicly undermine the president's choice to lead SDNY. I said that
we would consult with them, but we wanted "pen and podium"—
meaning control over what was written in briefs and what was said
in court.

We didn't get that. In civil litigation, DOJ rules provide for more oversight by Main Justice. We came to a compromise: we worked the case together, but Main Justice retained control and final authority.

THE CASE WAS HEARD by the US District Court judge Jesse M. Furman, who had this key issue in front of him: Was the contention that Commerce added the citizenship question at DOJ's request the truth or not? The answer would largely determine whether the question stayed in the census.

The government, as is routine in this type of civil litigation, was required to provide the plaintiffs with the administrative record, the documents relied upon by the decision maker in reaching the decision. This necessitates a kind of mining operation—a thorough search of files and emails to unearth relevant documents.

It's certainly not unusual for attorneys to be surprised by some of what they find—or for it to sometimes make their advocacy more difficult. It's less common for them to come across material that just blows their case up.

The review uncovered a 2017 email exchange between Secretary of Commerce Wilbur Ross and a top deputy that showed the citizenship question was first proposed by political staff and not—as the government claimed—the Department of Justice.

"I am mystified why nothing [has] been done in response to my months old request that we include the citizenship question," Ross wrote to his senior adviser, Earl Comstock, in May 2017.

We will "get that in place," Comstock assured Ross. "We need to work with Justice to get them to request that citizenship be added back as a census question, and we have the court cases to illustrate that DOJ has a legitimate need for the question to be included."

A different set of emails showed that Ross had spoken with Stephen Bannon about the citizenship question around the same time he traded emails with Comstock. Bannon had been Trump's campaign chief in the last three months of the 2016 campaign, and before that was chairman of the right-wing media site *Breitbart News*. He was known as an anti-immigration hawk. When Trump became president, he brought Bannon into the White House and gave him the title of chief strategist.

Bannon arranged a call between Ross and Kris Kobach, Kansas's secretary of state. Trump had named Kobach vice chairman of his Presidential Advisory Commission on Voter Integrity, which critics considered a group dedicated to voter suppression. He had long promoted the citizenship question as a way of reducing the number of congressional seats granted to blue states such as California, and he had pitched the citizenship question directly to Trump in early 2017.

Kobach believed some blue states' congressional-seat numbers were being inflated by the census data including undocumented immigrants—a point he reiterated in a July 14, 2017, email to Ross. He wrote that the lack of a citizenship question on the census "leads to the problem that aliens who do not actually 'reside' in the United States are still counted for congressional apportionment purposes."

Ross, a wealthy financier before entering government, was one of the lower-profile members of Trump's administration. A complicating factor for Ross in the census case was sworn testimony that he gave to Congress in March 2018 that DOJ had "initiated the request for inclusion of the citizenship question." He was asked directly by Representative Grace Meng, a Democrat from Queens who represents one of the most diverse districts in the nation, if anyone from the White House had ever discussed the citizenship question with either him or his staff.

Ross's reply: "I am not aware of any such."

THE EMAILS MADE CLEAR that the insertion of a citizenship question on the census was not initiated by DOJ to secure the voting rights of foreign-born citizens. Bannon's and Kobach's views were well established and had no overlap with efforts to protect minority voting rights.

Attorneys at Main Justice reviewed the emails, as did the AUSA working the case in New York, Dominika Tarczynska, who also shared them with her supervisor, Lara Eshkenazi. They were stunned. So was their boss, Oestericher. He called me immediately to say that the team had found "major emails" that would significantly undermine the Commerce Department's position that the census question was DOJ's idea.

The story that DOJ wanted the question for legitimate reasons appears to be a pretext, he continued. As a result, "the case does not look good for the government."

Attorneys in civil cases do not, of course, just bundle up discovery material and send it over to opposing counsel. They first take a close look to determine what may be privileged or confidential information, and therefore can be properly withheld. What they *cannot* do is conceal information just because it hurts their case.

The deadline for providing the documents to counsel for New York State was June 8, 2018. Line attorneys at Main Justice's Civil Division had reviewed the material for privilege and were prepared to send it. But at the last minute, more than seventy pages of documents were pulled by political appointees in Washington, among them a Deputy Associate Attorney General and two Deputy Assistant Attorneys General.

Our attorneys were told by this trio that the emails in question did not fall under the required preliminary discovery because they were subject to what's called the "deliberative process privilege"—which means, essentially, that they were part of the in-office narrative of how an agency reached a decision. We understood this exception and had asserted it at times, most commonly in response to Freedom of Information Act requests.

But in this instance, we did not believe it applied. In fact, we thought that Main Justice's argument was without support, and we told them so. What's more, there could not be more relevant documents.

The email written by Comstock demonstrated not only that the rationale for the citizenship question offered by the administration was false but that Ross omitted the real origins of the census question in his congressional testimony. Ross made the same omission in a memo he wrote to an undersecretary at Commerce in late March 2018. "As you know . . . the Department of Justice requested that the Census Bureau reinstate a citizenship question on the decennial census," he wrote to Karen Dunn Kelley, who as undersecretary for economic affairs had oversight of the Census Bureau. Later in the memo, he refers to DOJ's desire to have better census data in order "to enforce the VRA"—the Voting Rights Act.

The emails exposed this as nonsense. The citizenship question was being pushed from outside the Department of Justice, and not for anything having to do with voting rights.

Even if the deliberative process privilege applied, portions of the emails could have been redacted. But the political attorneys at Main

Justice did not suggest or propose any such redactions. They just pulled the emails in their entirety.

Our office was aghast when we received a copy of the discovery sent by Main Justice to plaintiffs. Oestericher called me, shaken. "In all my years at the Southern District, Geoff, I have never seen anything like this," he said. "They pulled the emails at the last minute without any discussion with our office or even their own trial attorneys."

JEFF SESSIONS WAS THE US attorney general when I began, and still was at this point. He had famously recused himself from any campaign-related investigations, which led his deputy, Rod Rosenstein, to appoint Robert Mueller as a special counsel to probe any ties between the Trump campaign and Russia. All of this enraged Trump, and the relationship between the president and his attorney general was fractured.

In my experience, Sessions largely respected the independence of US attorneys, much more so than the acting attorney general who served after him, Matthew Whitaker. And certainly more than Barr.

Sessions spent a lot of time giving speeches around the country, and I had no substantive interactions with him. I think most of my peers liked and respected him—in large part because he let us do our jobs. My contacts were mostly with Rosenstein, and he usually allowed SDNY to operate without interference. (He let the Cohen search warrant go forward and then took heat for it from the administration, and he was supportive of our bringing charges against Halkbank.)

I did not know then, and still do not know, who was really calling the shots on the decision to withhold the emails from the discovery process. Was it the political appointees at Main Justice acting on their own? Had someone from the White House reached in and exerted control?

It ultimately didn't matter. It was clear that we could not let this stand. We had an ethical obligation to the court to let it know these documents existed and to the plaintiffs so they could demand them. We were not counsel of record and not running the case, but if we had not pushed for involvement, the truth might have remained buried. It would have been a travesty.

I convened a meeting in an eighth-floor conference room. Oestericher and the team, which also included the executive assistant US attorney Neil Corwin, took us through the chronology of the emails, the misleading statements made by Ross, and the last-minute decision by DOJ to pull the smoking-gun emails.

We had three options. We could continue in the litigation and seek to change DOJ's position at some point later. We quickly concluded this was not tenable. The existing record misled the plaintiffs. Without correcting it, they might not know to ask for the critical emails, or if they were to make a request, it might be deemed a mere fishing expedition.

Our second option was to just withdraw from the case, but that didn't feel right. The plaintiffs would be left in the dark.

I chose the most confrontational course of action: tell DOJ that the plaintiffs had a right to know about the existence of the emails, even if they were privileged, and that we had an ethical duty to correct the record.

I told Oestericher to call his contacts at Main Justice to express our outrage at what had happened and to impress upon them the immediate need to correct the record. Either they would do it or we would.

FOLLOWING OUR ULTIMATUM, the nonpolitical leadership in the Civil Division at Main Justice, which originally supported our position, disengaged. It seemed as if they just wanted to get out of the way and take cover. What's called the Professional Responsibility Advisory Office at Main Justice, which had also backed us, did the same. Political appointees obtained an opinion from the deputy solicitor general that we were wrong and that no action needed to be taken.

In these types of disputes, the more allies the better. But soon after we voiced concern, we were alone.

To memorialize our position, Oestericher, Tarczynska, and Eshkenazi drafted an email for Oestericher to send to his counterpart at Main Justice. I told them to make it as strong as possible.

The email, which Khuzami, Strauss, and I reviewed before it was sent, stated that the failure of DOJ to provide complete discovery in the census case had been reviewed by me, and that the Southern District believed "remedial steps" must be taken to correct the record. That meant the government had to correct the misstatements made by Ross in his memo to Kelley that failed to make clear that political appointees had strategized about adding the citizenship question before DOJ was asked to become involved. They also needed to correct other aspects of their administrative record that had created, essentially, a fictional account.

SDNY did not have authority to release documents to the plaintiffs, but we believed that we could, over the objections of Main

Justice, let them know of their existence. They could then ask Judge Furman to require the government to turn them over.

Our objective was to pressure Main Justice to remediate and to let them know that if they didn't, we would. One way or the other, we were determined: the truths revealed in those emails were going to be daylighted.

Main Justice was furious, but our ultimatum left them with no option but to make the disclosure themselves. Having SDNY do it, when we were not even an attorney of record, would alert the plaintiffs and the judge to the internal dispute about the emails. DOJ did not want to bring attention to that.

It wasn't long after our email that Ross began to walk back his prior statements.

In a June 21, 2018, court filing, Main Justice added a "supplement" to the administrative record in which Ross acknowledged that the impetus for the citizenship question had not really come from DOJ.

"Soon after my appointment as Secretary of Commerce, I began considering various fundamental issues regarding the upcoming 2020 Census, including funding and content," Ross said in the filing. "Part of these considerations included whether to reinstate a citizenship question, which other senior Administration officials had previously raised.

"My staff and I thought reinstating a citizenship question could be warranted, and we had various discussions with other governmental officials about reinstating a citizenship question to the Census. As part of that deliberative process, my staff and I consulted with Federal governmental components and inquired whether the Department of Justice would support, and if so would request, inclusion of a citizenship question as consistent with and useful for enforcement of the Voting Rights Act."

Even after this about-face, Ross and his DOJ lawyers still refused to hand over the emails. They kept insisting that any emails prior to December 2017, which was when the DOJ made its formal request for the citizenship question to be added, were protected by the deliberative process privilege.

In a stunning rebuke, Judge Furman not only ordered additional discovery but scolded Ross.

"Secretary Ross testified under oath that the Department of Justice had initiated the request for inclusion of the citizenship question," Furman remarked during a July 3, 2018, pretrial hearing. "It now appears that those statements were potentially untrue.

"On June 21, this year, without explanation, defendants filed a supplement to the Administrative Record, namely a half-page memorandum from Secretary Ross. . . . In this memorandum, Secretary Ross stated that 'soon after' his appointment as Secretary, which occurred in February of 2017, almost ten months before the request from the Department of Justice, he 'began considering' whether to add the citizenship question and that 'as part of that deliberative process,' he and his staff 'inquired whether the department of justice would support, and if so would request, inclusion of a citizenship question.'

"In other words," Furman continued, "it now appears that the idea of adding the citizenship question originated with Secretary Ross, not the Department of Justice, and that its origins long predated the December 2017 letter from the Justice Department. Even without that significant change in the timeline, the absence of virtually any documents predating DOJ's December 2017 letter was hard to fathom. But with it, it is inconceivable to me that there aren't additional documents from earlier in 2017 that should be made part of the Administrative Record."

Furman ordered DOJ to produce discovery beyond the administrative record, and a few weeks later they did. Soon after, we withdrew from the case.

We did so for two reasons: First, we were confident that plaintiffs would receive all the emails to which they were entitled. Second, we did not believe the positions and arguments DOJ was taking in the litigation were appropriate and did not want to be associated with them.

With the help of that discovery, the plaintiffs went on to win in the district court. Furman's decision was absolutely withering. He described Ross's decision-making process as "a veritable smorgasbord of classic, clear-cut" violations of the statutes that govern how federal agencies develop and issue regulations.

The judge noted that Ross had been in numerous discussions with Bannon, with the then US representative Mark Meadows (who would later become Trump's fourth chief of staff), and with many others who favored adding the citizenship question long before he asked DOJ to request it—based on the ruse that the question was needed to enforce voting rights laws.

"The Court's conclusion is supported by the sheer number of ways in which Secretary Ross and his aides tried to avoid disclosure of, if not conceal, the real timing and the real reasons for the decision to add the citizenship question," Furman wrote. Among those efforts, he continued, were "the curated and highly sanitized nature" of what they initially turned over in discovery.

Furman also took note of our decision to withdraw from the case: "There are dozens of highly qualified lawyers and professional staff in the Civil Division of the United States Attorney's Office for the

Southern District of New York. The Court can only speculate why the lawyers from that Office withdrew from their representation of Defendants in these cases."

NINE MONTHS LATER, the US Supreme Court affirmed the decision to exclude the census question.

"We cannot ignore the disconnect between the decision made and the explanation given," Chief Justice John Roberts wrote in the majority opinion.

"Accepting contrived reasons would defeat the purpose of the enterprise. If judicial review is to be more than an empty ritual, it must demand something better than the explanation offered for the action taken in this case."

Part Two

FRIENDS AND ENEMIES

4

—————

It's Time for You Guys
to Even Things Out

On August 8, 2018, our office charged Chris Collins, a Republican congressman from New York, with insider trading and making false statements to federal law enforcement agents. It was just two weeks later that Michael Cohen surprised us by pleading guilty rather than face felony indictment.

These two events occurred as we were looking into possible criminal conduct by Greg Craig, a prominent DC lawyer, a Democrat, and the White House counsel for the first year of the Obama administration. We were still in the midst of a careful process to determine if there was a basis for charging him when Rob Khuzami got a call from Ed O'Callaghan at Main Justice.

This is the episode that I touched on briefly in the preface. Even as I think about it now, it remains no less stunning and disturbing, and in this chapter I'll give it the fuller exploration it warrants.

O'Callaghan wanted us to charge Craig as soon as possible, before the midterm elections that November, because we had recently prosecuted a couple of Republicans. "It's time for you guys to even things out," he said.

When Khuzami walked into my office right after this call to inform me about it, I asked Audrey Strauss to join us. After the three of us got through expressing our disbelief at the impropriety and outrageousness of O'Callaghan's demand, we talked about how to respond to it. We had no trouble agreeing among ourselves: it would have no weight in the decision we reached, and no influence on its timing.

What I could not know at the time was how determined Main Justice was to see Craig face a jury and the extremes they would go to in order to make that happen.

CRAIG WAS SEVENTY-THREE YEARS OLD in that summer of 2018. He still had a full head of gray hair and the patrician manner of a man who had been educated at Phillips Exeter Academy, Harvard, and Yale Law School.

By any measure, his career was distinguished. He worked in the office of Senator Edward Kennedy in the mid-1980s and later held a senior post at the State Department under Secretary of State Madeleine Albright. In his time outside government, he was a partner at Williams & Connolly, the high-powered firm founded by the DC legal legend Edward Bennett Williams. He had represented a long list of high-profile clients—among them, his former law school classmate Bill Clinton in the 1999 impeachment trial.

The conduct of Craig's that came into question occurred in 2012, when he was retained by the government of Ukraine to conduct an investigation into whether the trial of a former prime minister, Yulia Tymoshenko, had met Western standards of jurisprudence.

Tymoshenko had been a leader of what was known as the Orange

Revolution, and she favored Ukraine aligning with the European Union and NATO. Ukraine was led at the time by Viktor Yanukovych, who was considered an ally of the Russian president, Vladimir Putin. In a 2011 trial widely condemned in the West as politically motivated, Tymoshenko was convicted on corruption charges and sentenced to seven years in prison.

The relationships around this case in Washington were complicated. Yanukovych was a client of the political consultant Paul Manafort, whom he hired to improve his image abroad and blunt criticism of what was seen as a political trial. It was Manafort, who would later become Trump's campaign chief, who directed the Ukraine work to Craig, a beacon of the Democratic establishment.

Craig by then was a partner at another blue-chip firm—Skadden, Arps, Slate, Meagher & Flom. The 187-page report produced by Craig and his team at the firm on Tymoshenko's trial was not a total exoneration of the Ukraine government. But Manafort and others were able to use parts of it to put a positive spin on the story and try to advance the regime's cause in Washington.

It was what happened next—rather than the report's content—that caught DOJ's attention. Craig spoke to reporters about it. His interactions with the media raised a question: Had he gone beyond his role as a lawyer and acted in a public relations capacity for a foreign government? If so, he would have been required to register under the Foreign Agents Registration Act, which is known as FARA.

The purpose of the law is to ensure that the US government and public know the source of information meant to influence opinion on behalf of a foreign government. In essence, it is designed to be a shield against misinformation or propaganda flowing in across our borders. Craig's failure to register under FARA was, potentially, a crime.

His defense was as follows: In talking to reporters, he was not working on behalf of Ukraine but, rather, tending to his own reputation. The Ukraine government and its allies were exploiting the report for their own purposes, and he was attempting to let the media know that he had not produced a document that was a whitewash.

THE CRAIG INVESTIGATION came to us in March 2018 in a referral from Main Justice, arising out of an investigation from Mueller's office, which was looking into Manafort on Russia-related matters. The referral came from Ed O'Callaghan in a meeting with Ilan Graff (then co-chief of our national security unit). Mueller's team had come upon Craig's representation of Ukraine from half a dozen years earlier and the questions it seemed to raise. That had nothing to do with the special counsel's mission, so they handed it off to DOJ, which then brought us in.

Our line prosecutors Kristy Greenberg, Jane Kim, and George Turner spent the next few months thoroughly investigating the facts and analyzing the relevant statutes. In mid-August, they had conversations with Craig's defense counsel, William Taylor and William Murphy, of the firm Zuckerman Spaeder, and presented evidence in support of filing criminal charges. About a week later, we got a twenty-four-page letter with Craig's defenses.

This back-and-forth was not a special courtesy extended to Craig. In fact, these interactions are common. Defense attorneys, obviously, want to do everything they can to avoid having their clients indicted. But the process is helpful as well to prosecutors.

When we bring charges, we want to make sure they're warranted and, importantly, that what we have is strong enough to convince a jury. Hearing from opposing counsel gives us an opportunity to have our evidence tested and our theory of the case challenged.

About a week after sending the letter, the defense counsel came back in and made a presentation. It happened to be my first day back in the office after sitting shiva for my father, who had passed away in late August 2018.

It was a crowded meeting. I was in the room, along with Khuzami, Strauss, and Zornberg, as well as Graff and Michael Ferrara, national security co-chiefs, and Timothy Howard and Daniel Noble, who led the complex fraud unit. The three AUSAs working the case were there as well, and we had participation from Main Justice. One of the deputy assistant attorneys general for the National Security Division had traveled from DC to attend, as had an NSD trial attorney.

The tradition of the Southern District, and one I deeply believe in, is that everyone gets a say—from the most junior prosecutors on up. In almost every case, we were able to synthesize the views of everybody. If someone disagreed with a decision, they could respect it and know how it was reached. The final call was mine.

Craig's lawyers showed us documentary evidence that he sought legal advice from his own firm on whether he needed to comply with FARA and made a good-faith decision that it did not apply to the work he was doing.

His concerns that his Ukrainian client, the minister of justice, would distort the findings of his report—in concert with the justice minister's British public relations operative—were backed by evidence and documents. The client did ultimately falsely claim to the press that the Craig report found that the Tymoshenko trial was completely fair.

When Craig talked to a *New York Times* reporter, he said, "We leave to others the question of whether this prosecution was politically motivated."

His lawyers argued that this message was the opposite of what his clients in Ukraine wanted him to deliver, whereas the FARA statute requires registration if a person is acting on behalf of a foreign client. His point was that he couldn't possibly be acting as a foreign agent when he was at odds with the preferred talking points of his foreign client.

With respect to whether Craig lied to officials from DOJ's FARA unit when he was initially questioned about his work in Ukraine, his lawyers argued that the statements were literally true or there were no contemporaneous notes taken by the officials about what exactly Craig had said.

When Craig's attorneys left, I asked everyone in the room for their reaction. Adam Hickey, from Main Justice, was by far the most bullish for prosecution. Others were on the fence. Strauss was not on the fence. She felt strongly that a prosecution was not warranted.

I agreed with her. There was a marginal, at best, case to be made against Craig. If we prosecuted, I believed there was a good chance that a jury would find it hyper-technical or trivial. And it wouldn't help that a lot of time had passed since the alleged offense.

On the FARA charge, I believed that Craig was innocent because he was trying to protect his own reputation in talking to reporters, not the reputation of his Ukrainian client. On the potential false statement charges, if there was no credible FARA charge, would a jury really be moved by possibly false statements he made in relation to a noncrime? That seemed unlikely to me.

After the meeting, the NSD attorneys returned to Main Justice and no doubt reported to their superiors that charges against Craig were unlikely. It was soon thereafter that O'Callaghan told Khuzami, "It's time for you guys to even things out."

FAIRNESS TO DEFENDANTS and to those we are considering prosecuting was of vital importance to me. It has long been part of the ethos of the Southern District.

The training our rookie AUSAs receive is extensive, much of it focusing on their ethical obligations to provide defendants information that might help them fight the charges. I reinforced this duty at every swearing-in ceremony by quoting the Supreme Court justice George Sutherland's 1935 admonition that a US attorney "is the representative not of an ordinary party to a controversy, but of a sovereignty whose obligation to govern impartially is as compelling as its obligation to govern at all; and whose interest, therefore, in a criminal prosecution is not that it shall win a case, but that justice shall be done." To that end, a prosecutor "may strike hard blows" but never "foul ones."

In mid-December 2018, after further investigation by our team and discussion within our office, I told John Demers, the assistant attorney general for national security, that we were declining to prosecute Craig. I was in Washington for a press conference with Demers on an unrelated matter, so I let him know as we stood outside his office.

I explained that I believed Craig was innocent of any potential FARA charge because he had contacted *The New York Times* for his own personal reasons—to maintain his and his firm's reputation. I added that any potential false statement charges were weak, even with an underlying FARA charge; standing alone, they were unsupportable.

The next day, he called and said that the National Security Division still planned to charge Craig, and just had to determine what district would bring the case. I was flabbergasted.

I don't know of another case in which a US attorney's office went through a lengthy analysis of the facts and the law, concluded that no charges are appropriate, and the case was taken away by Main Justice and shopped out elsewhere. We had taken over cases from other offices where they were not excited about an early-stage investigation. They never really looked fully into it, and we saw potential and picked it up.

But this was far different. We had three tenacious and experienced prosecutors on it, as well as the involvement and full attention of SDNY leadership. We had investigated fully and come to a considered decision.

The next communication on this from Main Justice came on the last day of the year. An NSD supervisor called Graff to make sure we would not object to their sharing our work product on Craig with the US Attorney's Office for the District of Columbia.

In a call to me a few days later, O'Callaghan (with Demers also on the line) wanted to know if I had read the draft prosecution memo that our team initially prepared. Was I really familiar with the facts of the case? Would I look back into it and revisit our decision not to prosecute?

I held my ground. I said yes, of course I had read the memo and that I had been present in numerous meetings about Craig. I went back through the process that led to our decision and then assured them that we were not reversing it.

At that point, they changed their approach. What if another US attorney's office prosecuted Craig? Would I consider that improper?

I replied that if they charged him with a FARA violation, it would be improper for the simple reason that he's innocent of it. With regard to a possible false statement charge, I said it would not be improper; it would just be a really bad idea because the case was extraordinarily weak.

When a US attorney's office passes on a prosecution, after many months of consideration, that should be the end of it, especially when the subject of investigation is a friend or enemy of the president's. That calls for even greater distance between prosecutors in the field and political appointees in DC.

Main Justice peddled the case to the US Attorney's Office for the District of Columbia. That's a large office, even bigger than the Southern District, because it functions as both a local prosecutor for the city—everything from misdemeanors on up to murders—and a prosecutor of federal crimes. I had some familiarity with that office, having been detailed there as a special assistant US attorney for six months (misdemeanor unit) in order to get trial experience prior to working on an Iran-Contra trial.

Jessie Liu became US Attorney in DC in September 2017. She had worked as an AUSA in that office before serving in several high positions in Main Justice during the second term of President George W. Bush.

When I talked to her about Craig, I restated what I had told O'Callaghan and Demers: he was innocent of any FARA violation, and the potential false statement charges were trivial, at best, and not worth pursuing.

But my words had no impact. The train had left the station.

By April, Craig's lawyers knew that their client would soon be charged, and issued a statement. "This case was thoroughly investigated" by the Southern District, they said. "That office decided not to pursue charges against Mr. Craig. We expect an indictment by the D.C. U.S. Attorney's Office at the request of the National Security Division."

Craig's lawyers called the prosecution "a misguided abuse of prosecutorial discretion." A few days later, he was charged in DC with two felony counts related to alleged false statements he made when questioned about his Ukraine work. The indictment alleged that Craig did not want to register as an agent of Ukraine "at least in part because he believed doing so could prevent him or others at the law firm from taking positions in the federal government in the future."

It also alleged that he did not want to reveal that the law firm was paid by a private citizen in Ukraine for the report or the size of the fee—$4 million. You could look at the Craig case and have an interesting discussion about the ways of Washington, or about what kinds of business law firms engage in internationally, or about any number of other policy issues it might raise. But our job was to determine if any criminal laws were broken.

I rarely knew for sure who was pulling the strings when Main Justice acted in ways that seemed obviously political. When we first started getting pressure to go after Craig, Jeff Sessions was still the attorney general. I had no sense of whether or not he was involved when we were being pushed by political appointees under him in Main Justice. Nor did I know if those individuals were in direct contact with anyone at the White House.

Sessions was replaced by an acting attorney general, Matthew

Whitaker, and I never knew one way or the other about his interest or involvement in the Craig investigation.

The president's interest in Craig, however, was not a mystery. The day after the indictment, Trump tweeted out the news with evident pleasure, as well as *displeasure* that the media did not make more of it. "President Obama's top White House lawyer, Gregory B. Craig, was indicted yesterday on very serious charges," he wrote. "This is a really big story, but the Fake News New York Times didn't even put it on page one, rather page 16. @washingtonpost not much better, 'tiny' page one. Corrupt News!"

As HIS TRIAL BEGAN in the summer of 2019, Craig faced a single felony count of misleading federal investigators when they came to interview him (the other count was dismissed before trial). He was never charged with the alleged offense they had come to talk to him about—violating the FARA statute.

It was exactly the scenario I chose to steer away from: the criminal prosecution of an alleged lie about a noncrime. Federal prosecutors do not often lose cases—more than 90 percent end in either pleas or guilty verdicts—but this one seemed as if it could go in the other direction.

The government's case centered on Craig's having hand delivered a copy of his report on the Ukraine prosecution of Tymoshenko to David Sanger, a reporter for *The New York Times*. That was before an on-the-record interview he gave Sanger.

Craig took the relatively rare step of testifying on his own behalf. He said he spoke to Sanger and another journalist in order to make sure his report was accurately portrayed in the US media. "I did not trust Jonathan Hawker [a public relations person working with Paul Manafort] to give an accurate or honest description of the report we had written of the Tymoshenko trial," he said in the beginning of his testimony. "The headline about the report should be that this trial is flawed," Craig said.

The government alleged that Craig lied about his interactions with the media. He countered that he had no reason to, because he was confident that his underlying actions broke no laws. "If anybody was going to talk to *The New York Times*, it was going to be me," he said. "I was not acting in the interest of Ukraine. I was defending the integrity of the report."

The trial went on for two and a half weeks.

It took less than five hours for the jury to return with a verdict of not guilty.

Outside the courthouse, William Taylor, one of Craig's lawyers, spoke to the media. "Why, after the United States Attorney for the Southern District of New York rejected this prosecution, did the Department of Justice decide it had to hound this man and his family without any evidence and without any purpose?" he said.

"It's a tragedy. It's a disgrace. I'm glad it's over."

EVEN AS I WAS IMMERSED in the day-to-day work of the Southern District, I was understandably curious about the Craig trial and followed it by reading the newspaper accounts after each day's testimony. It wasn't always easy to get a real sense of how things were going—you have to be in the courtroom for that—but I never saw anything to suggest the government's case had become stronger.

I was in my office talking to Graff when the verdict came in. First, I got an email; then Audrey and others started walking in to talk to me about it. You always want to be proved right when you take a position that others have opposed. That's human nature. But my main response was one of relief.

The verdict felt like justice. Greg Craig should never have been prosecuted.

If people at Main Justice were not embarrassed by it, they should have been, because a jury dispensing with a case after five hours does not leave you anything to feel good about.

The Southern District has a reputation for being aggressive, but I'd like to think that our decisions were thoughtfully considered and based on a sense of fairness. We weren't reckless. When we looked into the Craig case and made the determination not to go forward, that should have been the end of it. After the acquittal, *The Wall Street Journal* editorial page made that same point.

"When the hang-'em-high Southern District won't prosecute," they wrote, "you know it's a bad case."

I assumed the verdict would send a message of deterrence about carrying Main Justice's water—that it would be a long time before another US attorney's office picked up a case that we declined to prosecute. I also believed, or at least hoped, that the Craig verdict might cool down the pressure we had been getting to prosecute yet another enemy of the president.

But that was naive on my part.

5

Next Up:
John Kerry

G reg Craig is a classic inside-the-Beltway figure—well known primarily within Washington's power corridors. I'm not sure how many people around the country were familiar with Craig before Trump started tweeting about him.

John Kerry's fame is of a different magnitude. He was a decorated Vietnam War veteran who became a high-profile critic of the war and then a US senator representing Massachusetts for more than a quarter century. He nearly became president. As the Democratic nominee, he was defeated in a close election when George W. Bush won a second term in 2004.

Kerry left the Senate in 2013 to become Barack Obama's secretary of state. In that role, he was the lead US negotiator for what became known as the Iran nuclear deal—the controversial accord in which Iran agreed to dismantle parts of its nuclear program and open certain facilities to inspection in exchange for the easing of harsh economic sanctions and cash payments of well over $1 billion.

(The formal name was the Joint Comprehensive Plan of Action, and the negotiations included other world powers, such as Russia and China.)

Trump opposed the deal and campaigned against it. About a year into his presidency, he pulled the United States out of it.

Kerry would have spent many hours in rooms negotiating with his counterpart, the Iranian foreign minister, Javad Zarif. After his tenure as secretary of state ended at the close of the Obama administration, Kerry publicly acknowledged that he would occasionally communicate with Zarif.

Kerry, who has since joined the Biden administration, later explained that it is common for previous secretaries of state, US senators, and others involved in international affairs to talk to and maintain cordial relations with diplomats and other officials from foreign nations. "Every secretary of state, former secretary of state continues to meet with foreign leaders, goes to security conferences, goes around the world," he said in a Fox News interview. "We all do that.

"And we have conversations with people about the state of affairs in the world in order to understand them. We don't negotiate. We are not involved in interfering with policy. But we certainly have reasonable discussions about nuclear weapons, the world, China, different policies obviously."

President Trump did not see it that way. On May 7, 2018, he tweeted, "The United States does not need John Kerry's possibly illegal Shadow Diplomacy on the very badly negotiated Iran Deal. He was the one that created this MESS in the first place!"

On May 8, he tweeted, "John Kerry can't get over the fact that he had his chance and blew it! Stay away from negotiations John, you are hurting your country!"

On May 9, the day after the second Trump tweet, the co-chiefs of SDNY's national security unit, Ferrara and Graff, had a meeting at Main Justice with the head of the unit that oversees counterintelligence cases at DOJ, which is under the National Security Division.

He said that Main Justice was referring an investigation to us that concerned Kerry's Iran-related conduct. The conduct that had annoyed the president was now a priority of the Department of Justice. The focus was to be on potential violations of the Logan Act.

THERE ARE SEVERAL things to know about the Logan Act.

One is that it is a very old law. It was enacted in 1799 by Congress and forbids private citizens to engage in unauthorized negotiations with foreign governments.

The statute was passed during tensions over whether the United States should become involved on the side of the French revolutionary government, which was still battling forces loyal to the beheaded Louis XVI.

Thomas Jefferson, recently returned from a five-year diplomatic stint in Paris, favored US intervention in the conflict. His antagonist, Alexander Hamilton, vehemently opposed it. (If you saw the Broadway show *Hamilton*, you probably remember Hamilton and Jefferson engaging in a comic hip-hop showdown over this, which George Washington tried to referee.)

In the midst of this political struggle (the real one, not the *Hamilton* version), a private citizen named George Logan traveled from his home in Philadelphia to France and met with government officials. Logan was a physician and farmer. His family were Loyalists, and he spent the Revolutionary War in England getting his medical degree. At least one historical text has referred to him as a "busy-body."

Logan succeeded in securing a French agreement to stop harassing and seizing US merchant ships, which they had been doing, primarily off the Eastern Seaboard and in the Caribbean. Logan's opponents, however, opposed his freelancing, and some considered it treasonous.

In response came the Logan Act.

It reads, "Any citizen of the United States, wherever he may be, who, without authority of the United States, directly or indirectly commences or carries on any correspondence or intercourse with any foreign government or any officer or agent thereof, with intent to influence the measures or conduct of any foreign government or of any officer or agent thereof, in relation to any disputes or controversies with the United States, or to defeat the measures of the United States, shall be fined under this title or imprisoned not more than three years, or both."

To say that the law has been sporadically enforced would be an understatement. In 1803, a Kentucky farmer named Francis Flournoy was indicted after writing an article, under a pen name, that advocated a new, independent state within North America that would become part of France. He was never actually prosecuted.

Half a century later, as a US-backed group of businessmen was seeking to build a rail line across a narrow stretch of land between the Gulf of Mexico and the Pacific Ocean—the area is known as the Isthmus of Tehuantepec—a US merchant living in Mexico tried to spoil the deal because he had his own ambitions to build the project. Jonas Phillips Levy was indicted under the Logan Act after writing a letter to the Mexican president asking him to reject a treaty proposed by Secretary of State Daniel Webster that would have smoothed the way for the preferred group to build the rail line.

That was the last attempt at a prosecution under the Logan Act—in 1852. Levy was never brought to trial.

It is worth mentioning one other thing about the Logan Act. It came up, peripherally, in a civil case—in 1964—in which one of the parties suggested that the other might have been in violation of the statute. A judge in the Southern District commented that the law, if ever put to the test, would likely be found unconstitutional because, as written, it is "vague" and "indefinite."

This is what we were being asked to consider using to prosecute John Kerry.

WHEN A POSSIBLE crime is brought to our attention, our obligation is to take it seriously. We don't set out to find reasons to disregard the allegations. Nor do we try to rush through the process. We investigate. We also, significantly, look at the conduct in terms of whether any laws were actually broken.

At that initial meeting, Ferrara and Graff were told that given the case's sensitivity, the National Security Division at Main Justice would be more involved than it typically is. Two days later, Ferrara and Graff briefed me and we agreed to accept the referral and explore whether a crime had been committed. They had already been in touch with their FBI counterparts, who would play a role as well.

It is important to note here that while Kerry was obviously aware of Trump's tweets, the former secretary of state did not know about this nascent investigation, and in the months that followed, he never learned of it. It never leaked into the media.

So, how did this investigation get started? Did Trump pass word down through Main Justice, which was then headed by Sessions, that he wanted Kerry prosecuted?

In a way, the question answers itself. No one needed to talk with Trump to know what he wanted. You could read his tweets. Anyone wanting to please him at Main Justice—from the attorney general down through the political appointees in his chain of command—could act on them.

An irony in the Kerry episode is that Trump himself was reported to have conducted foreign policy before he took office, during the transition between his election in November 2016 and his inauguration the following January. He opposed a pending United Nations resolution that condemned Israeli settlements on the West Bank. In order to prevent it from coming to a vote, Trump, still technically a private citizen, and in opposition to the still-in-office Obama administration, reached out to then Israeli prime minister Benjamin Netanyahu and Egyptian president Abdel Fattah el-Sisi, according to accounts in *The New York Times* and other media outlets.

From the outset, I was skeptical that there was a case to be made. I knew enough about the Logan Act to have strong doubts. Politicians from both sides of the aisle have talked about it from time to time, suggesting that some opponent is in violation of it. It never goes anywhere.

But I figured if they bring us a possible case, we'll do our best. We'll look into it. We brought a prosecutor from the national security unit, Andrew DeFilippis, into the investigation.

Trump, meanwhile, kept on tweeting. "John Kerry had illegal meetings with the very hostile Iranian Regime, which can only serve to undercut our great work to the detriment of the American people," he wrote that September. "He told them to wait out the Trump

Administration! Was he registered under the Foreign Agents Regis-tration Act? BAD!"

Trump's secretary of state, Mike Pompeo, joined Trump in his fixation on Kerry. After Trump's September 2018 tweet, Pompeo, referring to Kerry's conversations with his former Iranian counterpart, said, "You can't find precedent for this in U.S. history." He added that he would leave the "legal determinations to others."

The next step would have been to conduct an inquiry into Kerry's electronic communications, what's known as a 2703(d) order. That would have produced the header information—the to, from, date, and subject fields—but not the contents. I decided that before moving for-ward, it made sense to evaluate whether we would ever have a viable, appropriate charge that matched up with Kerry's alleged conduct.

At the risk of stating the obvious, under our system of law, pissing off the president is not a chargeable offense. I asked DeFilippis to conduct additional legal research into the Logan Act and other poten-tially applicable theories. "Look, we're talking about going to the next step here," I said. "But before we do any further investigation, I want to know what the law is on the Logan Act. Let's say we gather addi-tional documents—I want to know, how is that helping us?"

I wanted to answer the question, even if these things happened, was it a crime? Let's cut to the chase and find that out, because we've got plenty of other work to do and I don't want us to just be spinning our wheels on this.

For the next several months, DeFilippis conducted extensive re-search into the Logan Act as well as statutes relating to possible criminal ethics violations by former senior government employees.

On April 22, 2019, Trump tweeted, "Iran is being given VERY BAD advice by @JohnKerry and people who helped him lead the U.S. into the very bad Iran Nuclear Deal. Big violation of Logan Act?"

The tweet was in the morning. That afternoon, Ferrara got a call from Main Justice. He was told that David Burns, the principal deputy assistant attorney general for national security, wanted to know why we were delaying. Why had we not proceeded with a 2703(d) order—the look into Kerry's electronic communications?

The next day, Burns spoke to Ferrara, Graff, and DeFilippis and repeatedly pressed them about why they had not submitted the 2703(d) order. The team responded that additional analysis needed to be done before pursuing the order.

The pattern here is clear—and outrageous. In the beginning, we got pulled into this investigation by Main Justice after Trump started tweeting his displeasure about Kerry. And now, eleven months later, on the same day of another Trump tweet, one in which he's specific about what criminal act he believes Kerry committed, we were being pushed to move forward.

And they were asking us, basically, what's taking so long? Why aren't you going harder and faster at this enemy of the president? There was no other way for me to look at it.

By the time we got pressured in April 2019, on the same day as one of the Trump tweets, Bill Barr was the attorney general. He always insisted that he was his own man, running an independent DOJ. Trump didn't tell him what to do.

But Trump didn't need to tell Barr what to do any more than he needed to tell Whitaker or anyone else in DOJ who was interested in doing his bidding. All Barr had to do was read Trump's tweets—or follow the ubiquitous news coverage of them—to know that he wanted John Kerry prosecuted.

WE SPENT ROUGHLY a year exploring whether there was any basis to further investigate Kerry. Memos were written, revised, and thoroughly discussed.

Our deep dive into the Logan Act confirmed why no one has ever been successfully prosecuted under it in the more than 220 years it has been on the books: the law is not useful. It definitely does not prohibit a former US secretary of state from talking to a foreign official. We did not find that Kerry violated any ethics statutes or any laws having to do with the improper handling of classified material.

In September 2019, DeFilippis advised the National Security Division at Main Justice that we would not be pursuing the case further. He had earlier attempted to tell the specific NSD attorney assigned to the case of our decision, but he couldn't connect because that attorney was engaged in another matter: the Craig trial.

That's a pretty good coda to the Kerry episode: we couldn't close the loop and let the relevant Main Justice attorney know we were declining this bullshit prosecution because he was too busy with another bullshit case that we had declined.

This was, incredibly, not the end of it.

Shortly after DeFilippis's call, on September 19, 2019, the counsel for the attorney general, Will Levi, called me to say that Barr and the NSD expected to take the Kerry case to another district. It astonished me that Barr, about two weeks after Craig's acquittal, would follow the same failed game plan with the Kerry case. I told Levi that I stood by my decision not to prosecute.

The following April, I learned that the Kerry case had been reassigned to the District of Maryland. I received a call from Robert Hur, the US Attorney for Maryland, who asked about potential criminal charges against Kerry.

I went back through the whole thing, explained our reasons for declining, and urged Hur to do the same. Hur would come to the same conclusion we did, and the Kerry investigation just quietly died—as it should have.

6

Changes at the Top

I would ultimately serve under two attorneys general and one acting AG.

The first was Jeff Sessions, who, as I have mentioned, was not deeply engaged in the matters being run out of SDNY or, to my knowledge, any of the other districts. I think that was appropriate. Each case has its own history, intricacies, and pace, and for an AG to cherry-pick which ones he wants to put his imprint on is not a good idea. The effort itself can be viewed as political.

When Sessions stepped down on the day after the 2018 midterm elections, ending an icy, monthslong standoff with Trump over his recusal on Russia matters, the president named Matthew Whitaker as acting attorney general.

Whitaker was a former tight end for the University of Iowa—he played in a Rose Bowl—and a onetime Republican candidate for the US Senate in Iowa. In 2004, President George W. Bush appointed him US Attorney for the Southern District of Iowa. It was an unusual choice because Whitaker had no previous experience in law enforcement, but he reportedly had powerful supporters within Iowa's Republican establishment.

In September 2017, Whitaker became Sessions's chief of staff. When he stepped up to become acting attorney general fourteen months later, *The New York Times* headlined a profile of him "Matthew Whitaker: An Attack Dog with Ambition Beyond Protecting Trump."

The story quoted Robert Rigg, a defense lawyer and Drake University law professor who was once involved in a case with Whitaker, on the new acting AG's style. "He practices law the way he played football," Rigg said. "He's very aggressive. He's very passionate about what he believes in."

Matthew Strawn, a former chairman of the Iowa Republican Party, told the *Times* that Whitaker was "known inside Republican circles as someone you want on your side in a fight."

A couple weeks after his appointment, Whitaker decided to pay us a visit. I figured he was looking to elevate his stature and show that he had the gravitas to become the permanent AG. (He certainly had gravity on his side. The guy was six feet four inches and looked to be all muscle.) He wanted a little of our reputation to rub off on him.

But the qualities that SDNY is known for—independence, excellence—were precisely the ones that certain news outlets said he was lacking. Just days after he was elevated to acting AG, an exclusive story on the news site *Vox* reported that at the same time Whitaker was serving as chief of staff to Sessions, he was privately advising Trump on how to pressure the Justice Department to investigate his adversaries.

The official purpose of Whitaker's trip to New York was to give a speech to what is called the Joint Terrorism Task Force. The JTTF predates the September 11, 2001, terrorist attacks, but after them it was sort of supercharged. It is run by the FBI, but has people dedicated to it from dozens of federal and state law enforcement agencies. We have AUSAs and investigators embedded there, as does the Eastern District.

Whitaker asked me to set up a dinner the night before that would also include other US attorneys from neighboring districts. If his goal was to upgrade his reputation and how he was viewed, my hope over those two days was to stay as far away from him as possible because I didn't want to get tarred with what he was carrying.

I got us a place for dinner on the West Side of Manhattan that few people had ever heard of. It was a decent restaurant, a steak house, but I didn't want to be seen. I think there were half a dozen of us, all men in suits. We didn't have a private room, but they knew who we were and separated us, which wasn't difficult because there weren't many other people in there.

But midway through our dinner, a photographer was allowed into the restaurant. He walked up to our table and snapped photos. Whitaker's PR people had obviously arranged this, and at least one of the photos appeared in a media outlet the next day.

I figured if he's making me go to dinner, I'll try to get something out of it. At that point in time, the Halkbank case—the case of the Turkish financial institution involved in violating the Iran sanctions—was our top priority. Because of the nature of the case and the geopolitical elements involved, we needed to consult with Main Justice on it. The State Department had an interest in the trajectory of the case, as did Treasury.

But Halkbank's counsel was slow-walking every request we made. They were acting as if they held all the cards, and we're thinking, you hold the cards? No, you don't. That's not what the Southern District is accustomed to.

So, I said to Whitaker that night, "We want to indict Halkbank. We've run out of patience, and we have a case we can make."

He said to stand down. Just wait until we get more input from Treasury and State. I didn't have any idea where he had gained knowledge of this case, or whom he might be taking his cues from. I said fine, I get the message. But I didn't want to stand down for long. (I write in much more detail about the Halkbank case in a chapter later in this book.)

The next morning, Whitaker asked me to introduce him before his talk at the JTTF event. I'm thinking, what am I going to say? I kept it short, something along the lines of "Please join me in welcoming the new acting attorney general, who was formerly the US Attorney in Iowa. Let's give him a warm welcome."

And then I quickly exited, stage left, and gave him a handshake out of sight of any cameras.

WHITAKER DID NOT LAST LONG. In early December 2018, Trump nominated William Pelham Barr to be the nation's eighty-fifth attorney general. Barr had also been the nation's seventy-seventh AG, in the administration of George H. W. Bush.

In one marker of how much more polarized our politics have become, Barr's first confirmation hearing in 1991 was described at the time as "placid." He was approved unanimously by the Senate Judiciary Committee, then confirmed by the full Senate in a voice vote. When Barr's second nomination went before the Senate early in 2019, he was confirmed, but in a roll-call vote—with the 54–45 count mostly breaking down along party lines.

I was elated that we were getting somebody to come in to take

Whitaker's spot, and I had high hopes. The new boss was experienced and highly intelligent. He had a reputation as an institutionalist, someone who would respect the traditions and norms of the department. Most of all, I believed Barr would be a steady hand in turbulent times.

I sent him a handwritten note, relating that in his first tour of duty he had signed my certificate when I started out as a young AUSA. I said we had never had an opportunity to meet, but I was looking forward to that soon.

I added that he was "just what the doctor ordered." Like so many other establishment Republicans, I thought he would clean things up at DOJ and respect the rule of law.

THE ONE TIME that Barr met with me in my personal office at the Southern District involved an uncomfortable moment, and it was telling. It happened after he noticed a photo on the wall of me with Lawrence Walsh, the independent counsel in the Iran-Contra affair. It was signed, "Thank you Geoff, for all your good work."

Walsh indicted Caspar Weinberger, a secretary of defense during the Reagan administration, in June 1992, on charges related to the secret flow of arms to the Contra rebels in Nicaragua. He added another charge in late October of that year—on the Friday before George H. W. Bush would lose his reelection bid to Bill Clinton.

Bush was vice president when the events being investigated took place. The new indictment and the news it generated incensed Bush's inner circle, who felt it stopped momentum he was gaining against Clinton.

I did not agree with the timing of the second indictment. (I was no longer working for Walsh by then.) You don't take any action that would affect an election within sixty days of that election absent exceptional circumstances. That's the rule of thumb.

Four days later, Bush lost the election pretty soundly. The Electoral College count was 370 to 168, so it's pretty hard to argue that Walsh cost him a second term.

I had an abiding respect for Walsh and was proud of the work I did for his office. Barr despised everything about the Iran-Contra probe, and I assume he didn't think much of Walsh, either, who died in 2014 at 102.

Bush pardoned Weinberger and five others implicated in the scandal in the waning weeks of his presidency. It wiped away six years of the independent counsel's work. "In a single stroke," one news account said, "Mr. Bush swept away one conviction, three guilty pleas and two pending cases, virtually decapitating what was left of Mr. Walsh's effort."

Bush consulted with his Justice Department on pardons, which is how it is supposed to work.

His attorney general was Bill Barr.

In a 2001 interview for an oral history project at the Miller Center at the University of Virginia, which focuses on the presidency and political history, Barr explained his thinking at the time: "I asked some of my staff to look into the indictment that was brought, and also some of the other people I felt had been unjustly treated and whether they felt that they would have been treated this way under standard Department guidelines. I don't remember going through the pardon office, but I did ask some of the seasoned professionals around the Department about this, asked them to look into it. Based on those discussions, I went over and told the President

I thought he should not only pardon Caspar Weinberger, but while he was at it, he should pardon about five others.

"There were some people arguing just for Weinberger, and I said, No, in for a penny, in for a pound."

That day in my office, Barr fixed his gaze on the picture of Walsh and me. He looked at it for almost a minute straight without saying a word. Just stared with a sour look on his face. It was awkward as hell.

I'm just standing there, waiting for our meeting to start, and thinking to myself, "You know what, Geoff? Maybe you should have taken that picture down before he got here."

It was more than past history, or a lack of personal chemistry, that separated me from Barr. We had a philosophical divide.

His expansive views on presidential power—and his belief in what is known as the unitary executive theory—were well known and, arguably, well within the Republican and conservative mainstream. He expounded on them in 2019 while speaking at a Federalist Society event.

"I deeply admire the American Presidency as a political and constitutional institution," he said. "I believe it is one of the great, and remarkable, innovations in our Constitution, and has been one of the most successful features of the Constitution in protecting the liberties of the American people. More than any other branch, it has fulfilled the expectations of the Framers.

"Unfortunately, over the past several decades, we have seen steady encroachment on Presidential authority by the other branches of government. This process I think has substantially weakened the functioning of the executive branch, to the detriment of the nation."

He continued, later in his lecture, "I am concerned that the deck has become stacked against the Executive. . . . More and more, the President's ability to act in areas in which he has discretion has become smothered by the encroachments of the other branches."

There were critics—among them some lawyers who worked in prior Republican administrations—who felt that Barr soft-pedaled his views during the confirmation process and later acted in extreme ways on Trump's behalf. One of them was Donald Ayer, a highly regarded lawyer who served in the administrations of Ronald Reagan and George H. W. Bush.

In a 2019 essay in *The Atlantic*, Ayer wrote, "In securing his confirmation as attorney general, Barr successfully used his prior service as attorney general in the by-the-book, norm-following administration of George H. W. Bush to present himself as a mature adult dedicated to the rule of law who could be expected to hold the Trump administration to established legal rules. Having known Barr for four decades, including preceding him as deputy attorney general in the Bush administration, I knew him to be a fierce advocate of unchecked presidential power, so my own hopes were outweighed by skepticism that this would come true."

Ayer's piece appeared after the release of the Mueller report, which many believed Barr had both preempted and misrepresented. Ayer continued, "But the first few months of his current tenure, and in particular his handling of the Mueller report, suggest something very different—that he is using the office he holds to advance his extraordinary lifetime project of assigning unchecked power to the president."

Much of this political back-and-forth was beyond the scope of my concerns in the Southern District. I was a working prosecutor, and my focus was to lead the dedicated and hardworking public servants under me who came into work every day and busted their asses. My political views—and whatever my thoughts might have been on Barr's high-altitude insights into the Constitution—were beside the point.

But the fact was, Barr's top-down, unitary theories of power extended to how he viewed himself, how he ran the Justice Department, and how he felt about the people who worked for me. If Barr believed that the president could properly instruct the DOJ to take actions involving specific individuals, including his friends and enemies, that *was* a concern of mine.

Early in 2020, top Justice Department officials overruled the prosecution team in the case of Roger Stone, a longtime friend and associate of Donald Trump's, and recommended a more lenient sentence for crimes he committed to protect the president. This was another situation where the president's grievances and wishes could easily be discerned. Barr could say, "I don't take orders from above regarding sentencing," or "I don't talk to the president about it." But he didn't need to in order to know that Trump was enraged at what he considered the unfair treatment of Stone.

In protest, three of the prosecutors in the US Attorney's Office for the District of Columbia withdrew from the case. A fourth quit the office entirely.

Barr clearly had this uprising in mind in remarks he later made at a Constitution Day event at Hillsdale College in Michigan. "Name one successful organization where the lowest-level employees' decisions are deemed sacrosanct. There aren't any," he said. "Letting the most junior members set the agenda might be a good philosophy for a Montessori preschool, but it's no way to run a federal agency."

The people who worked for me at SDNY generally came from

elite law schools. They graduated top of their class. Most had clerked in the federal court system, some for Supreme Court justices. In terms of young legal talent, they were the best of the best. The AUSAs in districts throughout the country were similarly high achieving.

For Barr to have compared them to preschoolers was both outrageous and revealing.

7

TRUMP V. VANCE

W e prosecuted dozens of big cases during my tenure leading the Southern District, most of them without political interference. I couldn't be more proud of the work we did and the justice we won for victims. But *Trump v. Vance*—like the Craig case and the Kerry episode—demonstrates the importance of what we *resisted* doing.

Barr was atop Justice when our involvement in the matter began, and it fell squarely within his area of intense interest: presidential power and its limits—or limitlessness.

The roots of the case go back to 2018, when the district attorney's office in Manhattan began looking into what a grand jury subpoena called "business transactions involving multiple individuals whose conduct may have violated state law."

The investigation centered on the role that Trump and the Trump Organization played in payments made to Stormy Daniels and Karen McDougal before the 2016 election. The subpoena issued by the Manhattan district attorney, Cyrus Vance Jr., sought eight years of the president's business and personal tax records from Mazars USA, his longtime accountants.

Trump filed suit against Vance in September 2019, seeking a temporary restraining order and preliminary injunction to bar Mazars from turning over its records. The motion asserted that no state can criminally investigate, prosecute, or indict a president while he is in office because it would impose severe burdens on a president and distract him from his constitutional duties.

A few days later, I got a call from Joseph Hunt, the head of DOJ's Civil Division. He said that Main Justice intended to submit a statement of interest in support of President Trump's position, and it anticipated playing an active role in litigation. He requested our assistance in filing this in the Southern District.

Trump was represented by his private attorneys, but Hunt's suggestion, on the surface, was not improper. In this instance, DOJ would be representing the *institution* of the presidency, and by extension the United States, not the president himself. The government's interest would be to protect the powers that the Constitution imbues in the executive branch.

I went into this with my eyes wide open. I knew we were likely headed for conflict, but I never saw an advantage to being a roadblock straight out of the gate. A hard "no" from us on requests that presented, at least initially, as reasonable could easily be viewed as insubordination.

My strategy always was to take an incremental approach and let things play out. Maybe we come to a point of agreement. Or maybe the whole thing goes away for whatever reason. If either of those things happens, I've saved myself a confrontation.

I told Hunt that we could be involved in their first course of action, which was of no real substance. As I understood it, we were just going to ask the court for more time to give the government a moment to formulate its position.

They sent us a draft of the motion, and we edited it. It said the government was participating in support of the plaintiff—Trump—and we changed it to say the government was supporting its own interests. That may seem overly legalistic, but I wanted to make clear we were not Trump's personal lawyer in this matter.

We also deleted references to the state prosecutor's request for these financial records as "unprecedented" and took out language referring to his "venturing far beyond the traditional scope of state and local law enforcement." Main Justice accepted our changes, and the motion—stripped down to just the innocuous request for more time—was filed under the signature of SDNY's civil division chief, Oestericher.

The Department of Justice is massive, with 114,000 employees across all fifty states and a budget of about $30 billion. It employs attorneys involved in a wide range of cases. It oversees numerous law enforcement agencies, as well as the Bureau of Prisons, and fulfills an important role in national security. But this case—involving a president's alleged payoffs to mistresses and the dispute over who could see his business records—was clearly a high priority.

A couple days later, Oestericher and the AUSA Benjamin Torrance went down to Washington (with Sarah Normand participating by phone) for a large meeting that included James Burnham and representatives from the solicitor general's office and the Civil Division's appellate staff. It was clear that Main Justice wanted the imprimatur of SDNY—for the weight it carried with the judges in our district—while also wanting to control the substance of the filings.

The DA in New York was arguing that the case belonged solely in the state courts. We were comfortable in backing DOJ's position on jurisdiction—that in matters involving the president, the federal courts had a role to play. I believed in that, and I thought the law supported it.

But there was an additional argument on the table at Main Justice—one asserting that a president could not be criminally investigated, *in any way, by anyone*, while still in office. This would be an extension of the long-standing principle, though one never tested in court, that a sitting president could not be criminally charged. They wanted to push that to say that there should be limitations on a state grand jury's ability to even look into a president's conduct.

Ideas were exchanged at the meeting in DC. Oestericher reported back that a small majority of the meeting's participants seemed in favor of our approach—that we would go only so far as to argue that the case belonged in federal court. If the president's personal lawyers wanted to make broad claims about his immunity, fine, but we were not going to join them. Oestericher added, however, that "it appears that senior DOJ management will make the final decision."

WHENEVER A CONFRONTATION with Main Justice was imminent, it was usually preceded by some kind of signal—almost like when a warning light starts to flash on your dashboard. You know you're going to have to deal with something, even if you're not quite sure what.

In this case, the signal was Main Justice's stubborn insistence that we be the primary signatories on court filings. They wanted that because if a brief seemed to be authored only by DOJ lawyers in Washington, there was a greater chance it could be viewed as political. Main Justice's determination to put us front and center was my warning that they were headed in a direction we likely would not want to follow.

Oestericher told Burnham, Look, you're driving the bus on this and we're only contributing our input. As long as we're okay with the contents of a brief, you can put our names on the left—as the secondary signatures, indicating we're basically local counsel—and yours on the right. But that's all.

What we would not do in this case, or any other, was indicate to the judges of the Southern District that something was our work when, in fact, it was not.

Our message was heard, at least temporarily. The first filings were submitted to the court with us in the secondary position.

Trump's lawyers lost the first round. On October 7, Judge Victor Marrero issued a seventy-five-page ruling denying the president's request for an injunction to prevent the district attorney from obtaining the financial records. The judge wrote, "The President asserts an extraordinary claim in the dispute now before this Court. He contends that, in his view of the President's duties and functions and the allocation of governmental powers between the executive and the judicial branches under the United States Constitution, the person who serves as President, while in office, enjoys absolute immunity from criminal process of any kind. Consider the reach of the President's argument.

"As the Court reads it, presidential immunity would stretch to cover every phase of criminal proceedings, including investigations, grand jury proceedings and subpoenas, indictment, prosecution, arrest, trial, conviction, and incarceration. That constitutional protection presumably would encompass any conduct, at any time, in any forum, whether federal or state, and whether the President acted alone or in concert with other individuals."

Trump's private lawyers immediately appealed, and Main Justice informed us that they intended to file an amicus brief in support of his position. A draft of this brief was delivered to us—with a signature line for me—even though neither I nor any SDNY attorney had anything to do with crafting it.

The document amplified Trump's position. It argued, among other things, that Article VI, Paragraph 2 of the Constitution—commonly referred to as the supremacy clause—constrains a state grand jury from investigating a president. But the clause is typically interpreted to mean that the Constitution and federal laws take priority over conflicting state stautes; that states cannot interfere with the federal government's exercise of its constitutional powers.

It is generally understood that a president cannot be indicted while in office, but the relevant opinions from the Office of Legal Counsel at DOJ suggest other options. One is that you might be able to indict a president under seal. And you can certainly investigate a sitting president.

The argument by the president's lawyers seemed absurd. Trump was not the entirety of the federal government. And it was never clear how the functioning of the United States would be impaired if his accountants turned over records.

What we were being asked to support was an argument that a president may not have to respond to criminal service. That's a pretty extraordinary point of view—particularly for a Department of Justice that is, ostensibly, interested in the enforcement of criminal law.

We told Main Justice that we have an institutional responsibility here. We believe that when a criminal subpoena is issued, it gets responded to—whether it's Joe Schmoe or the president of the United States. That's the business we're in. We don't seek out excuses for people to hide from us, and we don't back any arguments on why they should be permitted to do so.

Our point was practical in addition to philosophical. Investigations have a life span. If you have to wait for a president's term to end before even looking into his conduct, the time clock may run out. You might have statute of limitations issues. Or people will throw their records out the window or erase their computer files. To say a president is beyond even being investigated really does put him above the law.

I instructed Oestericher to tell Main Justice to get my name off that thing. It's not our work product, and I want nothing to do with it. Oestericher sent an email that formally made the request.

Barr was sixty-eight years old when he became Trump's attorney general. He had a well-earned reputation as an old Washington hand and skilled inside player who knew how to exercise his power while keeping his hands clean. On *Trump v. Vance*, we dealt with others at Main Justice, on up to Jeffrey Rosen, the deputy attorney general. But I never doubted that Barr was pulling the strings.

The whole episode was a bit of a cat-and-mouse game right from the start. Their goal was to bring the full force of DOJ to Trump's side, which meant bringing SDNY along. We would never have supported the substance of their argument, but in the beginning, before that argument was shown to us, I couldn't just say, "Not interested."

That just immediately raises it to a Level 10 and puts me on the firing line. So I kept trying to take it one step at a time and make it about procedure, hoping that maybe there's an off-ramp somewhere and we avoid a collision. In the second week of October, we were told our name would be removed from the brief, as we requested.

One day later, Hunt called me and said it was back on. The final decision has been made, he continued, and it came down from Rosen, Barr's second-in-command. Hunt made it sound as if that were the end of the conversation. It was a direct order, and I just had to suck it up and follow along.

IT JUST SO HAPPENED that this exchange with Hunt coincided with a big moment—the day we announced the arrests and indictment of Lev Parnas and Igor Fruman. These were the Rudy Giuliani associates involved in shenanigans in Ukraine intended to influence US politics. In the United States, they had mixed with American politicians, among them Trump, and there were pictures of them with the president. (I write about this case in the next chapter.)

The rollout of the indictment had already caused a bit of a kerfuffle with Main Justice. Barr had a chief of staff by the name of Brian Rabbitt. A few hours before we were to announce the charges, Rabbitt asked me, "What are you planning to do for publicity for Lev and Igor?" I said, "I'm going to have a press statement," and he said, "Okay. Fine."

Later that day, we made our statement. It was in front of cameras, and it got huge coverage. When I got back to my desk, Rabbitt called me up, livid. "I thought you said it was going to be a press statement?" he barked.

I replied, "I didn't take questions. It was a press *statement*. If it were a press conference, we would have had questions."

I thought that was perfectly legit, but Rabbitt wasn't satisfied. The exchange with him was a little uncomfortable, but the Lev and Igor indictments came at a fortuitous time. (It just happened that way; we didn't intend it and couldn't have anticipated the international travel that prompted their arrests.) If Main Justice took action against me in any way, or even just got in a public flap, the media would have assumed it was retribution after we indicted these two individuals who moved in Republican circles. It would have played as blowback from the arrests.

After we got press attention on a big matter and our visibility was high, I always felt sort of bulletproof, at least temporarily. It gave me a couple more months of grace.

AFTER HUNT TOLD ME that my name would be on the brief, I reached out to Patrick Hovakimian, who worked for the deputy attorney general. It was more of the same. He said that it was "a directive" from Rosen that my name be on the document, it was staying on, and I should let it rest. There was no reason, he said, to go further up the chain to Rosen.

Trump v. Vance was important to Trump; therefore, it was important to Barr and his loyal underlings. I was supposed to follow orders and march in lockstep.

After the call, I emailed Hovakimian that he and Rosen should know that if my name or any name from my office appears in the brief I will have an obligation of candor to the court to let them know that we do not endorse the arguments in the brief.

INCREDIBLY, THEY KEPT PRESSING. After telling me I should not reach out to Rosen, Hovakimian reversed course and informed me that he had scheduled a call for me with the deputy attorney general later that afternoon. I sent an email in advance. It said that we're not

putting our names on anything that undercuts the power of a prosecutor to use a grand jury subpoena.

And by the way, it was not just that I couldn't abide that DOJ was
trying to put the president beyond the reach of law enforcement. It
was also that their legal reasoning made no sense.

I pointed out in my email to Hovakimian that the subpoenas
they were contesting were not even addressed to the president!
They went to Mazars USA, his accountants, which had no standing
to raise any constitutional issue. Was DOJ really suggesting that
not only couldn't you investigate a president, but you also had to
draw a big circle around his vendors and associates and leave them
alone, too?

The phone call with Rosen was tense. First of all, there were
quite a few people involved. He was in his office with Hovakimian
and a couple of others. I was huddled with Audrey Strauss, Ilan
Graff, Ted Diskant, and John McEnany, the ethics guru in our office. McEnany later joked that I was using him as a human shield,
which was not altogether inaccurate.

I shudder to think of the tax dollars that were expended on this
idiotic and ultimately fruitless quest to put Trump beyond the reach
of investigation. Finally, I said to Rosen, "Sir, if you put our name on
that brief, I will be compelled to send a letter to the court explaining
that we do not subscribe to its views."

That would have represented a huge and public blowup. The
media would have portrayed it as an open rebellion by the Southern
District.

"Your name will be off the brief," Rosen finally said.

It was and remains a mystery to me what qualified Rosen to oc-
cupy the second most powerful position at the Department of

Justice. He had never been a prosecutor and never worked in any capacity at DOJ. Rosen previously worked in the Office of Management and Budget. Directly before Barr brought him over to DOJ, he was the deputy secretary of transportation, a role in which he was credited with leading the Trump administration's initiative to scale back regulations that limited tailpipe emissions in new cars.

The reason I assumed Barr was calling the shots on *Trump v. Vance* was that Rosen had no background for any of it—not the legal issues involved or the norms on how the Southern District would deal with Main Justice.

After they relented and my name came off the brief, I was summoned to meet with Rosen in DC. It was a ritual dressing-down.

Rosen told me that he backed down only because of the urgency to get the amicus brief filed. He didn't have the time to keep fighting with us. But in the future, he said, he expected the Southern District to follow orders and sign whatever he put in front of us.

I fell back on my strategy of de-escalation—of being respectful without actually committing to anything. I heard Rosen out and then emphasized the long history of constructive partnership between my office and Main Justice.

Trump v. Vance had presented a unique set of circumstances, I said. What are the odds of them recurring? Why would we ever have this kind of disagreement again?

Rosen was clearly dissatisfied with my response, but that's how I left him.

TRUMP'S LAWYERS NEXT took their fight to the Court of Appeals for the Second Circuit, which had before it the Trump petition as well as the amicus brief that was filed and signed by Main Justice. (And not by us.) Less than a month after my meeting with Rosen, a three-judge panel unanimously ruled against the president.

The salient point in their decision was the one I expressed to Hovakimian: the subpoenas were addressed not to Trump but to an accounting firm, which could not possibly be construed as having some special constitutional protections.

His legal team then appealed to the Supreme Court. In explaining why this was necessary, one of Trump's attorneys, Jay Sekulow, framed the president's beef with a local district attorney in near-apocalyptic terms. "The issue raised in this case goes to the heart of our republic," he said.

In July 2020, the Supreme Court, in a 7–2 decision, ruled against Trump. "[N]o citizen, not even the President, is categorically above the common duty to produce evidence when called upon in a criminal proceeding," Chief Justice John Roberts wrote for the majority.

The court cited as precedent the 1807 treason trial of Aaron Burr, "the greatest spectacle in the short history of the republic," as one historian called it. People traveled to Richmond to watch, and some camped out on the banks of the James River.

Burr, three years after killing Alexander Hamilton in their duel, was accused of trying to detach territory along the Allegheny Mountains, then the American West, and set up a separate nation. To bolster his defense, Burr sought letters that had been sent to President Thomas Jefferson by a man named James Wilkinson, his alleged co-conspirator.

The prosecution, said to be "orchestrated" from afar by Jefferson, opposed the request. The judge in the case was John Marshall, the chief justice of the Supreme Court, sitting as the circuit justice of Virginia. After four days of arguments, he ruled that Jefferson had to turn over the correspondence.

What Roberts called the "bookend" to Marshall's ruling came in 1974, when President Richard Nixon tried to resist turning over materials requested by the Watergate special prosecutor, including tape recordings of Oval Office meetings. That, too, was rejected.

Trump's argument, Roberts wrote, was at odds with "200 years of precedent establishing that Presidents, and their official communications, are subject to judicial process."

8

LEV & IGOR

On the evening of October 8, 2019, I was not working, and I definitely should *not* have been working. It was Kol Nidre, the eve of Yom Kippur, and I was at Temple Emanu-El in Manhattan, observing this holiest day on the Jewish calendar, when my phone vibrated at about 7:00 p.m. I took a peek and saw that the call was from the public corruption unit co-chief Russ Capone, who I knew would not contact me on this night unless it was urgent.

Temple Emanu-El, on the Upper East Side, is one of the largest synagogues in the world. For once, I was glad that I was nowhere near the front of its vast sanctuary. I always have the same faraway seats, and this allowed me to leave the synagogue without being noticed and step outside to talk to Russ.

What he told me was that Lev Parnas and Igor Fruman had just bought airline tickets for travel the next day to Frankfurt, Germany—*one-way tickets*—and we had to decide whether to arrest them before they boarded the plane. The decision was not obvious. To arrest them meant that we had to obtain an indictment in less than twenty hours, which required us to finish thinking through the potential charges (campaign finance law violations) that had only recently been presented to us in a prosecution memo, draft and finalize an indictment, and present evidence to the grand jury with sufficient time to answer any questions the grand jury may have and allow for a vote.

Lev and Igor, as pundits came to call them, were émigré businessmen—Parnas was born in Ukraine, Fruman in Belarus—who had somehow ascended into the inner circle of Rudy Giuliani. Out of nowhere, they became players in Republican politics who showed up by the side of prominent party members, including Donald Trump.

In addition, they had traveled with Giuliani to Ukraine and were his confederates on two projects dear to him: trying to dig up dirt on Joe Biden's son Hunter and attempting to get the US ambassador to Ukraine removed.

We were in the midst of an active investigation of Lev and Igor that had developed substantial evidence of their crimes, and had entered their names on a list, kept by the Transportation Security Administration, of people who set off an alarm if they book international travel. We do not automatically arrest these individuals, or prevent them from flying, but we want to know if they plan to leave the country.

Did Lev and Igor know we were looking into their activities? Did they know how far along we were? Were they planning on returning, or was their intention to become fugitives and evade prosecution?

We had no definitive answers to any of these questions. All we knew for sure was that the two of them, both naturalized US citizens, were headed out of the country with no return tickets.

I left the synagogue, went straight back to the apartment, and began making calls to my team. I argued strongly that we arrest them before they could board the flight. I did not want to risk having them elude us.

It was quickly apparent to me that I was in a minority of one. I would describe one call as almost like an intervention. I answered and six people were on the line: Audrey Strauss, the chief of the criminal division, Laura Birger, Chief Counsel Craig Stewart, Ilan Graff, Russ Capone, and Ted Diskant. Every one of them said we should let them travel.

One of the arguments they made was that we did not have the time to draft a proper indictment and get it presented and voted on by a grand jury. Also, Lev and Igor were headed to western Europe, where we could have them arrested and extradited if it came to that.

The more we debated, the later it got.

After one of our group calls, I contacted William Sweeney Jr., the FBI assistant director in charge of the New York office. I needed a sanity test. Was I asking for the unreasonable? The impossible?

Sweeney, a former naval officer, is a big guy, tall and broad shouldered. His judgment is as solid as his stature. We had become close, and I often leaned on him for guidance.

He agreed that we should make the arrests. Why go through the cumbersome steps to get them back to the United States if we had the ability to control the situation and avoid all that? Why take the chance, however slight, that we might lose them altogether? Not every country in Europe makes it easy for us to extradite, and Lev and Igor were clever enough to cross through one of those borders.

I got everyone back on the phone and said, basically, that this is the Southern District and we have the capability to get it done. We have two of the most talented AUSAs in the office on the case—Rebekah Donaleski and Nicolas Roos—and the executive staff to back them up. "Now let's get to work," I said.

Donaleski and Roos came into the office at about 11:00 p.m., and I joined them with coffee I had made at my apartment. (The local coffee shops were closed.) They drafted the indictment through the night, with review and revision by others either in the office or from home. Because the charges included campaign finance violations, we needed sign-off from the career attorneys at Main Justice's Public Integrity Section. Diskant was on the phone with them at 4:00 a.m. and got the approval.

At 7:00 a.m., everyone came into the office for a final edit. At 9:00 a.m., the draft was finished, and Donaleski and Roos went before the grand jury. By 2:00 p.m., they returned an indictment. Time to spare! The speed at which the team worked took my breath away.

Later that day Lev and Igor showed up at Dulles Airport in Northern Virginia for an evening flight. They were early enough to park themselves in the first-class lounge of Lufthansa, where they indulged in free drinks and food. They were wearing T-shirts.

They gave no sign that they had an inkling what was about to happen. When the announcement was made for first-class passengers to board, they got up and began walking down the Jetway. Two law enforcement agents stopped them, checked their passports to confirm their identities, and then led them quietly out a door leading to the tarmac, where they were arrested. The arrest was handled flawlessly by the FBI; there were no cell phone pictures of the arrest by travelers at that busy airport.

The next day, they were arraigned in federal court in Alexandria, Virginia. A magistrate, agreeing that they were flight risks, released them on $1 million bond each and ordered them confined to home detention at their residences in Florida.

THE FOUR YEARS of the Trump administration will not be regarded by future historians as a time of high spirits and levity in America. There were two impeachments, unceasing drama, and a constant swirl of resentment and recrimination on all sides. The president communicated by tweet, a novelty, with his words often coated in rage.

Although there was nothing funny about what Lev and Igor were charged with, it's fair to say that for much of the American public they offered a glimmer of comic relief. Parnas had founded a company called Fraud Guarantee, which is what you would name a business if you intended for it to draw the attention of law enforcement.

The company's purported mission, according to its website, was to "reduce and mitigate fraud" and to serve as a watchdog to "recoup investment or consumer losses resulting from fraud." There's zero evidence it actually did that.

The revelations that followed their arrests—tales of them palling around in eastern Europe, either as a duo or with Rudy Giuliani in tow—seemed like the plot of a buddy movie, albeit a dark one, like something the Coen brothers might make.

Mug shots rarely do a defendant any favors. When the pictures of Lev and Igor were publicized after their arrests, they were still in their T-shirts, with dazed expressions on their faces. They looked like the last two guys you'd expect to find caught up in some high-stakes, international intrigue. But there they were—Lev and Igor—the latest bit players in this surreal narrative.

The case's origins went back to an independent group, the Campaign Legal Center, that monitors political giving. It was founded by Trevor Potter, an attorney and former chairman of the Federal Election Commission. (I got to know Potter a little when I volunteered for the 2008 presidential campaign of the Republican John McCain, in which he served as general counsel.)

In 2018, the Campaign Legal Center took note of a $325,000 contribution from a company called Global Energy Producers to America First Action, which was a political action committee, or so-called super PAC, that supported President Trump.

Global Energy Producers was "a blank slate," Potter would later tell National Public Radio. "The company hadn't existed. It had been formed literally a couple weeks before the contribution. It had no website, no history of political activity, so you're thinking this is most likely a company created to make this contribution."

Potter and his team did some digging and were able to link Global Energy to addresses in New York and Florida associated with Lev and Igor. They identified additional contributions the two had made to a Texas congressman, and reported it all to the Federal Election Commission as suspicious activity.

Our public corruption unit monitors complaints filed with the FEC for possible investigation. Nick Roos read the complaint and persuaded Capone and Diskant to open the investigation. Roos and Donaleski began to put the pieces together. We confirmed that Global Energy was nothing but a shell with no business and no capital investment. Lev and Igor ran foreign money through it for the purpose of contributing to political candidates and committees in the United States.

Part of these donations were to support their plans for a marijuana business. They put together a "multi-state license strategy" that contemplated pouring between $1 million and $2 million in foreign money into the US political system.

I KNOW THAT campaign finance violations are viewed by some as minor offenses, or technical in nature. Someone didn't fill out a form correctly or whatever. But those are not the types of irregularities that attract interest from the Southern District. We were drawn to intentional attempts to game the system and undermine our system of free and fair elections.

What Sweeney said on the day of Lev and Igor's indictment sums it up: "Campaign finance laws exist for a reason. The American people expect and deserve an election process that hasn't been corrupted by the influence of foreign interests, and the public has the right to know the true source of campaign contributions. These allegations aren't about some technicality, a civil violation, or an error on a form. This investigation is about corrupt behavior and deliberate law breaking."

Lev and Igor were not unintelligent. Igor had access to money; Lev was the details person. They had a lot of balls in the air. In both the United States and Europe, their activities were a mix of politics and business, and you couldn't separate the two.

As Potter later told NPR, we went well beyond what he ever imagined his initial tip might reveal: "To go from what . . . was a garden-variety FEC violation in a string of complaints we have filed to suddenly discovering that they were completely wrapped up in the White House actions, the Giuliani actions, what was happening in Ukraine and letters from members of Congress on the firing of the ambassador, is simply a very different scale than we had understood up until then in our work."

There were a couple of prongs to the indictment. The $350,000 contribution from Global Energy was part of a straw donor scheme. The company they created was used as a pass-through to funnel money from a foreign donor—illegal under US law—to the super PAC.

In campaign finance forms required by the FEC, Lev and Igor represented that Global Energy was in the liquefied natural gas business. That might have been an aspiration of theirs, but the company at that point existed only on paper, and it did not have the resources to make large political contributions.

The real source of the money was Andrey Muraviev, a Russian industrialist who was involved in the legal cannabis business they were trying to get licensed in Nevada. Another partner in this would-be venture, Andrey Kukushkin, was indicted with Lev and Igor for campaign finance violations. Muraviev was charged in March 2022 and remains at large.

Muraviev's money was also used to donate to statewide races in Nevada. In addition, Lev and Igor contributed money, also through straw donors, to Pete Sessions, who at the time was a congressman from Texas and chairman of the powerful House Rules Committee. The outreach to Sessions was connected to their effort to get Marie Yovanovitch fired from her post as US ambassador to Ukraine.

The day after Lev met with Sessions at his DC office, he posted a picture of himself with the congressman and captioned it "Hard at work!" On the same day, Sessions sent a letter to Mike Pompeo, the secretary of state, urging that Yovanovitch be dismissed. It said that he had "notice of concrete evidence" that she had "spoken privately and repeatedly about her disdain for the current administration."

Sessions subsequently put out a statement that his request for the ambassador's removal was unrelated to his meeting with Lev, which had focused on the strategic need for Ukraine to be energy independent. The information about Yovanovitch, he said, had come from "several congressional colleagues."

The indictment made reference to this meeting with Sessions. It included an allegation that Lev, at the request of a Ukrainian official, had sought the removal of the US ambassador to Ukraine and had met with a congressman (Sessions) to solicit his support for the removal. We were still exploring whether these allegations might later form the basis of a FARA charge against Lev and others who, through lobbying or media appearances, sought the removal of Yovanovitch at the request of a foreign official without registering as a foreign agent.

It's notable that the political activities of Lev and Igor took place not in secret but largely in daylight. Lev posted a picture of himself with Giuliani after a round of golf.

A week after the arrests, Giuliani acknowledged in an interview with Reuters that he was paid $500,000 for work he did for Fraud Guarantee. He said the fee was for consulting work and legal advice.

Yovanovitch's removal was a major goal of Giuliani's—and of other Trump allies—who believed that she was an obstacle to their efforts to unearth damaging information about the then presidential candidate Joe Biden and his son Hunter. The ambassador was considered an anticorruption advocate, and some Ukrainian officials—including those working with Lev and Igor—wanted her moved aside.

Lev and Igor, emboldened by their high-level connections in the United States, apparently carried themselves with a degree of audaciousness in Ukraine. Dale Perry, an energy executive based in Ukraine, became aware of their campaign against Yovanovitch and notified the US embassy. In an interview with NPR, he said, "I had never seen anybody in any part of the world where I've worked—and I've worked in some 30 different countries—never seen a business person to claim that they could see an ambassador removed."

It was, of course, impossible for me or anyone else to be unaware of how politically charged all of this was. The nation was in the third year of Donald Trump's combustible presidency, and the 2020 election cycle was underway. Two months after the indictment of Lev and Igor, the House of Representatives voted to impeach President Trump.

The first of the two articles of impeachment alleged that the president "solicited the interference of a foreign government" to take actions that would "benefit his reelection, harm the election prospects of a political opponent, and influence the 2020 United States Presidential election to his advantage." The foreign government was Ukraine, and the reference to Trump's being assisted by "his agents within and outside the United States Government" obviously would have to include Lev and Igor.

Impeachment is a political process. We had no role to play in it. All we could do in this case, as in every matter we took on, was to keep our heads down and follow the evidence and the law.

EXCEPT FOR THE CONCERN that we not have a press conference to announce the indictments, Main Justice and Barr did not interfere in the prosecution of Lev and Igor.

My sense, which I cannot know for sure, is that Barr viewed Giuliani as a rival. He was the other lawyer whispering in the president's ear.

Anytime there was a story about Lev and Igor, Rudy's name was in it. They were described as his associates. Or his business partners. After they were taken into custody at Dulles Airport, one headline read, "Rudy Giuliani's Fixers for the Ukraine Caper Just Got Arrested."

To the extent all of this tarnished Rudy, I think Barr was fine with it. But the case had tentacles. It raised other questions and suggested new areas of inquiry. It potentially led to other subjects.

And Barr certainly did involve himself in those potentialities. His goal, I think, was to contain and control whatever else might come of the Lev and Igor case and, more broadly, what came out of Ukraine that could either hurt or help the president.

Barr seemed always eager to be of service to the president—to be, as I said, the most valuable player in his cabinet. So, he wants to manage this situation. He has no way of knowing where it might go—and really, nobody does—but it looks to him as if it has the potential to spiral.

So in January 2020 he came up with a plan. He described this plan he had hatched as "an intake process in the field." That made it sound almost normal. The Department of Justice, in order to deal with the large influx of evidence, was going to employ this tried-and-true method in order to keep it all straight! But in all my years as a prosecutor and defense attorney, I had never heard of "an intake process in the field," and neither had my executive staff or Sweeney.

His plan was to run all Ukraine-related matters, including information that Giuliani was peddling about the Bidens, through two other districts. His choices were Rich Donoghue, the US Attorney for the Eastern District of New York, who sat in Brooklyn; and Scott Brady, the US Attorney for the Western District of Pennsylvania, in Pittsburgh. Donoghue would oversee all Ukraine-related investigations, and Brady would handle the intake of information from Rudy and his lawyer.

This scheme, notably, did not include me or SDNY, which, as the office running the Lev and Igor case, was well versed in all things Ukraine. Barr's implication seemed to be that with such a fire hose of material coming in from Rudy and his lawyer, we needed to spread the work out. And we had to have some kind of traffic cop to keep it all organized and flowing in the right direction—which was to be Brady in Pittsburgh.

All of this, of course, was utter nonsense. If somebody has information about an ongoing case, they typically hire a lawyer and approach the office that's involved. Regardless of the quality or veracity of the material, I wanted to see it. We were the office with the background to determine its value. And we certainly would have had our own questions for Rudy, because he was a close associate of the two guys we just indicted. What's more, our office was only a taxi ride away for Rudy and his lawyer—Pittsburgh was a 350-mile trip for them.

We could have handled whatever information Rudy had. With more than two hundred fully capable attorneys, I would have found a couple more to throw into the mix if it came to that. But that's not what was driving the attorney general's machinations. I believe it was really an effort by Barr to keep tabs on our continuing Lev and Igor investigation and keep us segregated from potentially helpful leads or admissions being provided by Rudy.

This became immediately clear to me and to Sweeney when we tried to access the information Rudy was providing. Rudy and his lawyer met several times with Main Justice and then with Brady's team in Pittsburgh.

There were FBI reports of those meetings, called 302s, which we wanted to review. So did Sweeney. Sweeney's team asked the agents in Pittsburgh for a copy and was refused. Sweeney called me up, livid.

"Geoff, in all my years with the FBI I have never been refused a 302," he said. "This is a total violation of protocol."

Sweeney asked Jacqueline Maguire, his special agent in charge, to reach out to the acting head of the FBI's office in Pittsburgh, Eugene Kowel, to request the 302s and related information. A few days later Kowel got back to Maguire and repeated what Brady had told him about the 302s: "It's not my job to help the Southern District of New York make a case against Rudy."

Of course, with Sweeney, they were starting up with the wrong guy. He pressed the issue with FBI leadership in DC and was ultimately provided with the 302s and related documents, months after he had initially requested them. He passed them on to us.

In addition, Donoghue, as part of his new role, was given a sensitive Ukraine investigation that I thought should have gone to us. I expressed my concern to Sweeney, who was working with the Eastern District on the case. He reassured me. "Don't worry, I have your back. If there is any information relevant to the Southern District, I will make sure you get it."

There were some press reports that Donoghue was supervising our Lev and Igor investigation. That was not accurate.

Donoghue did call me shortly after he received the appointment from Barr. He wanted to set a day to come to our office and get an overview from our team on our investigation. Instead, I offered to come to his office.

The next day I took the subway a few stops to Brooklyn and had an enjoyable afternoon getting a tour of his office and shooting the breeze. I spent a couple minutes giving Donoghue an overview, and he did not push for more. That was the first and last time I briefed Donoghue on our Ukraine investigations.

I DIDN'T KNOW Brady well, but I considered him a solid guy.

Donoghue and I were geographically closer than any two US attorneys in the nation. The Eastern District office is right across the East River in Brooklyn, no more than a ten-minute subway ride on the 4 or 5 train. In addition to Brooklyn, its territory includes Queens, Staten Island, and Long Island.

Donoghue had served in the US Army's Eighty-second Airborne Division. He was a paratrooper, a military judge, and later a longtime AUSA and criminal division chief in the Eastern District. He worked in the private sector as general counsel for a technology company.

He's a first-rate attorney. But he went along with Barr's machinations, even when that meant interfering in SDNY's cases.

Pittsburgh, no doubt at the direction of Main Justice, was boxing us out. The obvious reason to keep Sweeney out of the loop was that he was working with us.

The episode was one of the crazier things I encountered over the whole course of my tenure, which is really saying something.

ALMOST TWO YEARS after his arrest, Igor pleaded guilty to violating campaign finance laws. In court, he admitted that he and his Russian straw donor, whom he described as "an experienced investor in the cannabis space," gave money in order to help them secure licenses. He admitted that he knew it was against the law to contribute on behalf of a foreign national.

He did not agree to cooperate in prosecutions against anyone else. I think he just decided that he did not want to talk to the extent the Southern District would want him to. Every defendant makes his or her own calculations.

Lev decided to go before a jury and stood trial with a co-defendant, Andrey Kukushkin, in October 2021. (A fourth man involved in the campaign finance and Fraud Guarantee schemes, David Correia, had pleaded guilty previously.)

Lev's defense attorney, Joseph Bondy, argued that his client did not willfully break laws, but was bewildered by the complexities of the campaign finance regulations. "He was in well over his head," Bondy said. "But he had some good ideas."

After describing the scheme to the jury, Aline Flodr, one of the AUSAs on the trial team, said, "That is what secret foreign money infiltrating American elections looks like."

The jury came back with its verdict in five hours. Lev and his co-defendant were convicted on all counts. About five months later, in March 2022, Lev pleaded guilty to deceiving investors in Fraud Guarantee. He was sentenced to twenty months in prison.

I THINK BARR wanted to put the Ukraine probes into the hands of US attorneys whom he knew and trusted more than me. I had already engaged in the long push and pull with him over our involvement in *Trump v. Vance*, which he ran through Rosen but which I knew he was stage-managing. I had confronted him on Halkbank, which I will discuss in detail later in the book, and on our declination of the Kerry case. And going back to the beginning, we clashed in the aftermath of Michael Cohen's guilty plea.

Elements of his post-Cohen maneuvers can be seen as prologue to his attempts to manage the Lev and Igor material. In the Cohen case, he first questioned the basis of it and then raised the possibility that the conviction be reversed. Then, for two months, he put a stop to investigations that grew out of it. Finally, he attempted to put Donoghue of the Eastern District in charge.

That mirrored what was happening after we charged Lev and Igor: Barr sought to carefully manage the fallout.

My strategy to always steer away from huge blowups with Barr had been successful, for the most part. I was able to keep my job and maintain the integrity of the office.

But Barr and I were not close, and I was under no illusions that he liked or trusted me. He no doubt viewed me more as an obstacle than an ally.

The "intake process in the field" nonsense was clearly not driven by his sense that all that Ukraine material would be too much for the Southern District to handle. The only burden we needed lifted from us was the attorney general's improper meddling.

9

THE PARDONED

Much of what occurred during my tenure—and what I regarded as great accomplishments of the office—I believe were marked as demerits by my superiors. And I just kept racking up demerits.

I wouldn't fall into line. Not for various high-placed officials at DOJ who seemed to be taking orders from the White House, or possibly just cues from the president's Twitter account. Not for Whitaker.

And not for Barr, who you'll recall compared junior members of the Department of Justice—meaning everyone junior to him—to Montessori preschoolers. In his mind, I suppose, I was like one of those stubborn kids who would not behave correctly, no matter how many times he tried to corral me.

When we indicted Chris Collins, a Republican congressman from the Buffalo area, in August 2018, after I had been the US attorney for about seven months, that was an early demerit, preceding Barr, though he surely knew of it. It was one of the cases cited when we were later instructed to "even things out" and go after some

Democrats. Remember, this was as the 2018 midterm election was approaching.

Collins was one of the wealthiest members of Congress. The court would later value his assets at more than $13.8 million—including baseball card and coin collections worth more than $1 million each.

His crime—insider trading—was brazen. He served on the board of directors of Innate Immunotherapeutics, an Australian biotech company, and was one of its biggest shareholders. When he learned of a failed clinical trial of a drug in development by the company, he quickly alerted his son, who then dumped stock before the news became public.

Collins got word of the failed trial as he was attending the annual congressional picnic at the White House. He made the call to his son from there. We had a video of him talking on his cell phone at that moment—committing his felony right on the White House lawn.

THE DRUG TRIAL was a high-stakes gamble. Known as MIS416 (I assume it would have gotten a catchier name if it made it to market), the drug was intended as a therapy for multiple sclerosis. Because the company had no other significant products in development, a failure of its trial would amount to a big setback, or even a catastrophe, for Innate.

The company's CEO sent an email to his board members on June 22, 2017, and Collins looked at it on his phone while he was at the picnic. "I have bad news to report," it said. "The top line analysis would pretty clearly indicate 'clinical failure.'"

The trial found no significant differences in outcomes between MIS416 and a placebo. The CEO did not attempt to sugarcoat the disappointing result. "No doubt we want to consider this extremely bad news," he wrote.

Collins tapped out a response: "Wow. Makes no sense. How are these results even possible???"

He then attempted to reach Cameron Collins, his adult son. Over the next four minutes, they traded six missed calls between them. When they finally connected, he told his son about the failed clinical trial.

The congressman had been an evangelist for the company and its multiple sclerosis drug, and several other members of Congress also held stock in it. He owned millions of dollars of Innate stock. But he couldn't sell it. He was already under investigation by the Office of Congressional Ethics in connection with his holdings and his promotion of the company.

His son, however, also had substantial holdings in Innate. Based on the alert from his father, Cameron Collins began unloading stock the next morning. He sold almost 1.4 million shares before Innate publicly released the negative results of the drug trial.

The company's stock predictably tanked, losing more than 90 percent of its value. Cameron Collins, having received the heads-up based on his father's inside information, avoided $570,900 in losses.

Cameron Collins also passed on the information to his fiancée's father, Stephen Zarsky, who also sold his Innate stock before the test results became public. In all, the losses averted by Cameron Collins, Zarsky, and others who were passed along the news of the adverse results totaled $768,000.

One of the tough calls I had to make early in my tenure concerned the timing of the Collins indictment. We had the case ready to be presented to the grand jury by early August, with the midterms still three months away. There had been no leaks in the media. The team presented the issue to me: Do we indict Collins before the election—which would have a significant negative impact on his chances for reelection—or wait to indict until right after the election?

After all, an indictment contains only allegations, and Collins is entitled to a presumption of innocence. Indicting the case before the election could be perceived as an inappropriate political act on the part of our office.

In making the decision to move forward, I relied on the unwritten DOJ sixty-day rule—that you don't indict a case that will materially affect an election within sixty days of that election, absent exigent circumstances. I thought that Collins's constituents deserved to know about our charges, and he had over sixty days to present his side of the story.

On August 8, 2018, Collins, his son, and Zarsky were charged with securities fraud, as well as making false statements to federal agents when the FBI initially questioned them.

"Insider trading" is one of those bloodless terms that may not fully convey the seriousness of the crime. It amounts to gaming the system and cheating regular investors, who are at a disadvantage because they do not have the same information. They're like dupes at a rigged card game.

The fact that Collins was a congressman made it worse. He served on the House Energy and Commerce Committee, which oversees health-care companies. Paul Ryan, then the House Speaker, removed him from the committee after the indictment.

All three defendants initially pleaded not guilty. Chris Collins claimed the charges against him were "meritless." After first saying after the indictment that he would not seek reelection, he reversed course and reentered the race. The team and I watched his news conference live from my office and learned his plans along with the rest of the general public. He ended up winning a fourth term in New York's Twenty-seventh Congressional District.

It can be a little complicated to try a sitting member of Congress. The speech or debate clause in the Constitution gives lawmakers certain protections against having things they say or do during their official duties used against them in criminal or civil actions.

Other lawmakers have tried to use the clause when facing charges, almost always without success, and it certainly did not apply to our case against Collins, because his insider trading was entirely unrelated to his congressional duties. But his lawyers invoked it in a filing with the court, claiming we swept up protected materials during our investigation. It could have delayed the matter for some time. He likely had the right to appeal all the way to the Supreme Court before we could try him.

DAMIAN WILLIAMS WAS THE LEAD prosecutor on the Collins case. I met him for the first time when I became US attorney. He is brilliant, highly analytical, and, by nature, a consensus builder. During the Collins case, I elevated him to co-chief of the securities unit. Scott Hartman, Max Nicholas, and Bob Allen were also on the team and did a great job. They were deftly supervised by the chiefs Telemachus "Tim" Kasulis and Jason Cowley.

With the Collins case potentially delayed by his lawyers' tactical invocation of congressional privilege, our team made a pivotal decision suggested by Damian. They informed the judge that we would like to proceed to trial with the other defendants. This would force Collins to make a choice: confront the evidence against him in court, or bide his time on the sidelines while his son faced the music alone for a crime initiated by his father.

At the end of the day, the congressman could not stand to see his son face trial for something that was largely his fault and for his son to be convicted while he was still avoiding his day in court. Collins dropped his appeal, pleaded guilty late in 2019, and resigned from Congress.

His statement to the court was quite abject. "I regret these actions beyond anything," Collins, who was sixty-nine years old, told the judge, Vernon S. Broderick.

At his sentencing, he said, "People feel sorry for me. They shouldn't. I did what I did, and I violated my core values. . . . What I've done has marked me for life. I stand here today as a disgraced former member of Congress that will have that asterisk by my name."

Judge Broderick sentenced him to twenty-six months in federal prison and levied a fine of $200,000.

STEPHEN BANNON WAS INDICTED two months after I left the job, following an investigation that began when I was the US attorney. Barr knew about it because we filed what is called an urgent report, which is a DOJ requirement for all matters likely to generate wide public interest.

The Bannon case was without doubt another demerit for me. Like Cohen, Bannon had been a Trump insider.

As the chief executive of Trump's 2016 campaign and then, for a time, the chief White House strategist, Bannon was a driving force behind one of the animating features of both the campaign and Trump's presidency—the effort to stop immigrants from crossing into the United States from Mexico.

After leaving the White House, he participated in one of the most cynical criminal schemes I encountered in my time atop SDNY.

Taking advantage of Trump supporters who fervently believed in the cause of building a wall at the southern border—passions that he himself helped inflame—Bannon and three other men raised $25 million from donors in an online fundraising campaign to fund part of it privately.

Bannon and other leaders of the "We Build the Wall" campaign, as alleged in the indictment, told donors they were an entirely volunteer organization and pledged that all the money would go toward construction. Hundreds of thousands of Americans gave money.

Bannon allegedly then created another nonprofit, a shell company, to redirect some of the contributions to himself and the other organizers: Brian Kolfage, a US Air Force veteran of the Iraq War and a triple amputee; Timothy Shea, who according to *The New York Times* once marketed an energy drink as containing "liberal tears"; and Andrew Badolato, whose history included a string of failed businesses and unpaid tax bills.

Kolfage used at least $350,000 of the funds raised by We Build the Wall on home renovations, boat payments, an SUV, a golf cart, jewelry, cosmetic surgery, tax payments, and credit card debt. He pleaded guilty in 2022. Bannon, as alleged, spent hundreds of thousands of We Build the Wall funds on personal expenses.

Maybe it looked different to Barr, but we did not go out of our way to target Trump insiders. The Southern District would never do that. *I* would never do that.

The Bannon case came to us through a "suspicious activity report," or SAR, filed by a bank about the charity. Nick Roos, one of our AUSAs, was surfing SARs and spotted it. He brought it to Capone and Diskant, and we opened an investigation.

Bannon cast himself as a fierce American nationalist and a man of the people. He rarely wore business clothes, despite the high positions he occupied, preferring army-style jackets and the layered look of someone setting off on a hike in the wilderness. His long gray hair fell down to his shoulders, and he usually had a scruffy, two- or three-day beard.

He was arrested on August 20, 2020, when federal agents boarded a $35 million yacht in Long Island Sound that belonged to a friend of his—the Chinese billionaire Guo Wengui, who was a fugitive from China sought by Beijing authorities on corruption allegations. In the United States, three media companies tied to Guo paid $539 million to settle civil charges brought by the Securities and Exchange Commission connected to funds he raised from investors in his companies.

The name of the yacht was the *Lady May*. Bannon was arrested at 7:15 a.m. as he sat on the deck, reading a book.

After being arraigned in New York on charges that included conspiracy to commit wire fraud and money laundering, he was released on $5 million bail, which he secured with $1.75 million in personal assets.

I watched a video clip of him walking out of the courthouse. He stopped at a gaggle of cameras and reporters and gave a brief comment. "This entire fiasco is to stop people who want to build the wall," he said.

He was smiling, or perhaps smirking. He seemed relaxed. He didn't look like a man who was overly concerned with facing a trial and possible prison time.

A PRESIDENT CAN PARDON whomever he wants. It is an unlimited, essentially unreviewable power.

But there is a long-established process through which a person—normally one who has already been convicted, served time, and worked to rehabilitate him- or herself—has their case reviewed by a pardon attorney in the Department of Justice. The US attorney in the district where the person was tried has an opportunity to weigh in.

Trump was not the first president to ignore the process. But it is fair to say he was hyperaggressive in issuing pardons after he lost the 2020 presidential election. He did not appear to put many of the pardons through any discernible process, and the pattern of them certainly fit into the friends-and-enemies paradigm. A professor at Harvard Law School, Jack Goldsmith, examined Trump's pardons and found that 88 percent went to people whom he knew personally or who had furthered his political ambitions.

Three days before Christmas 2020, he pardoned two former Republican congressmen who had been convicted and sentenced to prison on corruption charges, Duncan Hunter of California and Chris Collins, and commuted the prison term of a third, Steve Stockman of Texas.

Collins was the first member of Congress to endorse Trump during the 2016 primary campaign. After the pardon, he said of Trump, "He is one of the most loyal people there has ever been."

A White House statement said Collins had been pardoned at the request of many members of Congress.

Collins had spent all of ten weeks at a minimum-security federal prison in Pensacola, Florida. He told *The Buffalo News* that he had formed deep bonds there with as many as ten inmates who would now be his lifelong friends.

He complained about prison guards who were unduly harsh—"a judge sends you to prison as punishment; he doesn't send you to be further punished by guards"—and said he came away from his short stay with many ideas for prison reform.

TRUMP PARDONED STEVE BANNON on January 20, 2021, just hours before he was to leave office. Notably, Trump did not pardon Bannon's co-defendants, nor did he pardon Collins's son or his son's future father-in-law.

A statement from the White House press secretary, Kayleigh McEnany, stressed Bannon's value as a political operative. "President Trump granted a full pardon to Stephen Bannon," it said. "Prosecutors pursued Mr. Bannon with charges related to fraud stemming from his involvement in a political project. Mr. Bannon has been an important leader in the conservative movement and is known for his political acumen."

It is an outrage that someone's political beliefs or their value as a political operative would figure into a pardon decision. But as I said, the Constitution grants extreme powers to a president on pardons.

Trump used them.

Part Three

PRIORITIES

10

BRINGING JUSTICE TO
SEX TRAFFICKERS

The Southern District brings enormous resources to its mission, enough for me to say with confidence that it is one of the most potent crime-fighting forces in the country and the world. In addition to its 220 prosecutors, it is one of the few US attorney's offices with a sizable staff of in-house special agents, led with distinction by Eric Blachman. Most of those working for us had served previously as NYPD detectives or came over after careers in federal law enforcement. They have a high degree of expertise and complemented our close working relationships with the FBI field office in New York, the DEA, and our other agency partners.

But our assets were not unlimited. We set priorities and made choices.

The office has long been known for its focus on financial crimes, often emanating from Wall Street, and for prosecutions of corrupt public officials. It prosecutes violent crime of all kinds, with special attention given to gang and gun-related violence.

In the last several decades, going back at least to the 1993 bombing of the World Trade Center, the 1998 bombings of the US embassies in Kenya and Tanzania, and the 2000 bombing of the USS *Cole* off the coast of Yemen, international terrorism has been central to the mission of the office. That focus, obviously, became even more intense after the 9/11 attacks.

Among our other priorities, and the subject of this chapter, was sex trafficking. I wanted these cases aggressively pursued because trafficking—especially when the victims are children or vulnerable young adults—is a scourge. It's an assault on our common humanity.

THE JEFFREY EPSTEIN prosecution is the trafficking prosecution best known to the public, but far from the only one we took on. One especially disturbing series of cases involved a sex-trafficking ring where girls, some as young as thirteen years old, were recruited from the child welfare system. Many of the victims lived at Hawthorne Cedar Knolls, a now-shuttered residence and treatment center for at-risk children in Mount Pleasant, Westchester County.

Some of these girls had been placed at Hawthorne after being rescued from the sex trade, and all were struggling with serious problems, including histories of physical and emotional abuse. These vulnerable girls became easy targets for a group of men who recruited them into their prostitution ring and sold them for sex by posting lewd photographs of the girls on Craigslist, Backpage.com, and other internet sites. The perpetrators forced the girls to turn over most of their earnings, and "compensated" them with food, clothing, and drugs.

The prosecutions, sensitive in nature because of the ages and vulnerability of the victims, were handled by the AUSAs Elinor

Tarlow, Mollie Bracewell, and Jacob Gutwillig, all in our general crimes unit, and expertly supervised by the co-chiefs of that unit, Hadassa Waxman and Brian Blais.

In 2018, the FBI's Child Exploitation and Human Trafficking Task Force began looking into numerous reports of missing and runaway children from the Hawthorne facility. Suspecting the girls had been forced into prostitution, they brought the case to our office, and we took it that day.

We learned that some girls were being forced to engage in sex acts between ten and fifteen times each day. We had to move quickly to shut down this sex-trafficking operation, but at the same time ensure that we had the evidence to make charges stick.

The AUSAs scoured social media sites for evidence that the targets were advertising the girls for sex and working together to traffic them. We obtained phone records showing contact between the targets, their victims, their co-conspirators, and the men who were purchasing sex. We identified the locations where the girls were forced to have sex, including abandoned buildings and motel rooms in New York. The whole thing was horrifying.

The team also interviewed young victims who had escaped, an especially challenging and sensitive assignment. These girls were traumatized from the abuse they endured and fearful of the perpetrators. Persuading them to share their stories and cooperate with the investigation took bravery on the part of the victims and empathy and perseverance from the AUSAs.

After a few months of investigation, in December 2018, we charged nineteen men with trafficking more than twenty minor girls and young women, many of whom lived at Hawthorne. Some of the defendants pleaded guilty; others fought the charges.

Hubert Dupigny went to trial. One of his victims described being directed into an abandoned house in Brooklyn to perform sex acts dozens of times a day and later being forced to turn over her earnings to Dupigny and his co-conspirators. Dupigny was convicted and sentenced to twenty-five years' imprisonment.

Another defendant, a man named Luidji Benjamin, advertised a victim by posting a graphic image of her performing oral sex on him. He transported this victim and others to the Bronx, Queens, and Manhattan, where they were made to perform sex acts for money—most of which Benjamin kept. Following a five-day trial, Benjamin was convicted and sentenced to seventeen years in prison.

Sean Merchant, who pleaded guilty to sex-trafficking charges, was sentenced to sixteen years in jail after the judge learned that he had forced three minor girls to have sex with strangers in exchange for money. Merchant took the money and plied the girls with illegal drugs. They became dependent on the drugs—as he intended, so that they could not resist his directions.

The defendants went by nicknames. Benjamin was "Zoe"; Dupigny was "Fox"; others went by "Dizzy" and "Panama." Incredibly, at least two of them were in prison for part of the time these girls were being exploited. They managed to communicate by telephone and text message—including one in which a defendant expressed displeasure that one of the girls had not been working frequently enough.

In the Hawthorne cases, the victims had come to the facility in need of healing. They were already vulnerable, many emotionally troubled, and the defendants sought them out and put them up for sale on the internet. It is hard to imagine more depraved and callous conduct.

THE TRADITIONAL WAY for a US attorney's office to become involved in a case is that it is brought to them by the FBI or another federal agency. Law enforcement agents come across possible criminal conduct through data analysis, an informant, a victim, or various other means and are often already investigating when they approach prosecutors.

We did not always have to wait for that. The Southern District's resources allowed us to be entrepreneurial, to proactively seek new investigations. I have already mentioned that our public corruption unit would scour complaints filed with the FEC. Similarly, our securities unit did not depend on the SEC referring us cases. We regularly reviewed SARs that banks are required to file and looked for what seemed like egregious violations. Or, through the use of sophisticated data analysis, we spotted patterns of possible white-collar criminal activity that invited more digging on our part.

Keep in mind that financial crimes always have victims, and the worst of them ruin people's lives. The reason we pored over those SARs was to make sure we were doing everything possible to identify financial predators. They didn't have to be as big as Bernie Madoff to severely hurt people.

In the realms that it makes priorities, SDNY has the capability to stop some really horrible human behavior. The goal is to bring justice to victims and—just as important—stop perpetrators from finding new ones. We want to get them off the streets before they can wreck more lives.

We investigated by units. Just as the AUSAs involved in prosecuting financial crimes read the reports filed by banks, I asked our supervisors to make sure the AUSAs were keeping their eyes open for anything in the media that might be relevant.

In the fall of 2019, the White House instructed federal agencies not to renew subscriptions to *The New York Times* and *The Washington Post*. The president, to put it mildly, was frequently unhappy with their coverage. His press secretary, Stephanie Grisham, explained that the edict was driven purely by a desire to save the taxpayers money. "Not renewing subscriptions across all federal agencies will be a significant cost saving," she said at the time.

Trump himself was more straightforward about the reason. "We don't even want it in the White House anymore," he said in a Fox News interview, referring to *The New York Times*. "We're going to probably terminate that and *The Washington Post*. They're fake."

Like anyone in public life, I had my occasional beefs with the press, but I certainly never considered it, as Trump said countless times, "the enemy of the people." I know it to be an essential part of our democracy, and paying attention to what was published in the media was an important tool in our work.

I ignored the instruction to cancel media subscriptions. In fact, I *increased* them during my time leading the office.

On April 29, 2019, *New York* magazine published a story under the headline "The Stolen Kids of Sarah Lawrence: What Happened to the Group of Bright College Students Who Fell Under the Sway of a Classmate's Father?"

I read this story. Others in our office read it. It was insane.

It's a normal reaction after reading a story about someone's venal behavior to ask, why is this person not charged with something? The difference, in our case, is we could do something about it.

As the article explained, Lawrence Ray worked on Wall Street in the 1980s. He co-owned a nightclub in Scotch Plains, New Jersey, and had worked in the insurance, construction, and gambling industries. He had a gift for bringing others into his circle, and not just college students. In fact, when he was riding high in the 1980s and 1990s, Ray was something of a Zelig-like figure around New York.

In 1997, when Mikhail Gorbachev visited the city, Ray arranged security and transportation for him and acted as a kind of unofficial host. After Gorbachev continued on to Los Angeles, Ray somehow brokered a meeting between the former Soviet leader and Robert De Niro, the actor. (De Niro told *New York* magazine that he found it odd that "this guy" was the person who had arranged it.)

Ray was close enough at one point with Bernard Kerik, New York City's fortieth police commissioner, to be the best man at Kerik's 1998 wedding.

But by 2010, Ray was just out of state prison in New Jersey on charges related to a child custody dispute. He was sleeping on an air mattress in his daughter's room on the campus of Sarah Lawrence, a private liberal arts school in Yonkers, or on a couch in the common room. She was a sophomore; he was fifty years old.

As described in the article, it was a big suite, with nine students in residence. Ray regaled them with tales of his career as a globe-trotting government agent, including his supposed role helping to broker a cease-fire in Kosovo. (There was often at least a shred of truth in Ray's stories; he did, apparently, work for a time for a US intelligence agency in Kosovo.) He talked a lot about the US Marines, though his own military service consisted of all of nineteen days of service in the US Air Force.

At "house meetings" and "family dinners," he lectured on a philosophy he called "Q4P," which stood for "quest for potential"—a prescription for living invented by a friend of his who worked in the Diamond District.

"He did all of our cleaning and definitely took on the dad role in the house in a big way," one of the suitemates said.

Ray lived with this cast of college students over the course of several years—on campus during the academic year and at an apartment in Manhattan during school breaks and holidays. The relationships and his control and abuse continued past their college years, for nearly a full decade. The behaviors described in the rest of the magazine piece are even more horrific.

He instructed two of the residents to have sex together, and either watched or sometimes participated. He once invited a friend (his landlord at the Manhattan apartment) to join them. His self-improvement sessions included interrogating individuals for alleged misdeeds in the residence—he called this being in the "hot seat"—after which they were sometimes made to sign confessions.

Ray had no medical or psychological training, but he diagnosed one roommate with schizophrenia. When one of the boys in the suite was questioning his sexuality, Ray counseled him, "Oh no, you're not gay. I can tell you that for sure." When the boy was still feeling unsure, he ordered him to put on a dress.

He accused this same young man of causing his daughter to miss a law school application deadline, and as punishment Ray "crushed pieces of aluminum foil into little balls and rolled them up inside a string of Saran Wrap, fashioning . . . a 'necklace' of metal lumps." He ordered the boy to "wrap the contraption around his testicles and penis, then Larry began twisting it."

There was, as reported in the article, an insidious financial aspect to Ray's predation. He accused his young roommates of causing damage at the apartment in Manhattan and demanded that their parents repay it. An itemized list that one of them sent in an email, under the subject line "Prices of Your Things I Damaged/Ruined," included more than fifty items and a bottom line of $47,726.79.

The victim threatened suicide if his parents did not come up with the money. The family paid Ray, though not the whole amount.

After their college years (some graduated; others did not), several of the suitemates traveled with Ray to his stepfather's house in Pinehurst, North Carolina, where they worked installing a drainage system in the yard. He claimed they had done damage there as well.

One family said they paid him more than $200,000. Another victim went to work as an escort, at an advertised price of $8,000 a night, and gave proceeds to Ray to compensate for the alleged property damage.

WHEN I READ THIS STORY, I had to wonder what the college's administrators were thinking for this to have been happening right on campus. It's a very small college, smaller than many high schools, with an enrollment of about thirteen hundred students.

How do you have a father living in a suite—a guy just out of jail—and nobody knows about it? It made no sense to me. The story included a statement from Sarah Lawrence that it "had no record that Larry Ray lived on campus at any time."

The one thing you can't ever do is look at these kinds of situations and blame the victims or question their judgment. The kids who fell under Lawrence Ray's control might have been more privileged than the girls from Hawthorne, but they were vulnerable in their own way and, in fact, were at that stage of life when some young people are especially at risk of being manipulated by a powerful adult.

Ray's high-end friendships around New York were testimony to his gifts as a con man. That he could get inside the heads of young adults, who had much less life experience, is not surprising.

By the time he ended up at Sarah Lawrence, he had burned through most of his old associations, including his friendship with Kerik, who was appointed police commissioner by the then New York City mayor, Rudy Giuliani, in 2000. Kerik was convicted in 2009 on felony tax charges and served more than three years in federal prison (he was later pardoned by President Trump). Ray was a cooperating witness in the investigation.

Kerik was quoted in the *New York* magazine story. "Larry Ray is a psychotic con man who has victimized every friend he's ever had," he said. "It's been close to 20 years since I last heard from him, yet his reign of terror continues."

The case was assigned to our violent and organized crime unit and investigated by the AUSAs Danielle Sassoon, Mollie Bracewell, and Lindsey Keenan, under the supervision of the co-chiefs Michael Gerber and Lauren Schorr Potter. We charged Ray on February 11, 2020, just short of a year after the article appeared in *New York* magazine. He was taken into custody at his home in Piscataway, New Jersey.

What we found in the course of our investigation went well beyond the initial magazine piece, and it was staggering and horrifying. According to the indictment, Ray's tactics in his "therapy" sessions included sleep deprivation, psychological and sexual humiliation, verbal abuse, and physical violence. He falsely accused a male victim of wrongdoing and placed a knife at his throat until he confessed. He

grabbed another young man around the neck until he fell uncon-
scious.

False allegations that the victims had damaged his properties or
possessions were at the heart of his schemes. In total, Ray was
charged with extorting at least five victims—for a total of approximately $1 million.

"The victims resorted to various measures to repay their supposed debts to Ray," the indictment states, "including draining their
parents' savings in the amount of hundreds of thousands of dollars,
opening lines of credit, soliciting contributions from acquaintances,
selling real estate ownership, and at Ray's direction, performing unpaid labor for Ray and earning money through prostitution."

For at least four years, one of the former Sarah Lawrence students worked as a prostitute at Ray's direction. He collected more
than $500,000 from her—the majority of her proceeds.

He was physically violent with this young woman, identified as
Female Victim-1 in the indictment. He saved explicit photos he had
taken of her and used them as coercion and constantly pressured her
to see a higher volume of clients in order to repay him the money he
falsely claimed he was owed.

WE TEAMED ON the Ray matter, as we did in so many others, with
the New York FBI. That combination added up to an extremely powerful crime-fighting engine. The third partner in the case, lending its
own formidable investigative capabilities, was the NYPD.

Ray was charged with multiple felony counts, including sex trafficking, extortion, and forced labor. When we announced the indictment, I focused on the particular stage of life these victims were in

when he chose to prey on them: "For so many of us and our children, college is supposed to be a time of self-discovery and newfound independence, a chance to explore and learn, all within the safety of a college community. Mr. Ray exploited that vulnerable time in these victims' lives through a course of conduct that shocks the conscience."

Ray's trial lasted nearly a month and several of his victims bravely testified. Danielle Sassoon told jurors, "He never thought they would have the courage to take the stand. To face the abuser they had been taught to revere and trained to fear."

After less than a day of deliberations, the jury convicted Ray on all counts. He faces possible life imprisonment.

His actions destroyed the lives of several young men and women. We cannot get his victims those years back, but we were able to take their tormentor off the street and, hopefully, give these young people a certain amount of closure, justice, and a path forward.

11

NYGARD

Peter Nygard, who is now eighty-one years old, loomed as a major figure in the fashion world for a quarter century. A native of Finland and a citizen of Canada, he founded a manufacturing, design, and retail empire, the Nygard Group, that had offices in Canada, New York, and California and big stores in Times Square and Brooklyn. The exterior of the Times Square store featured a massive billboard of Nygard posed in a tight short-sleeved shirt unbuttoned halfway down his chest. His gray hair is falling down to his shoulders, and his arms, crossed in front of his chest, glisten and appear weirdly muscled for a man of his age.

Nygard, an anti-aging enthusiast, was often seen with women a fraction of his age. He described his young companions as "the source of youth." His fortune in 2014 was estimated at $750 million. He reportedly has ten children with eight different women.

He owned a luxury estate in the Bahamas, a Mayan-themed site with massive sculptures of lions and other predators that he referred to as the eighth wonder of the world. Among its features was a so-called human aquarium where topless women swam in mermaid tails.

He held regular Sunday afternoon events at this property, big gatherings that he called "pamper parties," where underage girls and young women were offered free massages, manicures, and a steady stream of drugs and alcohol. Access was controlled; the women could not leave without Nygard's approval.

The actress Jessica Alba, who attended one of these affairs while on location filming a movie in the Bahamas, was later quoted as calling it a "gross" experience. "These girls are like fourteen years old in the Jacuzzi, taking off their clothes," she said.

A former personal assistant of Nygard's would later say that the girls were recruited in the Bahamas from shops, clubs, and restaurants and that Nygard, at one point, implored him to find poor girls who would be totally beholden to him. "One time, he was like: 'I don't know where you find these girls from, but there's pretty girls in the ghetto as well. You need to find pretty girls in need.'"

Nygard had faced allegations of sexual improprieties in the past, going back many decades. He was charged by police in Winnipeg in 1968, and again in 1980, but in both instances the women declined to testify. The FBI looked into allegations of sex trafficking in 2015 and 2017.

In February 2020, ten women filed a federal class-action suit in the Southern District against Nygard. (The list of plaintiffs has since grown to at least eighty.) It alleged that he "recruited, lured, and enticed young, impressionable, and often impoverished children and women, with cash payments and false promises of lucrative modeling opportunities to assault, rape, and sodomize them."

(Several months later, two of his sons filed their own lawsuit. It charged that their father had arranged for one of the women he

controlled to rape them when they were underage, fourteen and fifteen, respectively, in order to "make a man" out of them.)

The allegations contained within the women's lawsuit are ghastly.
The complaint claims that Nygard drugged and then forcibly raped
a fourteen-year-old, paid her $5,000, and turned her into a recruiter
to round up other victims. It alleges that he raped a fifteen-year-old
girl and then raped her fourteen-year-old cousin.

He raped some victims anally. He plied a minor with alcohol,
then instructed her to engage in sexual acts with another underage
girl. He requested a variety of deviant acts, including having girls
defecate on him.

Much of this took place in the Bahamas, where Nygard exerted
power and influence by giving generously to the island's political
leaders—by one account, as much as $5 million in contributions to
the ruling party. Top government leaders attended his "pamper parties," as did Bahamian law enforcement officials.

Nygard also took victims off the island, including to New York
and his apartment on Broadway, which was atop his big retail store.
They traveled in a private jet emblazoned with his name, and he was
said to confiscate their passports after boarding.

My role as US attorney was sometimes to counsel caution if I was
not fully confident that a case was ready. I wanted to know if we really had assembled everything we needed, and if we had considered
every eventuality—including arguments the defense would make—
before moving on to next steps. This could mean slowing things
down a little.

But there were other times when I wanted us to move more aggressively, and the Nygard case was one of them. The allegations

against him were horrific, and if the evidence supported them, I did not want him walking free a moment longer than necessary.

It didn't seem as though he had been particularly careful. There were multiple victims willing to talk and dozens or possibly even hundreds of possible witnesses from the so-called pamper parties. Because he traveled across national borders, taking his young victims with him, there had to be enablers (and possible witnesses) involved in his trafficking.

The case had some challenges, but they were not insurmountable. One was that the Bahamian authorities were not making it easy on us. They were neither quick nor thorough when we sought information or assistance. But we had faced more determined obstruction and, along with our FBI partners, knew how to work around it.

Another complication was that much of the damaging information about Nygard initially derived from a bitter feud he was engaged in with a neighbor in the Bahamas—a hedge fund billionaire named Louis Bacon. A common driveway connected the men before forking off to their respective luxury estates.

In 2009, a fire on Nygard's property, apparently caused by an electrical issue, destroyed several cabanas, a disco, and an area he called the "grand hall." When the government refused to let him rebuild, Nygard blamed Bacon, who had previously accused him of illegally mining sand to create a new beachfront.

From the time of the fire, Nygard and Bacon traded charges and countercharges. They spent what was reported as tens of millions of dollars and filed at least twenty-five lawsuits in five different jurisdictions. (They could well afford it. Bacon, chief executive of Moore Capital Management, was even wealthier than Nygard, with a reported net worth of $1.8 billion.)

Nygard accused Bacon of being an insider trader, a murderer, and, for good measure, a member of the Ku Klux Klan.

Bacon went to Bahamian authorities—and to numerous law enforcement agencies and media outlets in the United States—with information about the parties next door, the underage girls, and his neighbor's sex trafficking. He also alleged that Nygard was plotting to kill him.

We had to view skeptically any information that originated with Bacon. He had hired teams of investigators and lawyers to look into Nygard, and there were reports they had offered Nygard's associates incentives to help them, including money and jewelry.

But it's not as if confirming information were a new thing. We don't charge people based on media accounts or on dirt dug up by their enemies. We do our own work. This was no different in that regard.

The co-chiefs of our violent and organized crime unit, Lauren Schorr Potter and Michael Gerber, were overseeing the Nygard investigation, which was being run by three AUSAs, Jacqueline Kelly, Allison Nichols, and Celia Cohen. In October 2019, I called them in and asked them to move ahead as quickly as possible. "Devote the resources you need to it," I emphasized.

The investigation kicked into an even higher gear. In February 2020, we learned that Nygard was traveling into the United States for a few days on business. At that point, we were not yet ready to indict, but we did have probable cause for a search warrant. Our plan was to take his phone (with a warrant authorizing us to do so) and image it. We would also seize computers from his offices.

Two days before Nygard was to arrive in the country, I got word from James Margolin and Nicholas Biase in our press office that *The New York Times* was about to publish a story about Nygard and an ongoing federal sex-trafficking investigation. We feared that if the

Times published its story, Nygard would never travel to the United States and we would lose our opportunity to seize and mirror his phone. Also, he might instruct employees at his store to destroy records before the search warrant could be executed. After discussing our options with the team and the executive staff, I felt that I had no choice: I would need to request the newspaper to hold the story. I asked Jim and Nick to give the editors at the *Times* my number. I was at dinner on the second floor of a restaurant when my phone rang. I walked down the stairs and out to the sidewalk to have a telephone conversation with two editors at the paper.

I said, "Look, please don't run this story yet. Just hold it for a week. I can't tell you why, but it will endanger an investigation."

We talked for about five minutes. Without my having to say so, I'm sure they understood the stakes. We also knew that the final decision was theirs to make.

It was the only time I ever made that kind of request to a media organization. I think it's important to say that I was not asking them to kill a story. (Not that they would have.) I just asked them for time to let us do our jobs, and they agreed. Nevertheless, I felt uncomfortable making the ask but grateful that they agreed.

On February 25, 2020, FBI agents and New York police officers raided Nygard's Manhattan headquarters. The night before, federal agents and local law enforcement conducted a raid at his Los Angeles offices and also confiscated his phone.

Within twenty-four hours, Nygard announced that he would step down as chairman and divest his ownership in the company. Less than a month later, the privately held company filed for bankruptcy in both Canada and the United States.

Nygard had put it all at risk, but plenty of others paid a price as well. The company, according to *The Wall Street Journal,* operated 170 of its own stores in North America. It had 1,450 employees.

WE STILL HAD WORK to do: the painstaking examination of everything seized in those raids; finding witnesses and interviewing them; placing their accounts in the context of other evidence; a careful look at the relevant statutes to see what Nygard should be charged with.

On December 15, 2020, about nine and a half months after the raids on his offices, Nygard was indicted in the Southern District. The charges included sex trafficking of minors, money laundering, racketeering, and obstruction of justice.

One of the most stunning and disturbing aspects of what we learned about Nygard was the span of time over which his offenses took place: a full quarter century, from 1995 to 2020.

The indictment in the Southern District characterized the pamper parties as "victim recruitment events" where Nygard drugged and assaulted young girls. Many were lured by the ruse of obtaining jobs in the fashion industry.

When they arrived, they were screened to make sure their physical appearance would appeal to Nygard. If they met his standards, they were photographed and entered into a register that documented their names, contact information, weights, and physical measurements. Once inside, security prevented them from leaving without permission.

Those who fell into his web—traveling with him and recruiting other victims—he referred to as "girlfriends." He controlled them through threats, promises, and constant surveillance. When corporate funds were paid to them, it was noted on corporate accounts as payments to models, personal assistants, or "ComCor" employees, Nygard Group shorthand for those who worked in communications.

The system of abuse was elaborate and involved Nygard's friends, corporate employees, and business associates. According to the indictment, Nygard and others, including employees of the Nygard Group, used "force, fraud, and coercion to cause women to engage in commercial sex with Nygard and others, and to remain with Nygard against their will."

He was charged with racketeering because his corporation was so closely intertwined with his criminal pursuits. He enlisted his employees to intimidate possible witnesses who could reveal his sex trafficking by threatening to have them arrested and jailed in the Bahamas and vowing to sue them or smear their reputations.

We identified at least a dozen victims, including minors. Many came from disadvantaged backgrounds or had a history of being abused—or, in several cases, both.

Some were forcibly raped by Nygard or given cocaine, ecstasy, and other drugs and then assaulted. His friends and associates victimized them in the same manner. Some who resisted were beaten by Nygard or his friends.

Some of those who traveled with him accompanied him to swingers clubs in New York, Miami, Los Angeles, and Winnipeg, where he basically used them as trading chips—engaging in "swaps" with other men.

They also were expected to recruit new sexual partners for Nygard, approaching young women in Times Square and shops in Los Angeles and bringing them back to him.

By the time the office brought the charges in December 2020, I had been fired.

He was arrested in Winnipeg at the SDNY's request, by the

Royal Canadian Mounted Police. I was, to say the least, very pleased on the day that he was taken into custody.

Ten months after the SDNY charges, Toronto authorities charged Nygard with sexual assault and forcible confinement of numerous women in six different incidents between 1987 and 2006. About five months after that, in March 2022, Quebec also brought charges against Nygard. As I write this, he is awaiting trials in Canada and the SDNY.

12

EPSTEIN

The Epstein saga begins a long time before I took the helm at SDNY. Born and raised in Brooklyn, Jeffrey Epstein taught mathematics and physics at a private school as a young man before landing a position in finance, at Bear Stearns. He was fired from both of those jobs: at the tony Dalton School, in Manhattan, where he was said to walk the halls in a fur coat and gold chains, for poor performance; and at Bear Stearns, for running afoul of securities regulations.

These may not seem like the building blocks of grand success, but from there Epstein took off on his ascent to the top of Manhattan society. He began to privately manage the money of extremely high-wealth individuals, even without having distinguished himself on Wall Street. He squired beautiful and very young women around town, which was noticed, admired, and even envied. "He comes with cash to burn, a fleet of airplanes, and a keen eye for the ladies," a 2002 profile of Epstein in *New York* magazine said. The story was headlined "Jeffrey Epstein: International Moneyman of Mystery."

Epstein lived in a nine-story mansion at 9 East Seventy-first

Street, the Herbert N. Straus House, built by an heir of the Macy's fortune. It was said to be the largest private residence in Manhattan. He owned a seventy-five-hundred-acre ranch in New Mexico, a home in Palm Beach, Florida, a Paris apartment, and an entire seventy-acre island, Little St. James, in the Virgin Islands.

His circle of friends and associates included politicians, billionaires, academics, Nobel Prize winners, and royalty. He pledged tens of millions of dollars to create the Epstein Program for Mathematical Biology and Evolutionary Dynamics at Harvard.

The odd thing was, nobody seemed to know where his money or connections came from. It wasn't from his parents. Epstein grew up middle class in Coney Island. His mother was a school aide, his father a gardener for New York's Department of Parks and Recreation.

Despite his purported genius at investing and managing the money of billionaires, he was virtually unknown to others who dealt at *that* level. "The trading desks don't seem to know him. It's unusual for animals *that* big not to leave any footprints in the snow," a Wall Street insider told *Vanity Fair* for a 2003 story.

The *Vanity Fair* piece was more knowing than most of the Epstein press coverage, and its author, Vicky Ward, foreshadowed some of what we would later learn. It noted that Epstein's "best friend," Ghislaine Maxwell, organized his life and arranged parties at his home where the women greatly outnumbered the men, were far younger, and were not the types "you'd see at Upper East Side dinners." A cocktail party at his residence, populated with Russian models, was attended by Prince Andrew.

His more sedate social events went this way: "Guests are invited to lunch or dinner at the town house—Epstein usually refers to the former as 'tea,' since he likes to eat bite-size morsels and drink copious quantities of Earl Grey. (He does not touch alcohol or tobacco.)

Tea is served in the 'leather room,' so called because of the cordovan-colored fabric on the walls. The chairs are covered in a leopard print, and on the wall hangs a huge, Oriental fantasy of a woman holding an opium pipe and caressing a snarling lionskin. Under her gaze, plates of finger sandwiches are delivered to Epstein and guests by the menservants in white gloves."

What you see in the paragraph above, and in Epstein's grandiosity, is a mirror of Peter Nygard. Of Lawrence Ray. He might have been a little more refined, but he shared their instinct for cruelty and control.

With sexual predators, it is the same story over and over again. One of Epstein's victims would say years later, "Jeffrey preyed on girls who were in a bad way, girls who were basically homeless. He went after girls who he thought no one would listen to and he was right."

"Geoff, got a minute?"

I looked up.

Lisa Zornberg, chief of the SDNY criminal division, was standing at the doorway of my office. Behind her, waiting in the anteroom, were Capone and Diskant from the public corruption unit.

"Russ and Ted have something really important they'd like to discuss," said Zornberg.

"Sure," I said. "What's going on?"

They walked in and took seats. Capone spoke first.

"Geoff, have you been reading the *Miami Herald* articles on Jeffrey Epstein?" Capone asked.

Much of what we now know about Epstein began with the investigative reporting of Julie Brown, a veteran journalist with the *Miami Herald* who dug beneath the lore—the inventories of the gilded properties and fancy friends—and unearthed the ugliness at the core of it all.

I had read the stories. And they were shocking. Not just the crimes that were vividly described, but the shameful role that the then US Attorney for Miami, Alexander Acosta, had played in approving, for Epstein, the sweetheart of all sweetheart deals. It was a "non-prosecution" agreement—negotiated in secret with Epstein's powerful legal team.

We began strategizing how to put the full weight of SDNY behind his prosecution. But Acosta's decisions from a dozen years earlier greatly complicated our mission. Could we make a case against Epstein, or would the deal he cut with Acosta stop us?

As we started on our work, there was another factor on the periphery of the case. Acosta was now part of Trump's cabinet—his secretary of labor—and a rising star in the Republican Party. Was the Epstein matter something the Trump administration, or Main Justice, would have preferred we stay away from? I did not know the answer to that then—or even now. I also didn't care.

JULIE BROWN UNCOVERED an enormous trove of public records, and she interviewed Epstein's victims, at least eighty of them—"a revolving door of middle and high school girls" coming into his gated Palm Beach compound throughout the day and night.

The local police, and later the FBI in South Florida, had done the right things. In 2005, a fourteen-year-old girl reported that a friend and high school classmate at Royal Palm Beach High School had taken her to a mansion in Palm Beach in order to give the resident a massage in exchange for money. The homeowner was Epstein, who molested her.

Palm Beach police did what's known as a "trash pull," which is exactly what it sounds like. With a warrant, they sifted through Epstein's outdoor bins and found a telephone message for Epstein with the girl's name on it—a time that matched when she told the police she was there—and the names and phone numbers of other girls on scraps of paper.

That was the beginning of it all. Police interviewed multiple possible victims, Epstein's assistant, and his butler. It should have been obvious that this was a sprawling case. Witnesses and victims in a civil case brought against Epstein two years later would testify that there were hundreds of girls brought to his homes—some of them local, and others from Europe and Latin America. The evidence was out there for any prosecutor determined to go after it.

In June 2006, the local state attorney brought the case to a grand jury. He presented just one witness. One.

It was at this point, under pressure from the Palm Beach police, that the FBI became involved. Michael Reiter, then the Palm Beach police chief, said, "This was not a 'he said, she said' situation. This was a 50-something 'shes' and one 'he'—and the 'shes' all basically told the same story."

FBI agents expanded the investigation nationwide, interviewing victims and witnesses in Florida, New York, and New Mexico. By mid-2007, a fifty-three-page indictment was prepared and ready to go. This was when plea negotiations with Epstein's legal team began, with Acosta directly involved.

One morning in October 2007, he met with one of Epstein's lawyers, Jay Lefkowitz, according to the *Herald*. The meeting took place at a Marriott in West Palm Beach, about seventy miles north of Acosta's office.

This meeting in and of itself was highly unusual. We have a saying in the Southern District: the eagle does *not* fly. If there is a meeting on a case with the US attorney or the executive staff, it takes place at our offices. What was Acosta doing traveling to a Marriott? What was the meeting about?

If Epstein was tried and convicted on the charges in the federal indictment that had been drafted, he could have spent the rest of his life in prison. Acosta's office agreed to a deal: Epstein would plead guilty to state—not federal—charges. He would serve a sentence of thirteen months in the county jail.

This non-prosecution agreement was a gift not just to Epstein but also to his powerful friends and associates. As the *Herald* wrote, "The pact required Epstein to plead guilty to two prostitution charges in state court. Epstein and four of his accomplices named in the agreement received immunity from all federal criminal charges. But even more unusual, the deal included wording that granted immunity to 'any potential co-conspirators' who were also involved in Epstein's crimes. These accomplices or participants were not identified in the agreement, leaving it open to interpretation whether it possibly referred to other influential people who were having sex with underage girls at Epstein's various homes or on his plane."

As if all that weren't bad enough, Acosta agreed to keep the non-prosecution agreement secret. It was sealed. That meant that the victims could not come to court to oppose it for the simple reason that they had no idea it was taking place.

Even now, it is mind-boggling—and enraging—to look back on the seven-page document. If I had to pick out the most stunning passage, it might be this one: "The parties anticipate that this agreement will not be made part of any public record. If the United States receives a Freedom of Information Act request or any compulsory process commanding the disclosure of the agreement, it will provide notice to Epstein before making that disclosure." .

Epstein was a pedophile! This was a known fact to the person or persons who authorized the federal government to make this agreement. Nothing—nothing whatsoever—entitled him to be shown such deference.

Epstein's time in jail at the low-security Palm Beach County Stockade jail was an absolute joke. Most people know the phrase "doing hard time." If there's such a thing as extra-soft time, his confinement was the definition of it.

He had his own television in his unlocked cell. He was on "work release" almost immediately. At 8:00 a.m., his personal driver picked him up and drove him to the offices of a nonprofit foundation he had just established—the Florida Science Foundation—and returned him at 8:00 p.m. The privileges were part of a handwritten addendum to the non-prosecution agreement. (He would dissolve the foundation soon after his release from jail.)

A deputy accompanied Epstein when he was away from the stockade. He was required to wear a suit rather than a sheriff's uniform and drive an unmarked car. Epstein reimbursed the sheriff's office $128,136 for the deputies' time.

The deputies referred to Epstein as a "client." In one report, it was noted that he was "very happy" with the service he was being provided.

The chief deputy in the sheriff's office later explained the reasons for Epstein's treatment. "The precautions were because of his extreme wealth, his notoriety," he said. "His legal staff that he had was enormous."

After his thirteen-month stint in jail, Epstein served a year of house arrest in Palm Beach, which also included unusual privileges—frequent trips to New York, ostensibly to visit his lawyers, and getaways, via his private jet, to his private island in the Virgin Islands that were said to be for business.

ON THE DAY my team came to talk to me about Epstein, he had been out of jail for a decade, living again in polite society with a coterie of powerful friends. Epstein called himself a "science philanthropist" and spent time with leading academics across the country. He was still a free man. He still had his properties and his fleet of aircraft.

We felt a great sense of urgency. The SDNY investigation of Epstein was opened in December 2018, not long after the first of the *Miami Herald*'s investigative pieces appeared.

In any criminal case, you have to think several steps down the road. A strategy goes hand in hand with the investigation. How are we going to do this? In what order? Where are we potentially vulnerable, and how do we shore that up?

These questions were especially important with Epstein because of the set of issues raised by the non-prosecution deal. We did not have the power to reverse it. We had to make our own case and essentially build a wall around it.

We agreed that our case should not be a rehashing of the Florida investigation. It should focus on assaults committed at the New York mansion, and we should try to find New York victims who were not interviewed in the prior investigation. While the non-prosecution agreement did not bind the SDNY, because we did not sign it, the Miami US Attorney's Office was bound by it. If our case was somehow perceived to be a handoff from the Florida prosecutors or a carbon copy of that investigation, it might be thrown out. The last thing we wanted was to make a mistake and give Epstein another get-out-of-jail-free card. Thus, we agreed there would be no coordination with the Florida prosecutors.

There was another big issue to deal with at the outset: the rationale and basis of the Florida non-prosecution agreement. These were sensitive conversations, and not just because the guy who led the office in Florida was a member of Trump's cabinet. Even beyond that, it is highly unusual for one US attorney's office to investigate the actions of another. But, initially, we had to keep our minds open because it was such an inexplicable resolution. If there was potential criminality involved in it, we couldn't shut the door.

What we found out, rather quickly, was that the statute of limitations on any potential corruption charges related to the non-prosecution agreement had long since expired. The non-prosecution agreement was signed in 2007, more than a decade earlier. There wasn't much we could do. But at the urging of a Republican senator, Ben Sasse of Nebraska, the Justice Department's Office of Professional Responsibility did launch an ethics probe related to the deal.

Early on, Michael Osborn, the New York FBI's assistant special agent in charge of violent crime and the head of the branch overseeing the Epstein investigation, made contact with his FBI counterparts in Miami. He told them that we were not in favor of a joint investigation but we did hope for their full cooperation. They were willing, of course, but also skeptical, and I couldn't blame them.

They felt burned by the deal cut with Epstein in 2007. In the years since, some under-the-radar efforts to bring him to justice had produced nothing. The Miami FBI agent told Osborn, basically, we've been down this road before, and nothing has happened.

Osborn replied, "This is the SDNY. This time around, something will happen."

WE KEPT THE INVESTIGATION CLOSE. It had to be done quietly because we couldn't give the heads-up to Epstein or anyone connected to him. He had the means to flee the country, the intelligence to do so in such a way that could make it difficult to get him back, and a level of resources that could buy him a great deal of protection. The prospect of his settling comfortably in some nation not given to extraditing suspects back to the United States was a legitimate concern.

We brought in the AUSAs Alexander Rossmiller, Alison Moe, and Maurene Comey to investigate the case, and they were assisted by Abigail Kurland, the co-coordinator of SDNY's human-trafficking program.

Everyone got the same instruction: nothing about this case can be spoken of outside the office, and any discussions internally should be on a need-to-know basis.

I never briefed Barr on the investigation. The charges we were seeking did not need Main Justice approval, and I couldn't think of any way in which he would be of help. Keeping him out of the loop also meant that if he had any concerns or objections, we didn't have to deal with them.

The parameters emerged quickly: build an airtight, New York–focused case so that Epstein's powerful defense team could not claim we were violating the Florida deal.

Over the next weeks and months, a team of FBI agents, NYPD detectives, and our prosecutors scrambled to make that happen. This meant that they identified victims, interviewed them, and went about the sensitive task of getting them to agree to testify in open court against their tormentor. Without the voices of these young women—girls when Epstein raped them—there was not a case.

That our team accomplished these tasks without word leaking to Epstein or his lawyers that he was under investigation is a testament to their intelligence and deftness.

The New York victim in the Epstein indictment that we would ultimately file has never been identified in court. In the indictment, she was described only as "Minor Victim 1." Before we sat down with her, we had no idea what she would say.

But her full story—revealed publicly in the "Jane Doe" lawsuit that her attorney, Roberta Kaplan, brought against Epstein's estate on her client's behalf—was shocking and powerful. It mirrored what Epstein's other victims had told the *Miami Herald*—that Epstein operated a pedophilia Ponzi scheme in which underage victims became financially dependent on him and to keep getting paid had to recruit other young women to take their places.

The indictment that was ultimately drawn up described Epstein's mode of exploitation: Victims were recruited to give him massages, which were performed nude or partially nude. The sessions became increasingly sexual in nature. He typically masturbated during the sessions, asked victims to touch him while he did so, or touched the victims' genitals with his hands or sex toys.

That was the pattern, and it was repeated with dozens of girls at his mansion in Manhattan and estates in Palm Beach, the Virgin Islands, and New Mexico. They were minors, some of them as young as fourteen years old, which he knew because they told him their ages.

He paid the girls hundreds of dollars per massage and then paid them to bring him yet more victims. As the indictment stated, "When a victim would recruit another girl for Epstein, he paid both the victim-recruiter and the new victim hundreds of dollars in cash. Through these victim-recruiters, Epstein gained access and was able to abuse dozens of additional minor girls."

Epstein at times recruited these victims himself, but he also had substantial help, including from the person the indictment identified as "Employee-1." That was Ghislaine Maxwell—whom the *Vanity Fair* piece, way back in 2003, identified as the woman "who seems to organize much of his life." The victim-recruiters took direction from Maxwell, who sometimes instructed them to bring a specific girl for Epstein.

It was obvious to Epstein's employees that the girls were under-age. When the local police were investigating his activities at the Palm Beach mansion, one of his butlers described their diet when they were on the premises. "They would eat tons of cereal and drink milk all the time," he said.

Epstein's compulsion was such that when he was in New York, but preparing to travel to Florida, he would ask two other employees to schedule appointments with minor victims for when he arrived.

The pattern there was the same: victims turned into victim-recruiters. Their stories were heartbreaking, each in its own way.

The indictment of Epstein listed three specific minors whom he abused, a small fraction of the total number of victims. We knew that once the indictment became public, more victims would come forward.

But as in all cases, it is the quality, not quantity, of testimony that matters. We already had what we needed to put Epstein away for life.

IN JULY 2019, Epstein was staying at his apartment in Paris. He typically spent much of the spring there, sometimes into the early summer. From our point of view, it was not the ideal place for him to be.

In contrast to other countries in western Europe, France is

problematic when it comes to extraditing criminal defendants to the United States. The most famous example involves the film director Roman Polanski, who fled there in the late 1970s after being charged with raping a thirteen-year-old girl in Los Angeles and has been out of reach of American law enforcement ever since.

Obviously, I wanted to avoid anything like this with Epstein. We had not gotten this far, only to then be in a fight to get him back to face justice.

The FBI analyzed Epstein's travel history and found that he usually returned to the United States around the Fourth of July. To be prepared, we indicted him, under seal, on July 2. We knew that when he flew back, his private jet would always land at Teterboro Airport in New Jersey, and so the FBI quietly coordinated with Customs and Border Protection personnel at the airport and asked that when Epstein's name showed up on a manifest of passengers entering the country, the team immediately be called.

On the night of July 5, a Friday, word came that Epstein was on a manifest for a private jet that was scheduled to land the following day. I was with my family that Saturday visiting my mother on the Jersey Shore when Bill Sweeney called to let me know the plane was in the air. "Wheels up," he said.

We still could not be 100 percent sure that Epstein was aboard the aircraft. I remember sitting on the beach that day, looking east over the Atlantic Ocean, and hoping he was coming our way.

A team of FBI agents and NYPD officers waited at Teterboro, but it was critical that they not have a visible presence because Epstein's driver was there to shuttle him home to Manhattan. There was a possibility that if the driver noticed a law enforcement presence, he makes a call to Epstein and the plane stays in the air and flies off somewhere else.

I know that may sound far-fetched, but keep in mind this is a guy who has already gone to extraordinary lengths to avoid prosecution. He's not someone you take chances with.

The agents and officers stayed inside the Customs and Border Protection facility. They did not park their cars on the tarmac. When the plane landed, CBP officers boarded to check travel documents, which is standard procedure.

There were three people on the flight: two pilots and Epstein.

They walked Epstein back into the terminal, where FBI agents immediately read him his rights, handcuffed him, and transported him to the federal Metropolitan Correctional Center in lower Manhattan.

I had gone out for an early dinner with my family when Sweeney called again.

"We got him," he said. "And, Geoff, he had no idea. When Epstein saw our agents, his jaw almost hit the ground."

WE DID NOT WANT the victims we had been working with to read about the arrest in the media, so we alerted them just before the jet touched down at Teterboro. We asked them to tell no one.

There was another critical matter that had to be timed correctly—the search of Epstein's mansion. We couldn't do it in advance and risk having him learn about it. In that case, he likely would not have come back into the country. And if we waited too long after the arrest, he might reach out to trusted associates and ask them to destroy evidence.

At almost the same time he was arrested, FBI agents arrived at the front of 9 East Seventy-first Street—Epstein's limestone edifice at the edge of Central Park. The search was led by the head of the

FBI's Epstein team, Michael Osborn. The first thing they encountered was a solid-oak, fifteen-foot-high front door.

The agents knocked, shouting, "FBI! Open up!" (This is called knock-and-announce.) After another knock and no response, they pried the door open with a crowbar.

When they walked through, they came upon another set of doors leading to the mansion's interior, but they did not have to break those down. A housekeeper, who was inside preparing for Epstein's return, opened those doors and let them in.

As agents filtered in through the foyer, they passed by portraits of Epstein posing with luminaries and celebrities.

Various oddities were distributed around the residence, some of them eerie. A life-sized female mannequin hung from a chandelier.

In the kitchen, on a counter with barstools pushed up against it, the housekeeper had set out a single place setting. One plate, a knife, a fork, and a drinking glass atop a white paper doily—all laid out carefully in anticipation of Epstein's return. There was take-out food in the refrigerator.

The housekeeper told the agents that she planned to go home when her boss arrived. When they told her he wasn't coming back, she left.

The search of the mansion—forty rooms over several floors—was an immense undertaking. It would take fourteen hours to complete, until seven the following morning.

On the fifth floor, agents came upon the massage room. Its walls were lined with paintings and photographs of nude girls and women. The supposition—a correct one, I think—was that the artwork served to normalize the behaviors that took place in that room.

A safe was discovered in a closet, and an agent was sent back to

26 Federal Plaza to get a diamond-tipped saw to open it. It would take a long time to cut the safe open, and the smoke the sawing created set off a fire alarm. When Epstein's security service called into the house, they asked what the code was.

Osborn said, "We're here on a search warrant. We're the FBI; we're in the house, so you don't need to send anybody." But that was not good enough for the security company, and in a few minutes, in the middle of the night, two fire trucks pulled up and just sat outside until the FBI opened the safe.

A couple of lawyers who said they were representing Epstein's interests also showed up and were told they could not come inside. They wanted to wait outside. The agents said they would be a while and would give them a call when they were finishing up. At that point, the lawyers would get receipts for whatever was taken from the house, and they would be free to arrange for the mansion to be resecured. Some items were removed by the FBI, but for the most part they took pictures, hundreds of them, of everything in the mansion that might possibly figure in as evidence.

The contents of the safe: forty-eight loose diamonds, assorted other jewelry, $70,000 in cash, and three passports belonging to Epstein—from the United States, from Israel, and from Austria, which was expired.

On the top floor of the mansion, in a back windowless storage room, were binders containing computer disks. Out of an abundance of caution, we thought it prudent to get a separate search warrant, which was drafted by Alison Moe and signed by an SDNY magistrate judge in the middle of the night. These disks were part of the digital evidence seized.

The passports confirmed our fears that Epstein was an extreme flight risk. The Austrian passport appeared to have a photo of Epstein but a different name, and it listed a home address in Saudi Arabia. It had stamps for past travel into France, Spain, the UK, and Saudi Arabia.

His lawyer said in court papers related to his bid for bail that the passport was long expired and was for his "personal protection" against possible "kidnappers, hijackers or terrorists" who might want to target him because of his Jewish faith.

A financial disclosure form required after his arrest provided more confirmation of his potential to flee beyond our reach, at least for a good long while. He listed his net worth as $559,120,954, which included stocks, equities, a cool $57 million in cash, and six properties.

The last thing I would want is for anyone to feel sorry for Epstein. He was a serial pedophile. But what the agents observed, as it was related to me, did seem to reveal a man who was living a lonely existence in a big, creepy house.

In his closets, the clothes were lined up meticulously. There were polo shirts, all the same brand but different colors, evenly spaced. Slacks, sweaters, and jackets—the same thing.

There were just two televisions in the mansion, one in the workout room and the other in the staff's quarters. But there were books everywhere, thousands of them, including in a resplendent library with floor-to-ceiling shelves, maybe thirty feet high.

And on nearly every surface, beside wherever he might possibly sit or lie down, in every room in the house, there were reading glasses. Not just one pair, but multiple pairs on the same surface. In his office. In a parlor. In the workout room. There were hundreds of pairs of reading glasses.

Beside his bed, on each side, were napkins under a bottle of water, and alongside each of those, two more pairs of reading glasses.

EPSTEIN'S LAWYERS asked the judge who had been assigned to the case, Richard M. Berman (no relation), to release him on bond. They said he would hire private guards to keep him from fleeing. They offered his private jet and the Manhattan mansion as collateral. The judge refused, ruling that Epstein should remain behind bars until trial.

A couple weeks later, I was out with Joanne when I bumped into Reid Weingarten, one of Epstein's defense attorneys. He was with an investigator assisting him on the case.

I felt bad that Joanne had to step away while we talked. She is a highly accomplished lawyer and public servant, and I would have loved to have her input on various matters. But nearly everything I was dealing with was strictly confidential.

I had known Weingarten from way back when we worked together on the Iran-Contra investigation. He looked exhausted. We talked quietly.

He said that he had just come from meeting with Epstein at the Metropolitan Correctional Center and that his client was not happy. (Good! I remember thinking.) "I think my client might want to have an interesting conversation with your office," he said.

I had expected an overture. With Epstein facing forty-five years in prison—a life sentence for a man his age—it made sense for him to want a deal. But my openness to one was quite limited. He'd already been given the deal of the century in South Florida, buying him more than a decade of undeserved freedom.

Prosecutors, though, never foreclose the conversation. At minimum, you may get new leads, more victims to talk to, additional perpetrators. "The Southern District is always interested in having interesting conversations," I said.

I told my team to expect a call. A few days later, Weingarten reached out. He said that his client would come in for a proffer—an agreement between a defendant and a prosecutor's office in which the defendant agrees to share information with the understanding that his statements won't be used against him at trial. But Epstein had one condition: he wanted assurances that the SDNY did not see him as a rapist.

That was the end of that. He was a rapist, and we were not about to give him some other, more polite-sounding label.

EPSTEIN NEVER RETURNED to 9 East Seventy-first Street—or slept anywhere other than the Metropolitan Correctional Center.

At 6:30 a.m. on August 10, 2019, just a little over one month from when he was arrested, guards discovered him dead, with a bedsheet around his neck. He was alone because his cellmate had recently been transferred.

I received the call early in the morning from the US marshal. The news he delivered was so upsetting that I could barely process it at first. We had worked so hard to bring Epstein to justice. I remained silent for a while. My wife asked who had been on the phone.

"Epstein is dead," I told her. "They think suicide."

My despair quickly turned to anger. "The fucking MCC has one fucking job—to keep our defendants safe," I said. "And they can't even get that right with their most famous inmate."

I'm aware of all the conspiracy theories and have looked at them, searching for even a trace of plausibility. There isn't any. Epstein was not murdered. His death was ruled a suicide because it was a suicide.

First of all, he had attempted to kill himself at the prison once before, less than two weeks into his stay. He was inexplicably removed from suicide watch six days later.

His cleverness served him to the very end. After the first attempt, he told a prison psychologist, "I have no interest in killing myself," adding that he was a "coward" and "would not do that to myself."

The psychologist wrote, "He stated he lives for and plans to finish this case and to go back to his normal life." The report said he was "future oriented."

He had two cellmates over the course of his stay, and the second was someone cooperating with us on an unrelated case. We talked to him afterward, and he told us that from talking with Epstein, he knew he was suicidal. He had even told Epstein, basically, "Do me a favor, buddy, I know you've got a problem, but please don't do anything while I'm in here with you because you're going to mess up my deal with the government."

People who latch on to conspiracy theories often underestimate the role that rank incompetence plays in the events they want to attribute to some grand plan. Our office thoroughly investigated Epstein's death.

On the night he died, the guards who were supposed to be monitoring him surfed the internet and engaged in online shopping. Cameras appeared to show them asleep at times.

I personally reviewed footage from the prison. There is not a perfect picture of his cell area, but during the whole overnight I could verify that nobody went in or out of the block where he was being held.

THE EPSTEIN CASE is one of the prime examples of the baked-in, fierce determination of SDNY. It is a big part of what makes the office special.

He got himself a deal in Florida that was unprecedented, outrageous, and unjust. He had unlimited resources and high connections. The sheer scope of the case, with so many victims and locations, and the span of time in which the crimes occurred, made it daunting. The agreement granted by Acosta loomed as a real consideration, and I don't know that we would have been criticized if we determined there was nothing we could do about it.

But we were, frankly, incensed by it as prosecutors, as human beings, and, in many cases, as parents. We decided we would not let it stand, and we didn't.

13

EPSTEIN: THE AFTERMATH

I do not think it's too harsh to say that I do not mourn Epstein, the man. The world won't miss him. His death saddened me because he skipped out on the moment when he would face justice and denied his victims closure, for a second time. He was a bully, and like all bullies he ultimately revealed himself to be a coward.

I made a public promise on the day of his death—a vow that we would not give up.

"Today's events are disturbing, and we are deeply aware of their potential to present yet another hurdle to giving Epstein's many victims their day in court," I said. "To those brave young women who have already come forward, and to the many others who have yet to do so, let me reiterate that we remain committed to standing for you, and our investigation of the conduct charged in the indictment—which included a conspiracy count—remains ongoing."

The reference to the conspiracy was meant to be pointed: it meant that Epstein's enablers should not rest easy.

FEDERAL AGENTS WERE SCHEDULED to search Little St. James, Epstein's private Caribbean island, two days after the suicide. Sweeney wanted the search to go forward and called to ask whether I felt the same way. I said absolutely. In a way, the timing was good, because it sent an immediate and strong message that the investigation continued.

The search was a big undertaking, involving fifty-five FBI agents and nine NYPD officers. What they came upon was a tropical version of Epstein's gilded, twisted existence.

There was a big main house and, beside it, a couple of pools surrounded by well-appointed bungalows. An office, where we believe Maxwell worked, was missing its computer equipment; someone had seemingly removed it before the raid. Likewise, the erotic artwork that once decorated the walls had been taken away. (As if that might make the place seem more normal.)

Elsewhere on the island was a helipad, a desalination plant, and, oddly, an ambulance. The only way off the island was by boat or helicopter.

In New York, I gathered the team that had worked the Epstein case, thanked them for their extraordinary work, commiserated with them over what had happened, and set the path forward. Timing and secrecy required us to name only Epstein in the initial indictment, but we always planned that while Epstein was awaiting trial, we would continue our investigation into the role of his enablers. For the sake of the victims, I said, that investigation needed to continue with urgency. The evidence the team had collected to date, and the testimony we had of the victims, pointed to one person with the greatest culpability next to Epstein, the lady of the house, Ghislaine Maxwell.

Prince Andrew, the Duke of York, was friends with both Epstein and Maxwell. He had been at the New York mansion and on the island. He stated publicly that he would cooperate in the investigation, and we intended to give him a chance to make good on his word.

I FILED THE DEATH NOLLE—A document to withdraw charges because of a defendant's death—on August 19. It's normally a routine exercise. The judge signs it, the case is dismissed, and everyone moves on.

Judge Berman, wisely, announced that he would hold a hearing and invite the victims to speak. A week later, dozens of them sat shoulder to shoulder on his courtroom's wooden benches.

Even with all we knew, the sheer number of girls whom Epstein had victimized over the course of his adult life was staggering. If not for the short notice, even more of them would have been there that day. "I have in the courtroom today fifteen victims I represent and have represented over the years," Brad Edwards, a Florida lawyer, told the court. "There are at least twenty more who didn't make this hearing today."

One by one, the women testified. Jennifer Araoz said that Epstein began abusing her at age fourteen and forcibly raped her at fifteen. "He stole my chance at really feeling love because I was so scared to trust anyone for so many years," she told the court.

A common theme emerged, one that we knew from our own interviews with these same women: Epstein and his chief enabler, Maxwell, chose women who had previously been abused sexually, physically, or emotionally, or sometimes all three. He had an instinct, a cruel one, for defenseless girls.

A woman who was first invited into the New York mansion, and later trafficked to the island, said, "Jeffrey's abuse would continue for the next three years, and I allowed it to continue because I had been taken advantage of my entire life and had been conditioned to just accept it."

We invited the women to meet with us immediately after the hearing ended, and they made the short walk from Judge Berman's courtroom to our offices at 1 St. Andrew's.

Everyone gathered in the Pfeffer second-floor library. I wanted to have lunch or bagels or some kind of food, but our ethics officer told me that I couldn't do it. It could be seen as a gratuity, essentially paying for their cooperation. That seemed crazy, and I felt very bad about it.

It was extremely emotional for all of us. I gave remarks and told them how sorry I was for all they had endured. I thanked them for their powerful presence in the courtroom and their testimony. Sweeney followed me and gave his own thanks.

I'm pretty sure we both had tears in our eyes. But you have to keep it together, right? He's the head of the New York FBI and I'm the leader of the legendary Southern District. These women had been through enough. They didn't need to see us dissolving in front of them.

Also, while the morning had been a moment of catharsis, I did not want it to be only that. We still had work to do. It is sometimes said there is no healing without justice. I'm not qualified to say if that is a reality for everyone. My training is in the law. But to the extent there is truth in it, we could do our part.

I made a plea to the victims: Our job is not over, there is justice to be done, and we need your help. Epstein could not have done what he did without the assistance of others. We ask for your cooperation in our ongoing investigation into Epstein's co-conspirators.

The response was overwhelming. We conducted interviews that afternoon and in the days that followed. Over time, many other victims agreed to be interviewed. After the initial shock of Epstein's death, I could feel the team refocusing and reenergizing.

One big break was the cooperation of a victim, one of Epstein's first, whom Maxwell and Epstein had recruited at a summer arts camp back when she was just fourteen years old. She is now an actress and married with children.

She told us that Epstein and Maxwell approached her at the camp when she was fourteen. They took what seemed to her, at first, to be a genuine interest in her life and aspirations. Epstein paid for her voice lessons and some other arts instruction.

She had told no one about the abuse that followed, and specifically not her mother, who had naively believed that Epstein's interest was benign—that he was a kind, wealthy man helping her daughter reach her dreams.

It was difficult for her to come forward. She had never wanted her mother to feel guilty. (Her name, thankfully, has not been publicly revealed. Judge Alison Nathan, who was assigned the Maxwell case, allowed the victims to remain anonymous if they so chose.)

What she told us, and would later testify to, was that Maxwell was walking her pet Yorkie when she approached her at the camp. Epstein soon joined them and began asking questions. "He seemed very interested to know what I thought about the camp, what my favorite classes were," she said.

They stayed in touch, and at one point he took her to Victoria's Secret and bought her white cotton panties. Soon after, when she was alone with Epstein at his Palm Beach residence, he pulled his pants down, got on top of her, and masturbated. As she later testified at trial, "I was frozen and in fear. I had never seen a penis before. I was terrified and felt gross and like I felt ashamed." What followed were group sessions involving Epstein, Maxwell, and other women, which began with "Ghislaine or Jeffrey" summoning everyone to follow them to Jeffrey's bedroom or massage room. We continued to build the case and search for other victims. It was a long process. More legal research on the statute of limitations as it pertained to various offenses. More research on what constituted a sex act and what did not. We needed to establish venue—evidence that at least some of the criminal conduct had happened in the Southern District.

I asked if Maxwell had given testimony in the defamation case filed against her by Epstein's victim Virginia Roberts Giuffre. The team provided me and the executive staff with two days of depositions by Maxwell, from April 2016, that contained dozens of statements relating to her knowledge of the sexual assaults. For example:

Question: "Did Jeffrey Epstein have a scheme to recruit underage girls for sexual massages? If you know."

Maxwell: "I don't know what you're talking about."

Question: "List all the people under the age of 18 that you interacted with at any of Jeffrey's properties."

Maxwell: "I'm not aware of anybody that I interacted with, other than obviously [the plaintiff] who was 17 at this point."

Maxwell made these statements under oath, on video, and within the physical boundaries of the Southern District of New York.

I asked the team to include the perjury counts and then approved the indictment.

It was June 2020, and we were ready. But where was Maxwell?

THE JUSTICE BROUGHT in the Epstein case was never going to be enough.

We couldn't win victims their childhoods back. That's the sad and awful truth.

Justice was imperfect in other ways as well. We had sought forfeiture of Epstein's Upper East Side mansion, the scene of so much of his abuse, as part of the indictment. The money could have gone out to victims. But without a conviction, ownership reverted to his preferred heirs. The town house was later sold to a Wall Street executive for $51 million.

THERE WERE OTHER OUTCOMES worth noting on the periphery of the Epstein case.

Bill Barr did not call to congratulate us after the arrest and indictment of Epstein, and, as far as I know, he did not comment on it at the time. That was fine. I didn't need his help or any kind of slap on the back from him. But he was highly engaged after the suicide. He ordered a thorough investigation and peppered the FBI and others with questions.

Epstein's suicide called attention to a really horrid situation at the MCC.

The twelve-story, high-security Metropolitan Correctional Center housed mainly short-term inmates either awaiting or currently on trial. It is part of the Federal Bureau of Prisons, which is supervised by the Department of Justice in Washington. Our office had nothing to do with the running of the MCC.

It was Barr's job to keep it functioning, and it could not keep one of the highest-profile inmates in the nation alive. In a series of public statements, the attorney general blasted conditions at the prison and said that his staff had uncovered "serious irregularities" leading to the failure to "adequately secure this prisoner." He called it all "a perfect storm of screw-ups."

I would argue otherwise—that what took place did not require any extraordinary series of events, but, rather, could have happened any day of the week at that facility.

We charged the two guards on duty the night Epstein died with falsifying prison records to make it seem they were alert and properly monitoring him. The decision to hold them criminally accountable was not an easy one, or a unanimous call in the office, because they were doing essentially what every other guard in the place was doing: not doing their jobs. They were not highly paid. They didn't profit from their crime.

It may seem unfair, as though they were in the wrong place at the wrong time, but when someone dies, there has to be a consequence. It's like when a drunk driver kills someone. Yes, there were other drunks on the road, and some got pulled over, but there has to be a greater consequence when there's a death.

The office, after I left, agreed to dismiss the charges against the guards. As part of that deal, they admitted to willfully and knowingly falsifying records. They also agreed to perform a hundred hours of community service and cooperate with a continuing investigation by DOJ's inspector general.

In fairness, the problems at the Metropolitan Correctional Center long preceded Barr. Two years after the suicide, the Justice Department announced that it was closing MCC, at least temporarily, and transferring its inmates to nearby federal prisons.

David E. Patton, the chief public defender in New York, welcomed the shuttering of what he called "a long-standing disgrace."

I DID NOT NORMALLY MENTION anyone's name in relation to an ongoing investigation. Prince Andrew was an exception because he kept publicly saying that he was cooperating in the Epstein investigation, which was not true.

It started in November 2019, when Prince Andrew, following a disastrous televised interview about his association with Jeffrey Epstein, issued a press release stating that he would be willing to help in our investigation. "Of course, I am willing to help any appropriate law enforcement agency with their investigations, if required."

I asked our team to reach out to his lawyers to set up an interview. Alex Rossmiller and Ted Diskant spent about two weeks just trying to find out who his lawyers were. We tried calling Buckingham Palace, and they were not helpful. We tried the DOJ attaché and State Department, no luck. When we finally got to his lawyers, they had all these questions.

What kind of an interview will it be? Are there any protections? Is there this? Is there that? And where do you want it to take place? And we kept answering, and all that led to was further questions, and then they're saying, you know, "We'll consider it." It was an endless email exchange, and it was clear we were getting the runaround. He was not going to sit down for an interview with us, despite assuring the public that he was ready, willing, and able to cooperate.

In January 2020, when I was asked at a press conference on the steps of Epstein's mansion whether he was cooperating with our investigation, I said, "To date, Prince Andrew has provided zero cooperation."

My statement brought his lawyers to the table again. But it was more of the same. Repetitive emails back and forth with no commitment on his part. We said that if they are serious about cooperating, just name the time and place and we will be there. The lawyers never did.

We were getting nowhere with seeking Prince Andrew's voluntary cooperation. It was time to compel him. We sent what's known as an MLAT request through the State Department. It stands for "mutual legal assistance treaty," an agreement between countries to assist each other in criminal investigations. In practice, it means that your investigations are not going to get stopped at the borders; you'll get access to the people you need to talk to.

Because of our very good relations with the UK and Scotland Yard, we almost always got what we asked when we put in an MLAT request. And I think they got the same from us. But that was not what happened with Prince Andrew. We got absolutely nowhere. Were they protecting him? I assume someone was.

His lawyers later falsely accused us of pestering him just for the news value of it.

"They are perhaps seeking publicity rather than accepting the assistance proffered," a statement from them read in June 2020.

Just to be clear, there was no assistance proffered. The prince offered to send us some kind of written statement, but that's not how we do investigations, even for British royals.

I issued a statement of my own in response to the prince's lawyers: "Today, Prince Andrew yet again sought to falsely portray himself to the public as eager and willing to cooperate with an ongoing federal criminal investigation into sex trafficking and related offenses.

"If Prince Andrew is, in fact, serious about cooperating with the ongoing federal investigation, our doors remain open, and we await word of when we should expect him."

One newspaper story referred to the back-and-forth as "trans-Atlantic sniping," as if I were engaged just for the sport of it, but I believed it was important to set the record straight. Prince Andrew clearly knew Epstein and Maxwell. He was on the island. He was at the mansion in New York. He was in London with them. We had a lot of questions for him, and as of the day I was fired, those questions remained unanswered.

BARR, BY THE WAY, did indirectly involve himself in the Prince Andrew situation. He called me shortly after I made the "zero cooperation" comments on the steps of Epstein's mansion.

Barr said, "I really liked your comments on Prince Andrew. Could you keep it up?"

He went on to explain that he saw our request to talk to Andrew as sort of a chit in a dispute with the British involving a US diplomat's wife who had accidentally killed a nineteen-year-old British motorcyclist in an auto accident. The American woman was to be criminally charged with causing a death by dangerous driving, and the Trump administration, invoking diplomatic immunity, refused to extradite her. Barr told me that the public rift over Prince Andrew's refusal to sit for an interview was useful in this other case. It inflicted PR damage, was my impression, and made it more palatable for the administration to hold firm.

That all seemed kind of questionable to me, but it did not affect our approach with Prince Andrew. I still wanted to interview him, but it had nothing to do with Barr's agenda.

ALEXANDER ACOSTA RESIGNED as secretary of labor less than a week after we indicted Epstein. The president appeared with him on the South Lawn and said that he had been a "great, great secretary" and a "tremendous talent." Trump later tweeted about the "constant drumbeat of press about a prosecution which took place under his watch more than 12 years ago" that had caused him to resign.

After a twenty-two-month investigation—and sixteen months after Acosta's resignation—the Justice Department's Office of Professional Responsibility released its report on the secret agreement that Epstein benefited from in South Florida.

It absolved Acosta and others in the Southern District of Florida of professional misconduct. The investigation did not find that their decisions were based on "corruption or other impermissible considerations, such as Epstein's wealth, status, or associations."

OPR concluded that those were nonfactors in the non-prosecution deal. Rather than professional misconduct, it ruled that Acosta's resolution of the case constituted "poor judgment."

Acosta's disregard for Epstein's victims did come in for criticism: "Acosta failed to ensure that victims were made aware of a court proceeding that was related to their own cases, and thus he failed to ensure that victims were treated with forthrightness and dignity."

The victims' attorneys were outraged at the report. And Ben Sasse, the Nebraska senator, was withering in his response. "Letting a well-connected billionaire get away with child rape and international sex trafficking isn't 'poor judgment,'" he said. "It is a disgusting failure. Americans ought to be enraged."

Acosta viewed the report as an exoneration. In a statement issued after its release, he said the report "debunks allegations" that his office improperly signed a sweetheart deal with a serial rapist. He added that the "Epstein affair as understood today is vastly more sweeping and lurid" than he realized at the time.

I will withhold my thoughts on the report. I think I've written enough in the preceding pages for readers to come to their own conclusions about what occurred in South Florida.

GHISLAINE MAXWELL TRIED to keep out of sight. She was not traveling or using her phone and was living on a 156-acre property on a remote road outside Bradford, New Hampshire. She purchased it in late 2019 for about $1 million in an all-cash deal through an anonymous corporation.

At the foot of a long driveway leading to her home, a large rock was set on the ground. In big block letters on its surface were the words "Tucked Away."

The FBI initially thought she was living in Massachusetts. But they tracked her down, partly based on an analysis of her history and pattern of merchandise purchases and deliveries. She was arrested on July 2, 2020. (I didn't quite last all the way to that event, having been fired less than two weeks earlier. I celebrated it from afar.)

Four victims testified at her trial late in 2021. One, who testified using the name "Carolyn," was fourteen years old when recruited by Maxwell.

When she visited the Palm Beach estate for the first time, Maxwell had her disrobe, then touched her breasts, hips, and buttocks. She told her she had "a great body for Mr. Epstein and his friends."

The woman said she was a middle school dropout who became addicted to drugs during the time Epstein abused her. She had been sexually abused by her grandfather, starting at age four.

She had a child at age eighteen and returned to Epstein's house a few times because she needed money. "He asked me if I had any younger friends, and I said no," she said. "And that's when I realized I was too old."

The trial fully established the critical role that Maxwell played in facilitating Epstein's access to and abuse of these young girls. As an age-appropriate woman to be with Epstein, her presence provided the reassurance that normalized the situation for the victims.

As came out at the trial, Maxwell did a number of things that drew in and reassured the young victims. For example, she befriended the young victims by buying them clothing and taking them to entertainment venues, as a parent would. She also got them accustomed to touching and being touched by teaching them to perform massages on Epstein.

In an insidious and manipulative way, she was a reassuring presence, making it seem to the young victims that Epstein's approach was within normal bounds. Maxwell herself also directly engaged in abuse by touching the minor victims' breasts and involving one victim in a group sexualized massage.

The evidence at trial proved that Epstein had given Maxwell $30 million. It wasn't credible that he paid that simply to compensate her for managing his houses. The jury convicted Maxwell of five felonies of the six charges she faced, including the most serious of them—sex trafficking of minors. She was sentenced to twenty years in prison.

FOR ALL THE JOB'S CHALLENGES, it was, above all else, a rare chance to make the world a little safer and better. When we hit headwinds on some of the sex-trafficking cases, or other matters involving violent crime, Sweeney and I would remind each other, "Victims first." It would drive us forward.

14

A CEO as Drug Lord

As a prosecutor, what you encounter day after day is a great deal of horrific behavior and its consequences. You have to be dispassionate, to the extent it's possible, when building a case against someone like Epstein.

But, inevitably, larger questions intrude: How can some people heedlessly inflict such harm on other human beings? And how do they live with themselves?

There are never answers, and to dwell on those questions too long is not a great idea. I found it best to keep my head down and do the work. I stayed laser focused as we gathered evidence, interviewed witnesses, and went about the careful, step-by-step process of bringing cases.

Remorseless people wreck lives in numerous different ways. Sex trafficking, obviously, is one. Another plague that we dealt with, and one even more widespread, was drug trafficking.

The nation has gone through waves of drug addiction, involving different substances.

Meth. Cocaine. Crack cocaine.

Opioids are this era's poison.

One million Americans have died from drug overdoses in the last two decades, with the majority of those deaths attributed to oxyco-done, fentanyl, and other painkillers. Heroin overdoses also play a role, because some people who first get hooked on prescription opi-oids find they can no longer afford them and turn to scoring heroin on the street. In the years right before I rejoined the Southern Dis-trict, the opioid epidemic had reached staggering heights. In 2015, more people died from opioid overdoses than from guns or cars. By 2016, drug overdoses accounted for more deaths in one year than the Iraq and Vietnam wars combined.

The number of fatalities is only a fraction of those who have struggled, or are still struggling, with addiction and might still suc-cumb to it. And it doesn't account for the families of those whose lives have been destroyed by their dependence on opioids.

The difference with opioids, as opposed to substances abused in the past, is that they have a legitimate clinical use. There is, in fact, a great need for them. We can't just clear opioids off the streets.

This made prosecutions more complicated, though no less ur-gent. It also meant that we were no longer dealing only with people whose business was entirely criminal in nature—street-level dealers, their suppliers, and the drug lords atop the cartels.

We had to look at ostensibly respected individuals and entities: doctors; the companies involved in manufacturing and distributing medicines; your neighborhood pharmacy.

When I went out to speak in public, a family member of someone who died from opioid addiction would often approach me afterward and tell me their story. It was heartbreaking every time.

They spoke of children, parents, and siblings who were left behind. Whole families left broken. Tens or even hundreds of thousands of dollars spent on rehab.

The deceased did not lack the will. The drugs were just too addictive, and they were everywhere—dumped into every state, city, and small town in America.

Lots of the people who became addicted lived steady, productive lives before they fell into a spiral they couldn't climb out of. Their loved ones, quite literally, still could not comprehend what happened. They couldn't square the person they knew with the one they saw at the end.

I would listen compassionately and then say that I would do everything in my power to keep these drugs from taking loved ones from other families. And I meant it. I didn't want those to be empty words.

I knew we had to do more. And just as important, I knew that we needed to be more innovative. The old way of investigating drug trafficking was not going to work against this new scourge.

On April 23, 2019, I stepped to a lectern at the SDNY office in Manhattan to announce charges connected to the opioid menace. We didn't hold a press conference for many indictments, but there was no doubt we would for this one. Reporters and radio journalists set their microphones down on the lectern. At least a dozen cameras were pointed at me.

"Today, we announce the first ever drug trafficking charges against a pharmaceutical company and two of its executives for illegally distributing prescription drugs that help fuel the opioid epidemic," I began.

"Rochester Drug Cooperative, or RDC, is one of the nation's

largest drug distributors. From 2012 to 2017, it shipped tens of millions of highly addictive oxycodone pills and fentanyl products to pharmacies that it knew were illegally dispensing narcotics.

"Earlier today, my office filed a criminal information and civil action against RDC, charging it with unlawfully distributing oxycodone and fentanyl, defrauding the Drug Enforcement Administration, and failing to report suspicious orders to the DEA."

At this point, I gave an update on the status of the case. The company itself had agreed to pay a significant fine. A consent decree called for it to reform its practices and to be monitored going forward. One executive had pleaded guilty and was cooperating.

I then continued with news that I knew would send shock waves through the drug industry. You'll remember that after the collapse of the mortgage and financial markets in 2008, there was tremendous criticism that no top executives were criminally charged. They didn't go up the ladder. In this national crisis, we were taking a different approach.

"And today," I said, "RDC's former CEO is in custody and will be presented to a judge in the Southern District of New York this afternoon.

"Laurence Doud is charged with conspiring to distribute oxycodone and fentanyl and conspiring to defraud the DEA. Doud led the RDC during the entire period of the charged conspiracy, and as alleged, personally directed and profited from much of its criminal activity."

I continued, "Doud cared more about profits than the laws intended to protect human life. . . . He directed RDC to sell OxyContin and fentanyl to pharmacies that he knew were illegally dispensing them. . . . He routinely prioritized sales over compliance."

For the first time, a pharma executive was arrested and charged with conspiring to distribute drugs, the same type of charge used against notorious drug lords like El Chapo.

A TRADITIONAL DRUG INDICTMENT is a bare-bones document. It includes the charging language. It lists the names of the defendants and basically says these individuals willfully and knowingly trafficked, and conspired with others to traffic, say, five hundred kilos of cocaine in the Southern District of New York.

That's it. We tend to give no details of how the crime occurred, how they were getting the drugs, whom the drugs went to, and what they did with the money.

There are several reasons for this. Prosecutors do not want to disclose too much information about who their cooperating witnesses are and what other investigative methods were put to use. A drug case is typically part of an ongoing investigation. You don't want to give away too much and jeopardize those future cases.

But on some of our biggest priorities, we believed it was important to say more. In the case of Laurence Doud and the Rochester Drug Cooperative, we brought forward what is known as a speaking indictment.

Those still sometimes have some blanks—you'll see such language as "Confidential Informant-1"—because of the need to anonymize sources. But they tell a larger story that is meant to inform and educate the general public.

Over its twenty-five pages, the Doud indictment told several interconnected stories: the explosion of opioid abuse in America; the federal Drug Enforcement Administration's attempts to regulate the drugs and curb the epidemic; the corporate history of Rochester

Drug Cooperative; and, lastly, the role of Laurence Doud in running the company and causing it to violate regulations meant to stop the widespread abuse of oxycodone and fentanyl.

WE DID EVEN FEWER press conferences than speaking indictments. It had to be a case that was important to the country—potentially even something that the cable news networks might break into their coverage to carry live.

If you have press conferences on cases without great interest, and make a habit of it, the media loses interest. And then when you've got something big, worthy of their interest, you run the risk that nobody shows up, and you miss an opportunity to inform the public.

General deterrence is the name of the game, so we were putting out a message. In the case of Doud and RDC, the message was that we were willing to go up the chain—no matter how high that took us.

When we prosecuted doctors in opioid cases, we wanted to make sure that every physician who was violating the law or thinking about it took notice—that dirty doctors knew the feds in the Southern District of New York were on their tail and they should be concerned if their conduct even approaches what they see in this case we just brought.

With the Doud case, we were putting an industry on notice.

The press conferences were a whole other animal than the indictment itself. There was an element of theater in them, just as there is when a prosecutor tries a case in front of a jury. My presentation had to be short and powerful—just the essence of the case in as few sentences as possible.

An AUSA on the matter usually wrote up an initial draft, which would be revised by the unit chief. I would then work with the press office and the executive staff for a few days to winnow it down.

From my early days as a prosecutor, I realized that optics matter. We always had charts, and they also had to be simple and tell their own story. That took a lot of work as well.

The many talents of our press office's Nick Biase included visual design, and we had the capability to produce the charts in-house. Nick and I would go through various iterations on paper, and then he would photoshop on the computer and we would work from that.

I also had to prepare for questions from reporters. Even seemingly innocuous questions, if answered before having been completely thought through, could unnecessarily complicate or even jeopardize a prosecution or investigation. In advance of press conferences, I would typically spend an afternoon fielding questions from the team, executive staff, and press office.

All told, it took the better part of a week to prepare for a press conference—another reason we didn't have too many of them.

There were always going to be some defense attorneys who did not appreciate our presentations. But the US attorney's office is a public entity. We did our investigations with the utmost discretion, but our values and priorities were never meant to be secret. I don't think I was ever self-aggrandizing. It's just that there were times when I felt it was appropriate for me to step forward and help the public understand what we were doing.

The charges lodged against Doud and his company got the response that I hoped for. It was seen as a clear warning to others to clean up their practices.

"The pharmaceutical industry cannot ignore this case," one industry newsletter wrote. "Compliance officers and their staff, as well as executives, should view it as a wake-up call. It is the clearest example that the Department of Justice can and will hold individuals accountable for corporate misconduct."

The New York Times focused on the fact that we had regarded RDC as we would a drug cartel. "Law enforcement officials have long tried to stem the opioid crisis in America with criminal charges for street dealers and cartel kingpins who traffic in drugs like fentanyl and oxycodone," its story the next day said.

"Now, for the first time, federal authorities are bringing the same kind of felony drug-trafficking charges against a major pharmaceutical distributor and two of its former executives for their role in fanning the crisis."

I HAVE NOT YET written extensively about the attorneys in the SDNY's celebrated civil division. They worked in a different building and liked it that way. It was their own domain, distanced from "the brass," as everyone at SDNY calls the leadership. (When I announced in a speech to the office in November 2019 that the General Services Administration had received funding to design a new building at 1 St. Andrew's Plaza that would possibly have enough space to squeeze criminal and civil under one roof again, there were audible hisses from the civil AUSAs.) They had a certain amount of autonomy and treasured their independence.

There were roughly sixty of them, every bit as credentialed as their counterparts in the criminal division and some of the most tenacious, savvy litigators around. Everyone was on the same team.

The case against the company Rochester Drug Cooperative originated in the civil division, which had been looking into the company's compliance practices for several years.

RDC was the sixth-largest drug distributor in the nation. It bought in bulk from the pharmaceutical companies, and shipped drugs to more than thirteen hundred pharmacies. Its customers were community-based retail pharmacies, rather than the big chains like CVS and Walgreens.

Notably, RDC was collectively *owned* by the pharmacies that were its largest customers, which is why it was called a cooperative. They accounted for 75 percent of its business, and got dividends based on RDC's sales.

Between 2012 and 2016, a pharmacy in Woodbury, New York, was paid more than $10.5 million in dividends from RDC—making it the largest recipient of the cooperative's revenue. The same pharmacy was one of the nation's top dispensers of Subsys, a highly addictive fentanyl spray, and also a large provider of oxycodone.

The federal Drug Enforcement Administration has regulations in place for distributors that are designed to act as trip wires to slow the tide of painkillers flooding the nation. If a pharmacy is ordering too many opioids—if its orders dramatically increase—or if too many of its customers pay in cash or travel from great distances to make their purchases—that should set off an alarm.

RDC heard the alarms. But at the highest levels of the company, they were ignored. Several of its biggest customers raised all of the red flags, dispensing huge quantities of opioids, often to customers who came from afar and paid in cash—the telltale signs of people who did not have a legitimate medical need for painkillers.

Everything RDC did—and failed to do—was like a master class on how to evade and ignore important safeguards. In the four-year period covered in the indictment, it fulfilled 1.5 million orders for controlled substances to pharmacies—many of which were for highly abused drugs like oxycodone and fentanyl. The company reported a grand total of *four* of them as suspicious.

When it identified "orders of interest" because they contained too big a buy for opioids, instead of rejecting those orders, it just raised the threshold. Then the orders were no longer of interest; they were just filled.

The company maintained an internal list of doctors who had been arrested, had been investigated by state or federal agencies, or had been identified by RDC itself for suspicious prescribing patterns. But RDC went right on fulfilling orders for pharmacies dispensing prescriptions from these doctors—even as it was obvious the pharmacies were likely opioid clearinghouses, sometimes called pill mills.

Perhaps most tellingly, RDC did business with pharmacies that other distributors had cut off. It was a supplier of last resort. One of its biggest customers had been cut off by another distributor for a pattern of suspicious ordering. RDC filled its orders, even though half the pharmacy's customers paid cash for controlled substances.

Some employees at RDC were fully aware that the company was in flagrant violation of federal laws and tried to warn their superiors. One warned in an internal email that its continuing relationship with one troubling pharmacy was "like a stick of dynamite waiting for [the] DEA to light the fuse." Another wrote to the company's compliance division about the same pharmacy, asking that they consider "what evil lies within."

I was often confronted with difficult choices at SDNY, ones in which there was no perfect outcome. As part of an agreement, the Rochester Drug Cooperative admitted to its wrongdoing and paid a $20 million penalty.

But we made the decision that even as we pursued its chief executive, we would not pursue actions that would shut down the company. Instead, RDC submitted to supervision by an independent monitor, and it reformed and enhanced its compliance practices to comply with the Controlled Substances Act.

At the press conference, I was asked why we didn't move to shutter the company. It was a legitimate question.

But my reasoning was, if the criminal behavior at RDC was helping to tear apart the social fabric, we should not do social harm, in a different way, by putting people out of work. RDC employed about two hundred people in Rochester, a part of the country that was ravaged, like so many others, by the opioid crisis.

Our hope was that it could clean up its act and become a decent corporate citizen.

There were no solo practitioners at SDNY. Everything happened because of teamwork, and the drug cooperative case was a great illustration of that.

The civil part of the case was handled by Jacob Bergman and Jeffrey Powell in the civil division. Stephanie Lake, Louis "Tony" Pellegrino, Nicolas Roos, and Alexandra Rothman, all of the narcotics unit, were the attorneys involved on the criminal side. The case was supervised by Shawn Crowley and Ian McGinley, co-chiefs of the narcotics unit. We partnered on this case, as we did with so many, with the New York office of the Drug Enforcement Administration, which was led by Raymond Donovan. Ray was a great friend to our office and to me. We saw eye to eye on the big issues, which included the need to fight this raging opioid epidemic with every tool we had.

I received several presentations and briefings on the RDC cases over a period of about six months. New evidence and leads would develop and the case continued to get stronger. When I was briefed on the investigation in March 2019, in a room filled with the executive staff, criminal and civil AUSAs, and DEA agents, I had no hesitation over what we should do about Doud: bring criminal charges against him, as we would any drug kingpin.

There is a concept in criminal law called conscious avoidance. It is intentionally turning a blind eye to criminal conduct in order to not be held responsible for it. We believed that Doud's behavior met that standard and, in fact, exceeded it.

The evidence pointed to someone who was fully aware he was breaking the law, should have known the harm he was doing, and yet continued down the same path.

According to the indictment, he was repeatedly warned that one of the company's biggest customers, a pharmacy in Staten Island, appeared to be a pill mill selling massive amounts of painkillers—in particular, the highly addictive fentanyl spray Subsys. A compliance officer emailed him that the increasingly large shipments were taking RDC "to a point where we may not want to go."

Doud said to keep on selling to them. It was a big account.

The head of sales at RDC reached out with a more generalized alert about the pharmacies they were supplying. "We have some VERY suspicious customers," he wrote.

But nothing stopped Doud.

RDC's finances grew right along with the burgeoning opioid crisis. In 2013, its revenues were about $700 million. By 2017, they had increased to $2 billion.

Over the four-year period, sales of oxycodone pills increased ninefold, from 4.7 million to 42.2 million. Fentanyl went up even more, from 63,000 doses to 1.3 million doses.

Doud was financially rewarded. His compensation doubled in that stretch, to $1.5 million.

THE DAY AFTER I announced the RDC and Doud charges, President Trump spoke at the Rx Drug Abuse & Heroin Summit in Atlanta—a large conference held to address the opioid crisis. He touted his administration's actions to reduce the oversupply of opioids and highlighted the RDC case, stating that "earlier this week the United States filed criminal charges against the sixth-largest drug wholesaler for illicit distribution of opioids, because we are holding Big Pharma accountable."

RDC filed for bankruptcy in 2020 but continued to operate. According to the Rochester *Democrat and Chronicle*, legal fees associated with defending itself from multiple lawsuits filed by survivors of opioid deaths imperiled its finances.

The $20 million fine it agreed to in the settlement was among the obligations it was not meeting. It still owed half of that and had defaulted on a $2 million installment payment.

A company statement at the time said it had not been able to afford to buy "sufficient inventory to meet customer demand."

There was one element of its previous inventory of drugs it was no longer seeking to purchase at all: opioids. It already made the decision to stop selling them entirely.

Doud was tried in January 2022. One of the prosecution witnesses was an opioid addict, who poignantly testified through tears about her addiction, which began with prescriptions from a dirty doctor for oxycodone that she filled at an RDC-supplied pharmacy.

In his closing, Nicolas Roos argued that while RDC's drugs were making people sick, "what made Larry Doud ill was losing money." After a two-week trial and two days of deliberations, the jury convicted Doud of leading a drug distribution conspiracy and defrauding the DEA. He is facing up to life in prison.

15

Prescription
Payoffs

Another thing you come to understand as a prosecutor is that "respectability" is a relative thing. If you were ever overly impressed by its superficial hallmarks—wealth, professional status, the best neighborhoods—you get over it.

None of these things make people more law-abiding. And when individuals with those advantages do cross the line, you can argue it is less forgivable.

In 2018, our office charged five doctors for taking kickbacks from a pharmaceutical company to prescribe its drug to their patients. The doctors practiced on the Upper East Side of Manhattan. They held teaching positions at prestigious medical schools.

I have mentioned the drug, which goes by the brand name Subsys, before but will now discuss it in more detail. It is a fentanyl spray, and extremely powerful—fifty to one hundred times more potent than morphine. It is taken under the tongue and meant for patients who have cancer and are experiencing breakthrough pain despite already taking round-the-clock potent painkillers.

In other words, Subsys was a drug of last resort, and quite obviously a medicine to be prescribed with a high degree of caution. It was also quite expensive. Prescriptions cost thousands of dollars per month. Medicare and Medicaid reimbursed for it, as did commercial insurers.

It was developed by a Phoenix-based company called Insys Therapeutics whose founder, John Kapoor, is a chemist and entrepreneur who in 2015 appeared on the "Forbes 400" list with an estimated net worth of $3.3 billion.

Kapoor had a substantial personal investment in Subsys. At his direction, the company created a "speaker program" in 2012 that was purportedly meant to increase brand awareness of the fentanyl spray at lunches and dinners attended by doctors. The fiction created was that doctors with experience prescribing Subsys would educate their peers about its benefits for their patients.

In reality, the program was a sham. Its real purpose was to pay bribes to doctors, disguised as "speaker fees." The company recruited doctors and kept careful track of the volume of Subsys prescriptions they were writing.

On a daily morning meeting, known in-house as "the 8:30 call," Kapoor got updates on individual doctors. They were rated on whether they had a "positive ROI"—a return on investment that exceeded the bribes they were being paid.

Even though Subsys was a cancer drug, ample evidence emerged that it was being widely prescribed off label. The marketing of it—and the illegal kickback scheme—put it into the hands and bloodstreams of non-cancer patients.

In 2014, Symphony Health, a company that analyzes drug trends, found that just 1 percent of prescriptions for Subsys were being written by oncologists. The rest were written by pain specialists, general practitioners, neurologists, and even dentists and podiatrists.

"Almost overnight, a powerful new painkiller has become a $100 million business and a hot Wall Street story," *The New York Times*, which commissioned the Symphony Health study, wrote of Subsys in 2014.

What the Rochester Drug Cooperative case showed was that the opioid crisis is largely driven by money and greed. People become addicted, in part, because people are pushing substances at them.

The bad actors are predatory. They victimize vulnerable people.

GORDON FREEDMAN WAS one of the five doctors we indicted, and like the others his credentials were impressive. He was fifty-nine years old when he was charged. He lived in the village of Mount Kisco, in Westchester County, and had a private practice on the Upper East Side. He was an associate clinical professor at the medical school at Mount Sinai Hospital.

He received $308,600 in fees from Insys after agreeing to be part of the speaker program, making him the company's highest-paid speaker. His prescriptions for Subsys rose alongside the payments made to him. In one three-month period in 2014, he accounted for more than $1 million in sales.

After Freedman was given hockey tickets as an additional reward, a company employee wrote to his supervisors, "Freedo deserves this!" explaining that the doctor not only had been a top performer but also had turned down a junket from a rival maker of fentanyl spray.

At the same time Freedman was taking the kickbacks, he was distributing powerful prescription drugs to a patient with no legitimate medical purpose—a mind-boggling amount. Over one twelve-month period, he wrote prescriptions to this patient for 85,427 oxycodone pills—an average of 234 a day. (We can assume some were for resale.) He prescribed the patient fentanyl as well. The patient died in the spring of 2017 from an overdose of fentanyl, which Freedman had prescribed.

The speaker programs the doctors were paid to host—supposedly to educate other doctors about the fentanyl spray—took place at high-end restaurants. They had no educational value.

One of the defendants, Dialecti Voudouris, an oncologist and hematologist, frequently brought her husband and listed him on sign-in sheets with various titles, including chief operating officer of her practice. Another of the doctors, Todd Schlifstein, brought along his office staff for the free food.

Jeffrey Goldstein invited his accountant one night, and they talked about his finances. He sometimes appeared only briefly at the sessions he was being paid to lead before quickly leaving with take-out food. (He wrote to a company representative before one speaker bureau event, "Is dinner takeout or we expecting peeps?") During at least one scheduled speaker bureau event, Goldstein did cocaine in the restaurant bathroom.

Goldstein and Schlifstein, both osteopaths and partners in a Manhattan practice, went to a strip club with sales representatives of the company in 2013. The group spent $4,100 on a private room, alcohol, and lap dances. The bill was paid by Insys.

Schlifstein wasn't yet working with the company. But soon after the night at the strip club, he gave Insys a list of patients he would prescribe its fentanyl spray. He was enrolled in the speaker program after that and dramatically increased the number of his patients on Subsys.

Alexandru Burducea, an anesthesiologist at Mount Sinai Hospital, never prescribed Subsys before September 2014. In exchange for bribes and kickbacks from the speaker program, he became the fourteeth-highest prescriber of Subsys in the nation in the second quarter of 2015, accounting for $621,345 in sales.

THE CASE OF THESE FIVE doctors raises some issues that I suspect are not well understood by the general public. When there is a web of criminal behavior, involving multiple individuals, how do we sort them out in terms of culpability? Whom do we flip and turn into cooperating witnesses? Which ones get the best deals?

The first order of business, always, is determining whether you need a cooperator's testimony to make another case or cases. If you don't need the testimony, then don't make the deal.

Cooperation agreements are not free to the government; society pays a cost whenever a criminal receives a lighter sentence than he or she deserves. Second, you must ensure that the cooperating witness is going to tell the whole truth. A cooperating witness cannot hold back information about themselves or others.

To work with the Southern District, you can't lie to protect someone you still feel loyal to, for whatever reason. Finally, if you have a choice between two (or more) people as cooperators, and they offer essentially the same evidence and have similar credibility, offer the deal to the less culpable person.

Sometimes the culpability of an individual changes over time.

They may begin an association in an innocent enough way—indeed, they may even be a victim initially—but later take an active and knowing role in crimes against others.

In the Lawrence Ray case, all of the young adults who were living in the suite when he moved onto campus could be perceived as victims. But over time that changed for at least one of them. After I left the office, a superseding indictment added one of the young women as a co-defendant with Ray, charging that she had become his willing accomplice and helped him extort money from the former classmate he had forced into prostitution.

In these types of cases, our decisions on whom to charge are led, first and foremost, by our judgment about an individual's wrongful conduct. With respect to cooperation, our assessment turns on his or her willingness to acknowledge that conduct and be fully truthful. A person must, at some point, put their own interests first. They help themselves by working with SDNY.

In the Subsys case, there was no doubt about the identity of the person at the top of the criminal conspiracy. It was John Kapoor, the founder of Insys Therapeutics, which developed and distributed the drug. He was tried and convicted in a different jurisdiction, the District of Massachusetts, and sentenced to five and a half years in prison. Four other executives of the company convicted with him received lesser prison terms.

In our investigation in the Southern District, we had in front of us a different set of employees. They had to know they were pushing doctors to prescribe a drug that was potentially lethal. And they knew that some, if not most, of the recipients were not cancer patients in dire need of more powerful pain relief but addicts who had become dependent on opioids.

They sometimes labeled the speaker fees as "honoraria." But the Insys employees were fully aware the payments were bribes to induce the doctors to put more and more fentanyl in the hands of patients.

The physicians who wrote the highest volume of fentanyl prescriptions were referred to as "top docs." The correlation between the prescriptions and the bribes was explicit.

Jonathan Roper, a district sales manager, wrote to the sales reps under him, "Almost all of you have speakers, use that to your advantage and repeatedly inform them of one simple guideline for them to follow: NO SCRIPTS, NO PROGRAMS."

When he felt some doctors were underperforming, he wrote, "Where is the ROI??!!! WE invest a lot of time, $, blood, sweat and tears on 'our guys' . . . and dropping script counts is what we get in return? . . . This is a slap in the face to all of you and is a good indication as to why NONE of you are climbing in the rankings this quarter."

We charged Roper and a salesperson under him at the company with offenses related to the kickback scheme. They pleaded guilty and became cooperating witnesses. Others who participated in the scheme also cooperated.

But as reprehensible as their behavior was, our main interest was in the doctors. The employees at Insys were young guys. They weren't making that much in salary and were on commission.

Believe me, I'm not excusing what they did. It was awful. But you always go after the most culpable.

It was the doctors who took a solemn oath to care for people. To do no harm. And they violated it. They took tens and in some cases hundreds of thousands of dollars—plus outings to expensive restaurants, nightclubs, casinos, strip clubs, and whatever else—to basically sell out their patients. That was a much higher order of crime.

The other factor is one of deterrence. I wish these doctors were the only ones writing scripts for opioids for their own personal profit. But they weren't. So it's the prescribers we wanted to put on notice that we were watching them.

FOUR OF THE FIVE DOCTORS pleaded guilty, all of them on charges related to the federal antikickback statute. Three of them got substantial prison sentences, ranging from two years to fifty-seven months. One was sentenced to time already served.

Gordon Freedman pleaded not guilty and went to trial. He had taken the most money in speaker fees and prescribed the highest volume of opioids. In addition, he wrote prescriptions for the high doses of oxycodone and fentanyl, without a legitimate medical purpose, to a patient who had overdosed and died.

At his trial on the speaking fees, he testified in his own defense that there was no quid pro quo and that the patients needed the prescriptions. Like some other highly educated and credentialed defendants I saw, he thought he could fool the jury. It didn't work and he was convicted.

Freedman later pleaded guilty in a separate case for causing the overdose death of his patient Jeffrey Rosenthal. Rosenthal's mother wrote to Judge Kimba Wood at the time of sentencing, "When I received the phone call informing me that Jeff was found dead, my first thought was 'Thank God, he is finally at peace.' My second thought was that Gordon Freedman was involved in his death."

Freedman was sentenced by Judge Wood to seventeen years' imprisonment.

16

TERROR IN THE MAIL

Almost all of the important cases brought by the Southern District take months or, just as often, years to investigate. If a case is a quick hit, it may go to the Manhattan, Bronx, or upstate DA's offices. Some of the other straightforward drug or gun crimes are handled by the new AUSAs—the ones doing their yearlong boot camp in general crimes or refining their skills during a second intense year in the office's narcotics unit.

But the Southern District can move quickly when it needs to. Two cases in particular come to mind. The first is Cesar Sayoc. His domestic terror campaign (and that's what it was) spanned just five days in the fall of 2018. It was brief but intense.

On October 22, an employee at the Katonah, New York, home of the billionaire investor George Soros came upon a suspicious package with a Florida postmark in the mailbox. It was mid-afternoon on a Monday. The bomb squad of the Westchester County Police Department arrived at the scene and, after determining that the package was an explosive device, safely detonated it in a nearby wooded area.

The FBI and ATF quickly came in to investigate. It soon became apparent that the device at the Soros residence was the first in a series of explosive devices sent to locations all around the country, all to high-profile recipients.

The following day, a suspicious package addressed to the Chappaqua, New York, home of Bill and Hillary Clinton was intercepted. The Secret Service discovered it during their routine screening of the Clintons' mail.

Over the next three days, more suspected explosive devices, all sent through the mail, were found before they could do any harm. Some were addressed to current and former officeholders at their homes or offices, including the former president Barack Obama, the former vice president Joe Biden, Senator Cory Booker, and Congresswoman Maxine Waters. CNN headquarters in New York was evacuated after a device was sent to the former CIA director John Brennan, a commentator for the cable network.

Elsewhere, a package arrived at the Tribeca Film Center meant for the actor-director Robert De Niro. Another was intercepted in California before it could reach the billionaire Tom Steyer.

The sender clearly seemed to have a political intent. The intended recipients were either prominent Democrats, vocal critics of the president, or both.

The packages had been sent from Florida but landed in various jurisdictions—the first one being ours. It was not clear which US attorney's office would take the lead in the case, which isn't unusual.

SDNY HAS A REPUTATION among other US attorney's offices for being grabby. We're not the biggest office. Los Angeles and DC have more attorneys. Chicago is about the same size. But the reality is that we get a lot of cases partly because we are able to deploy quickly. We can charge quickly when that's appropriate.

Maybe the best way to put it is that the office has a New York metabolism. And, unfortunately, because of New York's history, we have more expertise in terrorism than any other office.

There were times we were in friendly competition with our counterparts in New York, the Eastern District. In those instances, it was always good to have input from the FBI and DEA. They help to keep the peace between the Eastern and the Southern Districts.

If it's a traditional mob case, the FBI will often want to direct it to the Eastern District because of their history with the Cosa Nostra. The financial cases often come our way. Some others were less clear, though we were usually able to work through challenges with a focus on what was best for a particular case.

The main office that wanted this investigation, besides ours, was the Southern District of Florida, based in Miami. Conflicts can sometimes be ironed out in conversations between the chiefs of two office's criminal divisions, and if that does not settle it, the respective US attorneys get involved.

The interactions were usually polite enough, though I did sometimes feel that other US attorneys occasionally sort of hid the ball, overstating the work they had done on a case or exaggerating the nexus between their office and the criminal conduct at issue. If the US attorneys could not resolve the dispute, it went up to the level of the deputy attorney general, who was the ultimate arbiter. The DAG's office determined that the Sayoc case was ours.

New York's Joint Terrorism Task Force is a national security institution. What began in 1980 as a partnership between the FBI and the NYPD has evolved into a thriving collaboration between dozens of state and federal agencies, and a model for the national JTTF program.

Every day, it hums with squads of agents and analysts tracking potential threats in New York City and around the world. The JTTF's depth of commitment and expertise fueled some of the most important terrorism prosecutions in recent decades. When there is an active threat to New York City, it ratchets up its intensity to an even higher level.

The JTTF launched an investigation after the first package arrived at Soros's home. When the delivery to the Clintons signaled a larger danger, a command center was opened, standard procedure when there's an active threat. It does not shut down until the threat subsides or is neutralized.

Our national security co-chiefs, Ilan Graff and Mike Ferrara, along with the AUSAs Emil Bove, Jane Kim, Jason Richman, and Samuel Adelsberg, embedded at the command post and basically lived there for the next five days.

I went over to get a firsthand look, and it was something to behold: dozens of workstations set up in a massive open space, each with a small sign identifying the agency and more than fifty agents and analysts at work, comparing notes and developing leads.

I thought I might witness some chaos, but I did not. I saw focused investigators working toward a common goal. It was why the JTTF was established decades ago, and thank God it was.

The SDNY table, in a far corner of the massive space, was a nerve center within a nerve center. Our attorneys drafted more than fifty warrants and subpoenas in a five-day period as agents in New York and across the country scrambled to identify who was sending these things.

In the midst of a frantic investigation, with hundreds of agents on the streets and involved in other ways, our team's phones never stopped ringing, and the team never stopped working. As soon as one affidavit or subpoena was out the door, they moved on to the next one.

And this was not just pro forma work. You have to establish probable cause for every warrant you're seeking. It goes before a judge. It has to be done right, or you can jeopardize a case right at the start.

Our team was also doing legal research, identifying the appropriate charges for these acts of domestic terrorism, and starting to build out a criminal complaint for when law enforcement identified the perpetrator.

I don't think there's another office that could have produced at the speed our people did. Even if we were resented in some quarters, that's why we were trusted with these kinds of cases.

A MASSIVE INVESTIGATION to find and stop the bomber grew in size each day as more explosive devices were discovered. It was coordinated out of the JTTF, with involvement from the FBI, NYPD, US Postal Inspection Service, ATF, and other federal agencies along with state and local police forces all across the country.

The devices themselves were taken to the FBI forensics laboratory in Quantico, Virginia—and in particular to what is called the Terrorist Explosive Device Analytical Center. The Quantico lab itself was founded in 1932 and is probably the foremost facility of its kind in the world.

The big break in the case came late that Thursday night, on the fourth day of the crisis. One of the lead FBI agents in the command center took Graff aside and quietly flagged that there had been a break in the case—one that the FBI wanted to act on before word could leak out.

Technicians at Quantico detected DNA and a fingerprint on the device that had been intended for Maxine Waters, the longtime California congresswoman. They were able to match what they found to a man named Cesar Sayoc, who had been arrested multiple times in Florida.

Sayoc was a loner and a bodybuilder who moved from job to job and was, at the time, working as a disc jockey at a strip club. He had played college soccer. He told people he was a member of the Seminole tribe of Florida, which wasn't true.

The past charges against him included fraud, possession of a controlled substance, assault, and theft. One was related to having made a bomb threat against the electrical utility Florida Power and Light, which he was in a dispute with over the size of a bill. He had been placed on probation but not sentenced to prison time.

Sayoc was living in a white van in South Florida that even before his arrest drew interest locally and had been posted on some social media accounts because it was so strange. A sticker on a window read "CNN Sucks." There was a picture on one window of Barack Obama, photoshopped to make it seem as if he were riding a tricycle. It had a target on it.

Pictures of Hillary Clinton, the filmmaker Michael Moore, and others had red targets or crosshairs over the images.

A general manager at a restaurant that had employed Sayoc as a delivery driver would later describe the van as "freaky-scary." Sayoc had reportedly once told another employer, a lesbian, that gay people and Democrats should be put on an island together and "nuked." His mother and sister would later say they had tried to get him to seek mental-health treatment.

After the fingerprint and DNA match, the FBI began scouring Sayoc's social media. They quickly came upon his political rants and another set of clues that were telling: his misspelling of names online—Hillary with one *l*, the US representative Debbie Wasserman Schultz as "Shultz"—matched the misspellings that he made on the packages.

At this point, the JTTF was confident they had the right guy.

Sayoc, the night before he was apprehended, was working his job from the DJ's booth at the Ultra Gentlemen's Club in West Palm Beach, selecting the music to which the dancers performed. He also worked there as a bouncer.

The next day, FBI agents and local law enforcement arrested him as he walked toward his van in the parking lot of an AutoZone store in Plantation, Florida. Three new packages were discovered in the mail that day.

They were similar to the others. Each had as its return addressee "Debbie Wasserman Shultz," six self-adhesive postage stamps bearing the American flag, and address labels printed on white paper with black ink in similar typeface and font size. Each contained an improvised explosive device, or IED, with approximately six inches of PVC pipe packed with explosive material, a small clock, and wiring. Some also contained shards of glass.

The van was not just where Sayoc had been living; it was also the bomb-making lab. (He showered at a gym or at the beach.) Agents found explosive powder and soldering equipment as well as stamps, envelopes, paper, and a printer.

ON THE DAY of Sayoc's arrest, our team swore out a criminal complaint against him before Magistrate Judge Katharine H. Parker in

Manhattan federal court. There were five counts—a preview of the thirty charges he would face when we indicted him a couple weeks later.

The document was a testament to how quickly and thoroughly the JTTF and other investigators had gone about their work. And it definitively tied Sayoc to the spree of mailings.

A laptop seized from his van contained addresses that matched where he had directed the IEDs. His cell phone showed that it had been used to search for the addresses.

Because the case was of such significant national interest, a press conference was scheduled for that afternoon in Washington, at the Department of Justice. I was with Bill Sweeney at the Joint Terrorism Task Force headquarters earlier that day, and I knew we were close to making an arrest. But as soon as it happened, it was like, hurry up, you guys all have to get down here fast.

Almost a year into the job, it was my first experience of having to travel to DC on such short notice.

I said to Sweeney, "There's a jet, right?" You hear all these stories about the FBI, I figure it has to have some kind of jet.

He said, "Yeah, we have a jet, but it's in Westchester. So by the time we can get on it, it's quicker if we just take the Delta shuttle." And I thought, seriously? What about a helicopter getting us out to Westchester? And what about O'Neill—James O'Neill, the New York City police commissioner—he's got like an army on the ground of fifty thousand cops and he doesn't have a way to get us to DC in thirty minutes?

We all ended up racing together to LaGuardia in an NYPD vehicle. It's here that I saw the true power of O'Neill. He had a phalanx of cops with him as we strode into the airport—in front of him, behind him, on both sides. We were in the inner circle, and we didn't stop. We didn't go through security. We just walked right onto the plane, at a very fast pace. It was the first time I experienced that at an airport.

I prepared my remarks on the plane with a draft emailed to me by Lisa Zornberg just before we took off. It was the first time I had even a moment to think about what I'd say.

When we landed in Washington, there were cars waiting. When we got to Main Justice, we walked directly onto the stage.

They had been waiting for us to start, although quite frankly I think they were waiting for O'Neill. It was a very back-the-blue, support-the-cops administration, and they wanted O'Neill standing next to them. O'Neill personified the tough cop; he was right out of central casting.

It was late October, but still a little humid in DC. And I am very quick to sweat. In my office, before a press conference, I would pump up the air-conditioning so it was like a freezer. But they did not do that at Main Justice. The lights were really bright, and it was hot on the stage. I had already perspired through my shirt, and I remember thinking that I just didn't want to sweat through my suit.

THERE'S A WAY these press conferences unfold, in terms of the order of speakers. First it's the attorney general, who was still Jeff Sessions at the time, then the deputy attorney general, the FBI director, and the US attorney of whatever district happens to be leading the case at hand.

I had no idea what anyone was going to say. There's usually some coordination, but this was put together too quickly.

The people who spoke before me were pretty nonspecific about who the targets of this had been. Someone mentioned Obama, but nobody gave a full list of names. It felt a little ambiguous and unusually muted.

At the lectern, I said, "The defendant mailed devices to those who currently hold or have held our highest public offices. President Barack Obama, former secretary of state Hillary Clinton, former vice president Joe Biden, former attorney general Eric Holder, Congressperson Maxine Waters, US senator Cory Booker, former CIA director John Brennan, and former director of national intelligence James Clapper."

I went down the list, naming every public servant who was known to us at that time.

AFTER HIS ARREST, one newspaper story described Sayoc as "a volatile nobody desperate to become a somebody." He succeeded at that—in the way that political violence in America, or attempted violence, has long been a vehicle for becoming known. Sayoc achieved a level of infamy and became a somebody.

The messaging and rhetoric on both sides of the political aisle was toxic then, and still is. You can find fault with it and argue that responsible people in public life should tone it down. I wouldn't disagree.

But I'm a firm believer in personal responsibility. This guy was a pathetic loser and he latched on to some poisonous messaging to give his life meaning. That was on him. He terrorized a nation and could easily have hurt or killed someone. There was no one else to indict for his actions.

Early in 2019, Sayoc pleaded guilty to sixty-five felonies related to sixteen devices that he mailed. The most serious charge, using a weapon of mass destruction, carried a potential sentence of life in prison.

In a filing before his sentencing, Sayoc's lawyers said that he suffered from untreated mental illness.

Our office requested a life sentence. The FBI had concluded by then that the IEDs, with ingredients that included fireworks, fertilizer, a pool chemical, and glass fragments, would not have worked as Sayoc had designed them.

The judge, Jed Rakoff of the federal district court in Manhattan, was swayed by the fact that none of them detonated. He said that he believed Sayoc had not meant them to work. He concluded that the flaws in the IEDs—inoperable fuse wiring, timers not set to go off—were intentional. "He hated his victims," Judge Rakoff said at sentencing. "He wished them no good, but he was not so lost as to wish them dead, at least not by his own hand."

He handed down a sentence of twenty years in prison. I never believed it was my role to argue with a judge's decisions in these matters, and a couple decades in a federal lockup is not a slap on the wrist.

I said after the sentencing that I remained thankful no one was hurt by Sayoc, whose actions "challenged our nation's cherished tradition of peaceful political discourse."

I was satisfied knowing that the investigation had moved at lightning speed. The perpetrator was identified and arrested within five days of the discovery of the first IED, quickly charged, and then sentenced to a lengthy time in jail.

17

AVENATTI

On March 25, 2019, the lawyer Michael Avenatti was arrested on a complaint issued in the Southern District after attempting to extort millions of dollars from Nike, the giant shoe and sports apparel company. We had learned of his conduct just one week earlier.

SDNY prides itself on thorough and meticulous investigations. But, like the Sayoc prosecution, this case was another illustration of the office's ability to move at lightning speed when necessary.

The Los Angeles–based Avenatti gained a degree of fame during his representation of Stormy Daniels, the adult film star who alleged an affair with Donald Trump. Avenatti was brash and flamboyant. He raced sports cars and even competed at the famed 24 Hours of Le Mans, in a Ferrari, with a Saudi prince as his driving partner. He talked about running for president in 2020.

But his professional and private lives were turbulent and messy. His law firm had been in bankruptcy a couple of times. Not long before we charged him, Los Angeles police arrested Avenatti over an alleged episode of domestic violence. (He denied the allegations and the district attorney did not bring charges.)

Ted Diskant came to my office on March 18, seven days before we would charge Avenatti. It was 6:30 p.m.—but normal for the place to still be buzzing at that time. Few people went home early at SDNY.

"Where is Capone?" I asked, referring to Russ Capone, his co-chief. They were a team and almost always came to my door in tandem.

Capone was on a well-deserved vacation. It may not reflect well on me that I was soon thinking that he picked a bad week for it.

Diskant said that he had just gotten off the phone with Pete Skinner, a partner at the law firm Boies Schiller Flexner and former SDNY organized crime prosecutor. Skinner told him that the firm represented Nike and had just received a call from Michael Avenatti that they perceived as an extortion attempt.

Diskant related the broad strokes of the alleged plot to me: Avenatti represented a supposed "whistleblower," a youth basketball coach who he said had information that Nike was funneling cash to the families of star high school players to influence their decisions on where to play in college. All the major college teams are sponsored by one of the big shoe companies; they become known as "Nike" or "Adidas" or "Under Armour" schools depending on which company they affiliate with.

The wrongdoing Avenatti was alleging mirrored the college basketball case that we brought the previous year involving a rival company, Adidas, and some of the biggest college basketball programs and coaches. Diskant was one of the lead prosecutors on those cases.

But Avenatti was not referencing an actual federal case or investigation. He appeared to just be threatening to smear Nike with his own allegations unless it paid him a huge amount of money.

It was a shakedown. And the clock was ticking.

Avenatti told Nike's lawyers he was going to quickly hold a news conference on the eve of the company's quarterly earnings call and just as the annual NCAA basketball tournament was to begin and tens of millions of people would be paying attention to "March Madness." Instead of solely focusing on the games (and their betting brackets), basketball fans would also be hearing news of a scandal involving the sport's biggest supplier of shoes and apparel.

Avenatti warned them if they did not act quickly, Nike would suffer grievous economic harm.

I asked Diskant if Nike's lawyers had recorded the conversation. They had not. In investigations of extortion, the exact words of a conversation, and the tone, are critical to making a case. This is especially true when the alleged perpetrator is an attorney.

After all, the attorney could later argue that it wasn't extortion; it was simply zealous advocacy. For better or worse, there are plenty of lawyers who raise their voices, yell, and promise all kinds of catastrophic consequences if adversaries do not give them what they want. It may not be pretty (or effective), but it's usually not criminal.

Without Avenatti on tape, I feared that we would not be able to assess criminality. I questioned Diskant about the level of cooperation we could get from Nike's lawyers. Would they agree to be wired up?

That would be a big ask. We wire up witnesses and confidential sources all the time, and sometimes even ask victims of schemes like extortion to make a tape. But I had never asked a lawyer to wear a wire.

To get Avenatti on an audio recording and on video, our investigators would need to access conference rooms in the law firm. It would be disruptive to their business. And it would make the attorneys themselves witnesses to a crime.

We also needed access to the Nike lawyers' mobile devices so we had Avenatti on tape when he talked to them on their phones.

Diskant said he would find out. An hour later, he was back in my office. David Boies, the law firm's founder, had personally signed off. With time being of the essence, we made heavy use of our extraordinary in-house investigators to set it all up, working in close coordination with the FBI.

There is another point I should make here. We had gotten criticism and a fair degree of pushback within the Department of Justice for prosecutions of people who were perceived to be friends or supporters of the Trump administration. But here we were swiftly ramping up an investigation against someone who was a major irritant to Trump.

All of this was immaterial to me. I didn't care where anyone stood politically. But the Avenatti case did demonstrate that we went about our business the way we were supposed to, without fear or favor.

ONE OF THE THINGS you learn as a prosecutor is that there are a surprising number of people in the world who enjoy talking like mobsters when they're behind closed doors.

Avenatti was demanding $22.5 million to undertake an "internal investigation" of Nike's practices. In return, he would not hold a press conference to publicly make allegations about its supposed payments to players, which would endanger the players' amateur status and put the college teams at risk as well.

That was the shakedown. He was weaponizing his law license.

His contention was Nike had to pay him, because otherwise his allegations would cause the company's stock price to crater.

"I'm not fucking around with this, and I'm not continuing to play games," he said in one of the phone conversations we taped with the consent of the Nike lawyers. "You guys know enough to know you've got a serious problem. And it's worth more in exposure to me to just blow the lid off this thing. A few million dollars doesn't move the needle for me.

"I'm just really being frank with you. So if that's what's really being contemplated . . . then let's just say it was good to meet you and we're done. And I'll proceed with that press conference tomorrow."

He repeatedly stressed that it was going to take lots of money to stop him, not just a few million bucks. "So if you guys think that, you know, we're gonna negotiate a million five, and you're gonna hire us to do an internal investigation, but it's gonna be capped at $3 or $5 or $7 million, like let's just be done. . . .

"And I'll go and take $10 billion off your client's market cap. And I'm not fucking around."

Every evening that week, I would walk down the hall of the eighth floor to Diskant's office to listen to the most recent recordings, along with the AUSAs on the case, Matt Podolsky and Rob Sobelman. It was a highlight of my day. Whatever worries I had that someone could claim we were entrapping Avenatti were quickly allayed.

It was clear that no one put words in Avenatti's mouth. There simply wasn't the opportunity. A few times I turned to the team and asked, "Did he really just say that?"

"The company will die—not die, but they are going to incur cut after cut after cut after cut, and that's what's going to happen as soon as this thing becomes public," he told Nike's lawyers at the firm's office.

His price tag kept changing, but it never went down. He said he would need a $12 million retainer, which was to be paid immediately and deemed earned when paid, a minimum guarantee of $15 million in billings, and a maximum of $25 million—"unless the scope changes."

Alternatively, he said he would take $22.5 million just to drop the whole thing. He wouldn't do any work, but he wouldn't hold a press conference to damage Nike.

On some level, you had to appreciate his audacity. Why just ask for pocket change, a couple million bucks, when you can try to shake somebody down for ten times that? Go big or go home, right?

Avenatti told Nike that he was representing the interests of his client Gary Franklin Sr., who coached one of the top youth clubs in the nation, the California Supreme. The team was sponsored by Nike, receiving about $70,000 a year, but the company had recently ended the relationship.

But at the same time he was seeking money for himself, Avenatti was selling out his client. His disregard for clients was something our office was already investigating. He represented Stormy Daniels in a book deal, and a couple months earlier she had referred a case to us, claiming that Avenatti had improperly taken $300,000 of her advance from the publisher.

By the Friday of that week, just five days after getting involved, we knew we had enough to charge and convict Avenatti. He had a meeting set up for the coming Monday at Boies Schiller, Nike's law firm. We planned to arrest him after he arrived.

That weekend, we worked on the complaint, the related search warrants, and a plan for the arrest. We arranged for an FBI agent to park outside Franklin's house to be ready—right after Avenatti was in custody—to interview the coach to determine what, if anything, he knew about his lawyer's threats to Nike.

The answer, it turned out, was that he didn't know anything. The coach wasn't involved in the plot.

When we informed Main Justice about Avenatti's imminent arrest, as we typically did with anything likely to generate media attention, it turned out there was one other matter we had to deal with. Federal authorities in California were a year into a tax and wire fraud investigation against Avenatti, and I was told to coordinate with Nicola Hanna, the US Attorney for LA.

We could not initially come to an agreement, and Ed O'Callaghan in Main Justice told me that we should stand down until the turf issue got settled. Our interactions with Main Justice had been strained, to say the least, and I thought O'Callaghan might have just been punishing the Southern District. But over the weekend, I was able to reach an understanding with Hanna: if we arrested Avenatti on Monday, Hanna would announce their charges as well.

The meeting at the law firm was scheduled for 1:00 p.m. Avenatti arrived on time, but was waiting to be joined by Mark Geragos, another well-known LA lawyer, who was to be part of the meeting. (Geragos was not charged.)

The FBI agent outside the coach's house thought he had the go-ahead to proceed at 1:00 p.m. New York time. After he knocked at the front door and introduced himself to Franklin, the first thing the coach did was text Avenatti to tell him he had a visitor at his house—an FBI agent.

Avenatti immediately fled the Boies Schiller waiting room and walked into the massive Hudson Yards complex. The agent who was supposed to have eyes on him lost him. In the meantime, we see that he's tweeting that he intends to hold a press conference at 2:00 p.m.

In retrospect, it's funny, a true comedy of errors. In retrospect. That afternoon, I was in Diskant's office with Podolsky and Sobelman following the blow-by-blow, and the humor had yet to register. Finally, we got word that one of our in-house investigators, Deleassa Penland, tracked him down in Hudson Yards, arrested him, and took his phone. We notified Los Angeles that we had him, and they executed their search warrant and announced their indictment of him that day.

I had been so intensely involved in the preceding days that I couldn't miss the presentment. When Avenatti walked into the courtroom, I was struck by how diminutive he looked. He was no more than five feet eight and very thin.

The court proceeding was fast. He pleaded not guilty and posted bail. On the way out, he walked up to Penland, who had arrested him.

"I wish we had met under different circumstances," he said.

IT WAS A BREATHTAKING FALL for someone who had spent a couple years as a ubiquitous figure in the media and seemed as if he were on top of the world.

Avenatti was convicted of extortion in February 2020 following a jury trial (Daniel Richenthal joined the team for the trial) and several months later sentenced by the US District Court judge Paul G. Gardephe to a prison term of two and a half years.

Before he was sentenced, Avenatti, addressing the court, said, "All the fame, notoriety, and money in the world is meaningless. TV and Twitter, Your Honor, mean nothing. I and I alone have destroyed my career, my relationships, my life. There is no doubt that I deserve to pay, have paid, and will pay a further price for what I have done."

In February 2022, two years after his extortion conviction, Avenatti was convicted again in the Southern District for stealing money from Stormy Daniels. He was sentenced to an additional two and a half years of imprisonment.

Part Four

NEAR
AND FAR

18

NYCHA

As prosecutors working in the Southern District, we were in New York, and I also felt, very strongly, *of* New York. We had an obligation to help keep the city safe. And we were one of the many public institutions called upon, in whatever way we could, to make life better for its citizens.

The official number of people who live in the city's public housing is about 400,000. If those who crowd into units off the books were included, the count would rise to an estimated 600,000 (or greater)—more than the populations of several major American cities, including Cleveland, Miami, and Atlanta.

We were sworn to serve these residents every bit as much as the wealthier and more privileged inhabitants of the city.

One of the first things I was hit with when I came in to lead SDNY—I think less than a week into the job—was a request to sign off on a civil complaint against the New York City Housing Authority, widely known as NYCHA.

As quickly as possible, I learned about our investigation. The work done by our AUSAs Robert Yalen, Mónica Folch, Jacob Lilly-white, Talia Kraemer, and Sai Mohan was extremely impressive and comprehensive. I closely read what had been put in front of me. It made for a compelling and righteous lawsuit. Yet I determined, against the wishes of many in my office, that I was not yet ready to affix my signature to it.

To be clear, the complaint itself, all eighty pages of it, was thorough and forceful. It was the product of a yearslong investigation that revealed shameful deficiencies in the city's public housing that urgently needed to be addressed.

The situation was deplorable and had been for many years. To give just a sampling of the persistent, nightmarish conditions that residents were forced to endure:

Patches of mold in some NYCHA buildings were measured at a hundred square feet.

The heat failed constantly, leaving residents freezing in their apartments on some of the coldest days in winter. Over one four-month period in 2017 and 2018, more than 323,000 residents, 80 percent of NYCHA's official population, experienced at least one outage. The average duration was forty-eight hours, meaning that some buildings went without heat more than two nights—in some cases, probably considerably longer.

Elevator failures were routine, and they often occurred with people in them. In 2016, nineteen hundred breakdowns left someone trapped inside, and it took an average of two hours to rescue them. It was so common for all of a building's elevators to be malfunctioning at the same time that NYCHA had its own terminology for it—a "double header."

Elderly and disabled residents found themselves shut-ins inside their apartments during these multiple breakdowns, or if they arrived back and found the elevators out of service, they spent nights sleeping in the lobby. Often a cold lobby.

Lead paint was everywhere, long after it had been identified as a danger to children and a potential impediment to their intellectual development. Some children showed elevated levels.

Rats were so numerous that one internal report described a "labyrinth" of rat burrows in the basement of a complex in the Bronx. A work order described a unit in Harlem as "overcome by rats." Despite the known problems, NYCHA abandoned routine extermination programs for a four-year period between 2012 and 2016. Only tenants who complained got services; meanwhile, because routine pest abatement had been abandoned, the problems exploded.

WHAT CAUSED—and compounded—all of these problems was NYCHA's institutional culture of lying and taking shortcuts. It provided its maintenance staff with explicit instructions on how to gloss over violations, some of which were enshrined in a manual of "quick-fix tips"—in reality, a how-to guide on how to trick inspectors.

The inspectors came from the federal Department of Housing and Urban Development, as part of the Public Housing Assessment System. The goal was to conceal problems from PHAS inspectors, as they were known, or to stay one step ahead of them.

A single layer of plywood was recommended to quickly build out false walls to conceal dilapidated rooms.

Rather than repair or replace damaged ceiling tiles, the quick-fix remedy was to use painted cardboard that mimicked the tile color and tack it up in a way that would not be noticed.

If mailboxes were damaged, the guidance was to cover them up for the day. Hazardous materials left in the open, like gasoline cans stored in basements, were removed and then put back as soon as buildings were clear of inspectors. Signs would be posted in common rooms with dangerous or unsanitary conditions that said, "Danger: Do Not Enter," then removed when inspectors left.

If there were leaks in buildings and inspectors were due to arrive, the brilliant quick fix was just to turn the water off.

The complaint that our office had drafted and was ready to file represented one part of an integrated effort to take on the agency's horrible problems. The second step, agreed to by NYCHA's leadership, was that they would sign a consent decree admitting all the wrongdoing uncovered in the investigation.

In addition, NYCHA agreed to be overseen by a federal monitor as it went about making fundamental reforms to remedy its many problems.

That was all good. But I had a question: Where are they getting the money for all this? I mean, we've identified all of these awful problems. It's billions of dollars in desperately needed improvements. Where in the settlement were the funds coming from?

NYCHA was in need of a culture change. Its management had to stop coaching employees to lie. But you couldn't ignore the money aspect.

When I asked where the money would be found, the people in our civil division said, basically, we don't know. NYCHA itself doesn't have it because its money from rents and from HUD is already obligated for necessary work. It doesn't have enough to take on anything transformative.

I then asked, what about the City of New York? And they said, well, we had a meeting with New York City's counsel, and he said, "You're not getting a dime out of the city." (We could not directly sue the city because NYCHA was a separate legal entity and the city did not control its day-to-day functioning.)

It was at this point that I said, until we have money to back it up, we can bring all the complaints we want, but we're just making noise. We might embarrass some people and get small donations from the city for patchwork fixes, but what's that do? It's just name and shame, and then everybody moves on and we've still got all these people, all these residents who work hard and pay their rent, still living in miserable conditions.

In my mind, they were victims—just like the victims in so many of our other cases. They were vulnerable and, in essence, preyed upon by more powerful forces.

But in this instance, there were at least half a million victims— every resident of public housing in the city. That was more, by many factors, than any other case that came our way.

The discussion with my team in the civil division wasn't easy. They had poured countless hours into this case and thought filing the complaint was the only path toward any improvement at NYCHA. They told me that there were deadlines and we were going to miss them, that I didn't understand the time pressure to get this done—the care that had gone into putting it together and the possible consequences of a delay.

I stood my ground. I said that what I'm looking at right now isn't really going to help anybody, and I'm not signing it.

THE POST OF US ATTORNEY for the Southern District of New York, or any district, is not a political job. Or it shouldn't be. But there's a difference between being political and having some political sense.

I'm not sure how successful I would have been overall—and in particular on the NYCHA case—if I did not have a feel for the local political landscape.

NYCHA is a public development corporation, the sort of entity that is sometimes referred to as a quasi-government agency. A seven-person board, all appointed by the mayor, runs it.

It's gigantic. With 326 developments, 2,462 residential buildings, 175,000 apartments, and an annual budget of $2.3 billion, it is larger than the next eleven public housing agencies in the nation combined.

Troubled public housing agencies in other cities have in the past been taken over by HUD. That conceivably could have happened in New York, but the reality was that NYCHA is too big for anyone else to want to truly take ownership—even the federal government.

It was no secret that the mayor at the time, Bill de Blasio, and the governor, Andrew Cuomo, detested each other. The US attorney normally wouldn't talk to either one of these people. With politicians, you keep your distance: you never know when you might open an investigation into their conduct. But if I were going to get real money to start to fix the city's public housing, it would have to come from one or both of these guys.

I initiated a series of conversations with de Blasio and Cuomo, separately, about NYCHA. Their hatred for each other was palpable. They couldn't talk to me without trashing each other. My hope was to leverage their hatred into something good for the residents.

With Cuomo, I emphasized that he had an opportunity to help solve a problem. The state had money. It could invoke emergency powers to take over the city's public housing, and that could be a golden opportunity.

If he did it in conjunction with the federal government, it would one-up the mayor. He'd be saying, "This was your problem, de Blasio. You couldn't solve it, so now I'm riding in to fix it."

I didn't use those words with Cuomo, but I didn't need to. I could almost see him turning them over in his head.

I didn't overtly go through these possibilities with de Blasio, but I'm certain that it got back to him through his sources that the state was talking to the US attorney about NYCHA. He knew Cuomo was hovering, and if he didn't get serious, the governor might try to assert control.

That's when we started talking turkey about the city putting up real money.

Just filing the civil complaint, absent an agreement with real teeth, would have been Kabuki theater. Words on paper. Our office could have told itself we got something out of a three-year investigation. But after I went back and forth with Cuomo and de Blasio for several weeks, we got to real substance.

For starters, NYCHA signed a consent decree admitting to its failings. We insisted that it not be some kind of generalized sorry-we-screwed-up apology. It had to be specific about the problems with heating, mold, lead paint, broken elevators, rats, and all the rest—right down to numbers and dates.

"NYCHA's data reflects more than 260,000 work orders for roaches between 2013 and 2016," the final document said. "For the same period, there were more than 90,000 mouse work orders and nearly 36,000 rat work orders."

The consent decree acknowledged numerous examples of the "quick-fix" deceptions, including this doozy: "In one 2013 email, a NYCHA superintendent wrote to staff members, 'We're hiding four big pails of oil behind your containers for our PHAS inspection to-day. We'll get them after it's over.'"

It was the money that was most critical to me. In the agreement we hammered out, and settled on in June 2018, de Blasio committed the city to additional spending of $1.2 billion over the next five years and $200 million every year after that—indefinitely—to begin to fix NYCHA's dilapidated buildings and crumbling infrastructure. The state pledged $550 million. The federal government, which had cut funding to NYCHA and other public housing agencies over the last decade, did not provide more money.

The new money from the city was certainly not enough to fully address capital spending needs—no one knew that number—but it was a start, and a big step up from "not a dime."

The agreement went to Judge William H. Pauley III for his ap-proval. To our surprise, he rejected it. He did not believe that it was appropriate for the court to be supervising this type of consent de-cree and monitorship, which was to continue indefinitely until the problems were fixed.

The following January, a final deal was approved that did not involve the courts. It was not substantially different. De Blasio agreed to the appointment of a federal monitor to watch over NYCHA's compliance and its spending of the new money. There would also be a new leader at NYCHA. It was not a federal takeover, but it shifted oversight and a good degree of power to forces outside NYCHA and away from the mayor's office.

NYCHA, UNDER ITS NEW LEADERSHIP, has made progress. But there is still much work to be done to ensure that the residents live in de-cent, safe, and sanitary housing, as is their right.

As the monitor has correctly pointed out, NYCHA needs more money than what the settlement called for. A culture of shoddy work and dishonesty that festered for so long will be very difficult to change, and it won't happen quickly.

I'm immensely proud, however, that the Southern District's investigation shined a light on the shame of NYCHA and that I was able to work some levers to get politicians to commit money.

It was an important start.

19

Nine Trey

Clearing the streets of violent, murderous drug gangs brings with it an obvious gain in the city's quality of life. The Southern District had to be concerned with what was happening on its home turf, which at times meant chasing down and putting away some really bad characters.

That was more or less the job description of our office's violent and organized crime unit, which worked with the NYPD, FBI, Homeland Security Investigations, ATF, and other federal and local law enforcement on investigations of some of the city's most dangerous criminals.

As attorneys in the office were working on NYCHA, and, of course, hundreds of other cases, prosecutors in violent and organized crime were closing in on a gang that called itself the Nine Trey Gangsta Bloods.

Nine Trey members engaged in murders, assaults, and kidnappings in Manhattan and Brooklyn. They sold a wide array of drugs, including heroin and fentanyl. (If you looked at the long list of substances they peddled, you might wonder if there were any street drugs they *didn't* sell.)

The violence they perpetrated was sometimes to protect their business from encroachment from rival gangs. At other times, it was just senseless and indiscriminate: A Nine Trey member fired a gun in a corridor inside the Barclays Center arena in Brooklyn. It happened at a night of boxing matches when he and his cohorts ran into a rival crew they were beefing with on social media.

It's no secret that there is sometimes a crossover between violent rap music, or gangsta rap, and actual violence and gangsters. A young man named Daniel Hernandez became part of the Nine Trey crew. He was variously described as a rapper and an "internet troll" because his notoriety came from his outrageous persona and his taunting of other figures online.

As a performer, Hernandez was known as Tekashi69. Or, alternately, as 6ix9ine (pronounced "Six-Nine").

One of the things I've always enjoyed about being a litigator is the ability to become a mini-expert in whatever you happen to be working on at the time. When the case is over, you move on to something else, but for that moment you're immersed.

I had never heard of Hernandez, and when I was first briefed on the investigation, I went home and asked my daughter, who was in high school then, "Have you ever heard of the rapper Six-Nine?" She said, "Of course, everyone's heard of him. He's huge. Why?"

I think I said something like "Oh, somebody I know is going to a concert of his." I'm not sure who that would have been, but we left it at that.

The AUSAs on the case, Michael Longyear, Jacob Warren, Jonathan Rebold, and Sebastian Swett, sent me Hernandez's music videos so I could get a look at him. His hair was rainbow colored, and his teeth were capped with so many colors that his mouth looked like a crayon box. His face was tattooed. I later learned that one of the many tattoos on his body, the one that read "SCUM," was meant to stand for "Society Can't Understand Me."

I'm far from a prude, but his music and his act were just repulsive. At least to me. His big hit, "GUMMO," quickly went platinum; the video for it has been viewed more than 400 million times.

In the video, a crew behind him, many of them members of Nine Trey, wear red bandannas and point guns at the camera. Bags of what appear to be drugs are visible on top of a car hood.

The lyrics are violent and repetitively misogynistic, featuring such lines as this:

Man that's really all I use her for, I kick her out the door
I don't want her, you can keep the whore
She fiendin' for some more.

Believe it or not, the rest of the song is far worse. I won't repeat any more of it here. You can find the more than thirty lines of the lyrics to "GUMMO" online, though I don't recommend it.

It may not be surprising that in real life Hernandez was not all that fearsome. He stood five feet six and weighed about 130 pounds. He never made it past the tenth grade. He had been treated for depression and post-traumatic stress following the murder of his stepfather.

Before he became a rap star in his early twenties, he worked the counter at the Stay Fresh Grill and Deli in the Bushwick section of

Brooklyn, near where he grew up. A story in *Rolling Stone* referred to him as "Danny the deli clerk."

He was said to have a deep Christian faith, and according to the *Rolling Stone* piece he would walk the streets of his neighborhood saying to himself, "Please, God, change my life. Please, God, make me famous."

Nine Trey is one of the most violent crime organizations across New York's five boroughs. Its roots date back to the early 1990s and Rikers Island, the notoriously violent city jail complex set down between the Bronx and Queens, on an island in the East River.

Gang members released from Rikers established the gang in some of the city's most disadvantaged neighborhoods, working at first out of uninhabited buildings. From there, they recruited new members and claimed territory up and down the East Coast, where they engage in drug dealing, prostitution, and sex trafficking.

Hernandez and the leaders of Nine Trey both got something out of the relationship. He wanted the association with them to gain the street cred he lacked and to elevate his career.

He was first introduced to Nine Trey members by his former manager and sought to integrate their "aesthetic," as he put it, into his visual style. Before the "GUMMO" video, he purchased three dozen bandannas for them to wear. The video made him famous, and his internet stardom crossed over into more mainstream stardom—to the extent that he was collaborating with more established hip-hop figures like Nicki Minaj, Kanye West, and 50 Cent.

"I got the street credibility. I would say I got my career," is how he would later describe the benefits of his relationship with the gang. "I knew I had a winning formula for my music videos: repeat the gang image. That's what people liked."

His videos and fame went global. He was said to be a cult figure in eastern Europe. He had upwards of fifteen million Instagram followers.

What Nine Trey gained from Hernandez was their own enhanced level of fame. They were no longer just anonymous street thugs engaged in the seamy business of dealing drugs and trafficking women; with the growing fame of Hernandez, or 6ix9ine, they now had a big hip-hop star as a front man.

Hernandez, though, was in way over his head. He officially became a member of the gang, and as he became more successful, the proceeds from his music helped fund the organization. He participated with them in an armed robbery of a rival crew in midtown Manhattan, just off Times Square, helping to direct it while also filming it from a nearby car. He dealt heroin. He was present when the shot was fired inside Barclays Center. (It was directed at another rapper, who went by the name Casanova, but it did not hit him.)

On November 19, 2018, we indicted six members of the Nine Trey Gangsta Bloods, including Hernandez, who was then twenty-two years old. The others were Jamel "Mel Murda" Jones, Kifano "Shotti" Jordan, Jensel "Ish" Butler, Fuguan "Fu Banga" Lovick, and Faheem "Crippy" Walter.

They were among the gang's leaders. Several were hardened, veteran criminals. Hernandez was charged with the same serious crimes they were, including attempted murder, drug dealing, and racketeering.

He had recently given a radio interview in which he said he feared only two things: "God first, and the FBI."

Confronted with the possibility of spending the rest of his life in prison, Hernandez flipped almost immediately. He agreed to give information and testify against his fellow gang members and became a model cooperating witness—in fact, almost a dream witness.

I ALWAYS TRIED to make it into at least a part of every jury trial taking place. I never entered the courtroom with an entourage. I usually walked in alone and quietly slipped into the back row to see how a case was going.

I think it was appreciated by the judges in our district and by the AUSAs. I was sometimes able to give some advice, but usually my comments consisted of just telling them what a great job they were doing.

Knowing what I did of Hernandez's crimes and his associates—and having watched his videos—I found it almost mesmerizing to sit in the courtroom and watch him. He had pleaded guilty and was testifying against the other men with whom he had been charged.

His hair was no longer rainbow colored, and the colorful caps on his teeth were gone. He was slight, soft-spoken, and introspective. He gave an impression of being artistic. He looked fifteen years old to me.

Under questioning by Michael Longyear, he patiently described the meanings of the slang in his songs.

"What is blicky?" he was asked.

"Blicky is another word for gun," he said.

His fellow Nine Trey members told him he had to "feed the wolves," which he explained meant that he had to financially support them. That included paying for their weaponry. "It was for the homies . . . to take care of them. I was the [one] eating. I was okay. I was making money. My understanding was, make sure they are good financially, you know, stable."

Shotti—Kifano Jordan, his former gangmate and one of the men who pleaded before trial—"was always big on equipping himself with the right artillery, guns, and everything. If we had to be ready for war, you know, we will have that."

Asked about the meteoric rise of his music career, he said the gangster persona he adopted as a pose—and then inhabited in real life—was behind his success. "That's what people like . . . it was just a formula, a blueprint that I found that worked."

I have written earlier about the level of cooperation the Southern District demands in order to recommend leniency for defendants. Hernandez's assistance was extraordinary. In addition to his testimony, he talked to prosecutors more than two dozen times.

Despite his fame, he was relatively low in the chain of command. He wasn't planning the crimes, directing the drug trafficking, or making big decisions. But he knew how the gang worked. He could explain its hierarchy.

His decision to help us came with considerable personal risk.

He is the only cooperator I am aware of who slept over in our offices. We were so concerned that he might be killed traveling to the courthouse from the outside, or leaving from it, that he stayed in a conference room, outfitted with a cot, on the ninth floor. He was guarded at night by agents who stayed with him inside the conference room and by our investigators, who were stationed outside the conference room. He walked across a private bridge between us and the courthouse during his three days of testimony.

Before his sentencing, the AUSAs who had debriefed him wrote to the judge, Paul A. Engelmayer, that Hernandez provided "critical insight into the structure and organization of Nine Trey."

He had done some really bad stuff, nothing to be proud of. My hope was that underneath all the outrageousness of his act, he has a decent character. He apparently has some talent. With age, you want to think that his judgment improves and he gets on the right track. But at a certain point, we could only do what we do. We were prosecutors, not psychologists or social workers.

Hernandez was sentenced to two years in federal prison, far less than he could have received. He was credited for the thirteen months he had already served.

The judge noted he had signed a new $10 million record deal. He was not interested in entering the witness protection program.

On the day of sentencing, Longyear referenced the implications of that decision. "Certain things people take for granted—going into a store, going to the movies, things of that nature—Mr. Hernandez will have to think strategically about," he said. "He'll have to look over his shoulder."

Hernandez received the majority of the media coverage, but the importance and impact of this prosecution went far beyond his cooperation and sentencing. Before we brought this case, Nine Trey was one of the most violent, powerful, and influential gangs associated with the East Coast Bloods, or as they are otherwise known, the United Blood Nation. They had a seat at the "Council," the ruling body of the United Blood Nation.

Jamel "Mel Murda" Jones, our main defendant, had been somewhat untouchable. He had a relatively modest arrest record despite his years of involvement with the gang. He was known on the street as "The Godfather," the one in the background calling the shots. Our office targeted him and the others in an attempt to cripple the gang by decapitating its leadership.

It is fair to say that our efforts were largely successful. Nine Trey, while still active, is not the menace it was. Jones and the others were convicted and received lengthy sentences. And, as a result of our prosecutions, Nine Trey is no longer playing a leading role within the United Blood Nation, which has itself been significantly diminished.

20

A RENOIR COMES HOME

W e brought justice to drug dealers. Dirty doctors. Corrupt
politicians. Many others. The reach of the office extended
across the city of New York, across America, and into pretty much
every corner of the world.

It was incredibly satisfying work. I understood the power of the
office every day I walked through the doors of 1 St. Andrew's. It
could never be used as a cudgel to threaten or bully. But I was never
unaware of our enormous capabilities, and I wanted to use them to
do good in every way possible.

On a late-summer day in 2018, we welcomed Sylvie Sulitzer to
New York. She had traveled from her home in the South of France,
and we referred to her, respectfully, as Madame Sulitzer.

Her family was the victim of a crime—the theft of a painting. It
occurred in Paris in 1941.

ONE OF THE MANY AWFUL ironies of the Nazi era is that at the same
time Hitler and his inner circle were planning and perpetrating the

murder of six million Jews and the brutal conquest of Europe—and the slaughter of many more, including at least half a million Roma people—they were searching out and looting the Continent's art. As they carried out their inhumane acts, they coveted these symbols of a civilized society—all the Picassos, van Goghs, Monets, and anything else they could rip out of homes or thieve from secret storage facilities and bank vaults.

As many people know, the Third Reich systematized and documented nearly everything. An agency was created to coordinate the theft of art and catalog where it was stored. It was called the *Einsatzstab Reichsleiter Rosenberg*, or *ERR*—named for Alfred Rosenberg, a Nazi theorist and Hitler's adviser on art and culture.

The *ERR* was also meant to "study" Jewish life, which in reality was a pretext for looting Jewish property and assembling yet more information to be used in anti-Semitic propaganda. (Alfred Rosenberg was convicted of crimes against humanity at the Nuremberg trials and executed in 1946.)

General Dwight David Eisenhower, the supreme Allied commander, was acutely aware that as his troops fought to liberate Europe, the Continent's artistic legacy was one of the stakes. "Shortly we will be fighting our way across the continent of Europe in battles designed to preserve our civilization," he said two weeks before Allied troops stormed the beaches at Normandy. "Inevitably, in the path of our advance will be found historical monuments and cultural centers which symbolize to the world all that we are fighting to preserve."

As the war proceeded, and especially near its end, Allied troops, sometimes guided by curators and other art experts, made a concerted effort to recover art looted by the Nazis and return it to the private owners or museums where it came from. But in all, the Nazis stole hundreds of thousands of artworks, and much of it could not be found.

Thousands of paintings in the decades that followed seeped into the world's art market—their rightful owners in many cases having died in the war or of natural causes, leaving their heirs with no idea what happened to the artworks.

ALFRED WEINBERGER WAS A PROSPEROUS Jewish resident of Paris and an art collector. Madame Sulitzer is his granddaughter and sole surviving heir.

After the Nazis invaded France and asserted control in Paris, Weinberger and his wife, Marie, fled into the Alps. He became a *maquisard*, a rural resistance fighter. He left his art collection behind, storing it in a vault at a Paris bank.

One of the canvases was a small painting of two women, both of them in colorful dresses and surrounded by flowers. Called *Deux Femmes dans un Jardin* (Two Women in a Garden), it was painted by Pierre-Auguste Renoir. Alfred Weinberger purchased it in 1925 from a dealer who had acquired it directly from Renoir's estate.

On December 4, 1941, the Weinberger collection was seized from the bank vault by the Nazis. On September 10, 1942, they transferred his paintings to a museum controlled by the *ERR*. The exact dates are known because of the Nazi habit of writing everything down.

The Weinbergers survived the war, and Madame Sulitzer lived with them for part of her childhood. Her grandfather spent decades trying to recover his stolen art.

He registered a claim for various works with French restitution authorities in 1947 and, a decade later, another claim with a German agency searching for looted art. Alfred Weinberger would live a long life, dying in 1977 at eighty-nine. Some of his paintings came back to him, but he never saw the little Renoir again.

Maybe *Deux Femmes* had been transported somewhere and was lost in the rubble of the war, or it had been shipped to Germany and kept, quietly, in private hands. Alternatively, it could have been in an attic or basement of someone who did not know its value and someday would turn up as one of those important works purchased for twenty bucks at a flea market.

It could have been in Kansas City. Maybe Scranton.

Or maybe it was out there in the world's vast art market, floating between auction houses, dealers, and private buyers, and no one had yet traced it back to its rightful owners.

THE FBI HAS AGENTS with experience in recovering Nazi-era stolen works. They are part of a team that investigates art-related cases of all kinds, including forgeries and thefts in the high-dollar world of dealers, galleries, and collectors. In our office, the go-to attorney for these cases was Andrew Adams, co-chief of the money laundering and transnational criminal enterprises unit.

The art cases are another example of how SDNY's location comes into play. Other cities—London, Paris, and Tokyo, among others—are important in the art world. But New York is very much the center of it all in a way that I did not fully understand until getting involved in these cases.

First of all, the city is a mecca for artists themselves. After World War II and after the Holocaust, there was a massive exodus from Europe of many of the world's foremost artists. Some, but by no means all, were Jews. They came to New York and fostered a scene that did not previously exist on the same scale.

In addition, New York has a concentration of some of the great museums in the world. It has galleries, dealers, and auction houses that do business globally, and also some other critical infrastructure that people wouldn't normally think of. The biggest insurers of artworks, and the companies involved in the logistics of shipping works, are based in Manhattan.

Just as we are the custodians of the rails of finance because of the big banks in the Southern District, the same is true for the art market. At the highest end, virtually nothing of significance takes place that does not go through our jurisdiction.

Cases in which we attempt to repatriate art to its rightful owners—or more typically, the heirs of those who once owned it—can go one of two ways. Often, people do the right thing and the cases are amicably resolved. Other times, it gets contentious.

AT THE SAME TIME we were working to return *Deux Femmes* to Madame Sulitzer, the office was involved in a similar case. It involved a 1639 painting by the Dutch artist Salomon Koninck, called *A Scholar Sharpening His Quill.*

The piece looked like a Rembrandt and, at times during its nearly four-century history, was mistaken for a Rembrandt. The artist, in his time, was considered a Rembrandt imitator, but his works are in the collections of the Louvre in Paris and the National Gallery of Art in Washington.

The painting was quite valuable. And it had a very dark history.

A woman in Chile had owned it for many years after inheriting it from her father. When she decided to sell, she asked the Chilean branch of Christie's auction house to handle the transaction.

They shipped it for treatment and appraisal to Christie's in New York, where serious art historians look at such works. They quickly suspected it was problematic and called the FBI. We soon joined the investigation.

Through the work of Christie's, the FBI, and our office, the provenance of *A Scholar Sharpening His Quill*—and its World War II and postwar transit history—were established.

At the outbreak of the war and through the first several years of the Nazi conquest, the painting was held by the children of Adolphe and Mathilde Schloss—French Jews whose vast art collection was one of the most important in Europe. Adolphe made his fortune owning department stores. After his wife died in 1938 (he had passed away decades before), their four children inherited hundreds of valuable old-master paintings.

Fearing for their safety, they fled Paris at the start of the war and moved to the countryside in the South of France. They took hundreds of paintings with them and settled in an area that had become a haven for Jews fleeing the Nazi onslaught; local residents hid them or in some cases helped them transit to neutral Switzerland.

Because of the value and significance of the Schloss collection, the *ERR*—the same agency that seized *Deux Femmes* from Madame Sulitzer's grandfather—made a concerted effort to locate it.

In 1943, Nazis found the Schlosses in a château where they were hiding—along with 262 paintings. Each one was photographed and then entered into a log with the name of the painting, name of the artist, its date of composition, and its dimensions.

The paintings were first transported to a museum in Paris the

Nazis had commandeered. It was more a depot than a museum. The best works were sent off to Germany. Most of the Schloss collection, at least 230 paintings, was transported to the *Führerbau*—Hitler's headquarters in Munich.

Nazi functionaries put together two leather-bound, gold-tooled albums with photographs of each of the looted Schloss paintings. The albums were presented to Hitler and are now in the National Archives in Washington.

The photograph of *A Scholar Sharpening His Quill* is plate number 119 in the albums.

EXACTLY HOW THE PAINTING FIRST got onto the open market is not entirely clear. In the days after the fall of the Third Reich, but before Allied troops arrived at Hitler's *Führerbau*, German civilians looted the building. They took many of the paintings, including some of those stolen from the Schlosses.

After the FBI and our office got involved, the Chilean woman who consigned the painting to Christie's in 2017 was told it was not hers to sell—that it was, in fact, stolen property.

She replied that it had come to her from her late father, who purchased it in Chile in 1952. She knew who sold it to him: Walter Andreas Hofer.

That was a name familiar to art historians with knowledge of World War II–era art theft. Hofer was the purchasing agent for Hermann Göring, an architect of the Holocaust and a zealous consumer of stolen Jewish art. "I fully admit I had a passion for collection," Göring said on the witness stand at Nuremberg.

Göring was sentenced to death, but committed suicide the night before his scheduled hanging. Hofer was convicted in absentia by a French military tribunal on charges related to art looted from Jews. He was sentenced to ten years in prison, but never served the time.

Until his death in 1971, he lived openly in Munich, working as a seemingly respectable art dealer. Somehow, he came into possession of *A Scholar Sharpening His Quill.*

And sold it to a man in Chile.

ONE OF THE QUIRKS of the art cases is that when a person holding a looted painting resists giving it up, and we must go to court to get them to forfeit it, the painting is the defendant. It makes it seem as if we were suing a piece of art.

The complaint to get this particular work back into the hands of the Schloss family, filed on October 19, 2018, was *United States of America v. The Painting Known as "The Scholar Sharpening His Quill" by the Artist Salomon Koninck.*

The FBI was holding the painting, having seized it after Christie's raised an alarm. There could be no doubt to whom it belonged.

On April 1, 2019, after the court ruled, it was returned to the Schloss heirs.

The exchange, and a short but emotional ceremony, took place at the French consulate in Manhattan.

THE RENOIR OWNED by Madame Sulitzer's grandfather was quite small, just twelve by fifteen inches. The artist painted it in the last year of his life.

It went on its own twisting journey after the war—across at least three continents—traded between auction houses, dealers, and private buyers without being identified as a work pilfered by the Nazis. It would ultimately come to America and into the possession of a gallery that specialized in staging art auctions on board cruise ships.

The Southern District became involved in 2013, when a private owner brought *Deux Femmes* to Christie's in New York in order to have them sell it. When the auction house listed it for sale, Madame Sulitzer was informed of it by her lawyer. She was born after the war and long after the theft of the painting. She had only ever seen a photo of it.

In combination with the FBI and various art experts, this is what we were able to learn about its travels:

Deux Femmes turned up in a sale at a London gallery in the early 1970s, its first known appearance in the market since the war. In 1975, it was sold by Sotheby's in Johannesburg. Two years later, it was back in London and up for auction again, by Sotheby's. A year after that, Christie's listed it.

In 1999, it was offered for sale in Zurich. In 2005, it surfaced in New York, where it sold for $180,000 at Sotheby's. The buyer was Park West Gallery, based in Southfield, Michigan—the outfit that sells paintings on cruise ships.

"Everything about that transaction felt, smelled and sounded normal," a lawyer for Park West would later tell *The New York Times*. Park West held the painting until 2012, when it sold it to a buyer—not on a cruise ship, but in Michigan—for $390,000.

Both Christie's and Sotheby's (and other reputable auction houses around the world) have gotten far better about trying to identify art brought to them that might have been looted during the war. For obvious reasons, it is not good business for them to deal in those paintings. They don't want to lose the trust of customers or risk lawsuits and the possibility of lost income.

There are various registrars of stolen art, but somehow *Deux Femmes* slipped through the cracks. Lucian Simmons, a vice-chairman at Sotheby's, told the *Times* that the firm's researchers would have checked a list of paintings kept by the French government "because it's the kind of artwork a typical French collector would have had."

One of the best databases of looted art, however, did not go online until 2010—after Sotheby's and Christie's had the piece in their possession.

But after it came back to Christie's yet again, when the buyer from Park West wanted them to sell it, the Southern District was able to definitively identify its rightful owner—Alfred Weinberger's lone surviving heir, Madame Sulitzer.

Park West refunded the $390,000 to its private buyer. And Christie's relinquished *Deux Femmes* to the FBI.

THERE WERE SATISFYING DAYS in the Southern District, but it's hard to say there were many happy ones. Happiness is a relative thing when you're dealing with the likes of Jeffrey Epstein, Cesar Sayoc, and Laurence Doud, or fighting with Main Justice just to be able to carry out your sworn duty.

September 12, 2018, when Madame Sulitzer visited us in New York, was a happy day. I arranged to return the painting to her in a ceremony at the Museum of Jewish Heritage, an incredible space on the southernmost tip of Manhattan. The building's six-tiered, louvered roof is meant to be a reminder of the six million Jews who died in the Holocaust. The view extends out to the New York Harbor and Ellis Island and the Statue of Liberty.

I was passionate about these art repatriation cases. We were returning something beyond property. The paintings were emblems of our common humanity. They were the remains of a lost civilization, the once vibrant Jewish communities of Europe. Our work on these paintings was a demonstration of SDNY's ability to reach across borders and even into past eras to redress wrongdoing.

The room was packed. It was a great honor that among the guests that day was Robert Morgenthau, the longtime district attorney of Manhattan (and former SDNY US Attorney), who pioneered the use of the legal system to take back art looted by Hitler's forces. (Morgenthau, a founder of the Museum of Jewish Heritage and its longtime chairman, passed away the following year, ten days short of his one hundredth birthday.)

Deux Femmes rested on an easel near the lectern where we were to speak, with a white piece of fabric draped over it. Madame Sulitzer, fifty-nine years old at the time, stood between Sweeney and me. She was vigorous looking, with a big, open smile.

I imagine that her grandfather, with his art collection, must have been a wealthy man. But Madame Sulitzer was not a person of great means. A trained chef, she owned a small restaurant.

When I lifted the fabric off the painting, she looked at it for a moment and then extended her arms and enveloped me in a big hug. She patted my back once or twice and held on for a long time.

She had let us know beforehand that she was not proficient in English. Maybe she would be able to communicate a few words. But her English was very good, and she was eloquent and moving.

"When you're just a Frenchwoman living in the South of France and you hear that the FBI is investigating, well, you can imagine, it's a shock," she said. "For us, the FBI is such a huge institution. Working for me, a little thing in France, it is a lot of emotion, because you really realize how people are concerned about what happened, because it is so easy just to say, okay, it is the past. But we'll never forget. We can't forget.

"It's very important that we—me—as a human being, as a Jewish person, to consider that you have people who work for justice.

"It was a huge emotion, to be honest, not specially for the painting—but for all that it means. It brings me back to when I was a young girl, living with my grandfather, my grandmother, my mother, and her brother. It is more the symbol of the life I had with them. The symbol of justice after the huge work everybody did to make this day today possible."

At the lectern, I said that I hoped the return of *Deux Femmes* brings some measure of justice. But I spoke only briefly because there was very little that anyone needed to add.

The tableau of Madame Sulitzer standing beside a painting stolen so long ago—and her beautiful words—were enough.

21

HALKBANK: A BREAKING
POINT WITH BARR

I was happy to keep a respectable distance from Bill Barr, and I think he felt the same way toward me. It suited us both just fine. But I always understood that our relationship, cordial enough on the surface, was almost certain to reach a breaking point. It was just a question of when and over what.

Two days before I became the US attorney, a Southern District jury convicted a Turkish banker named Mehmet Hakan Atilla on charges that he had participated in a scheme to help Iran evade US economic sanctions. This was just one part of an ongoing, sprawling investigation that would be a point of bitter contention with Main Justice for much of my tenure.

On one level, the matter—which would become *United States of America v. Turkiye Halk Bankasi, a/k/a "Halkbank"*—was incredibly complex. It involved billions of dollars stashed in bank accounts, laundered through various means, and moved between national borders. There were gold bars transported by cargo planes. Cash stashed in shoeboxes. And a large cast of characters, some of them quite colorful.

But when broken down to its essentials, the case was not hard to grasp. The bank and its executives, with help from senior Turkish officials, were all deeply involved in helping Iran dodge US efforts meant to stop its development of nuclear weapons. SDNY and the FBI caught them at it. In the process, we revealed a web of corruption at very high levels of the Turkish government.

We wanted to bring criminal charges against the bank itself; Main Justice kept trying to stop us.

As was often the case in my dealings with Barr and others in the DOJ hierarchy, I could not say with 100 percent certainty what was motivating them. But I could look at the forces in play and try to connect the dots, which was not difficult when it came to the interference we faced on Halkbank. The players, and their motivations, seemed to line up neatly.

Donald Trump was close with the Turkish president, Recep Tayyip Erdoğan. Trump had a property in Turkey—Trump Towers Istanbul. Erdoğan attended the official opening in 2012.

The Turkish president adamantly objected to all aspects of our probe and did not want the bank charged.

He made that case directly to Trump.

Barr, always eager to please his boss, appeared to be doing Trump's bidding.

This would ultimately lead to a big blowup in his office between the two of us. I wouldn't call it a shouting match, because it was only Barr raising his voice.

I sat there and listened and calmly but firmly held to my position.

THE HALKBANK CASE involved a large measure of what is sometimes known, colloquially, as international intrigue. Reza Zarrab was one of the primary actors—an architect of the scheme, and later a cooperating witness against the banker Atilla.

Zarrab was a dual Iranian-Turkish citizen and a gold trader—a "swashbuckling gold trader," as one press account described him. He married a big pop star who was like the Beyoncé of Turkey. The couple's exploits—including their lavish shopping excursions in Istanbul—were documented by the Turkish press and caught on camera by paparazzi.

Zarrab could have been expected to have at least an inkling that American law enforcement was interested in him. But on March 21, 2016—about two years before the Atilla trial—he inexplicably showed up with his wife and daughter in the United States. The FBI arrested him as they were en route to Disney World.

Thirty-two years old at the time, Zarrab was charged by my predecessor Preet Bharara with money laundering, bank fraud, and various other counts connected to the scheme. He tried to stay out of jail by offering to post a bond of $50 million. His lawyer said he would stay in a luxury Manhattan rental, wear a GPS device, and pay for guards to watch over him twenty-four hours a day to make sure he did not flee. A judge denied the request.

A brief explanation of sanctions and how they work, or are designed to work, may be helpful here. The US dollar is still the default currency around the world. In many industries, it is the only acceptable form of payment.

Nations facing US financial sanctions can be severely handicapped economically. An overseas bank of any size cannot afford to be sanctioned and left without access to the US financial system.

Iran had long been under a variety of US economic sanctions, which were eased after former president Obama signed the Iran nuclear deal and toughened again after President Trump withdrew from the agreement.

As early as 2012, Zarrab began his scheme to help Iran evade sanctions—primarily by laundering billions of dollars of Iranian oil proceeds deposited in Halkbank through transactions involving the buying and selling of gold. Much of the gold transited through Dubai.

The complex transactions created, in essence, a massive slush fund that allowed Iran to use money that otherwise could have been put to use only for humanitarian purposes. Zarrab's cut of the action was substantial—hundreds of millions of dollars.

His co-conspirators included Zafer Çağlayan, who at the time was Turkey's economic minister, and Süleyman Aslan, the chief executive of Halkbank. He paid bribes to both of them—including regular deliveries of cash that came to Aslan's house stuffed in shoeboxes.

The nation of Turkey benefited from the conspiracy. The gold transfers out of the country were so large—about $20 billion—that they artificially inflated Turkey's export statistics and made its economy look stronger than it really was. (The bank is publicly traded, but its majority shareholder is the government of Turkey.)

A year after Zarrab was arrested on his way to Disney, another big break in the investigation occurred when Atilla, Halkbank's deputy general manager, entered the United States. He was on bank business, a road show to make presentations to various US banks. After the Southern District learned he was here, FBI agents arrested him as he attempted to fly out of JFK Airport.

Zarrab testified over the course of six days at Atilla's trial. He said the scheme reached to the top levels of Turkey's government and that Erdoğan himself had given it his approval.

The case was of intense interest in Turkey and followed closely by its media outlets. After Atilla was convicted, a big question loomed: What would we do about the bank?

ATILLA WAS HALKBANK's deputy general manager for international banking. Evidence at the trial showed widespread complicity among several other Halkbank officials. As a legal matter, it meant the bank had participated in criminal activity and could be charged.

What normally happens in these kinds of sanctions or money laundering cases is that a conviction of top executives sets off negotiations between the bank and the Department of Justice on how to resolve the financial institution's criminal liability.

But such alternatives to criminal charges are not some kind of corporate slap on the wrist. The Southern District requires a frank and detailed admission of the crimes that were committed, and it usually seeks substantial fines as well as other measures to ensure that the bank's criminal conduct does not reoccur.

Halkbank did not seem to feel any of that was necessary. More alarmingly, it seemed to believe it could get away with stonewalling us.

It acted as if it had an ace in the hole, or two aces: a friend in the White House, and a back channel to Main Justice.

Erdoğan and others in the government repeatedly attacked the fairness of Atilla's trial and, by extension, the entire US justice system. "If Atilla is going to be declared a criminal, that would be almost equivalent to declaring the Republic of Turkey a criminal," Erdoğan said in an interview with Bloomberg News.

After Atilla was sentenced to thirty-two months in prison, the Turkish Foreign Ministry said that the sentence was handed down "after an entirely feigned process which is inconsistent with the principle of a fair trial." The process, it claimed, had relied on "forged evidence and false statements."

I'm no expert on Turkish jurisprudence, but I know how our system works. Atilla was convicted. If they had some evidence he was wrongly convicted, we'd look into it, but they did not.

The pushback from Turkey was so extreme that the judge in the case, Richard M. Berman, ordered the transcript of Atilla's sentencing to be posted on the court's website. "The idea is so that everyone will know exactly what was said here, and so that everybody can evaluate the outcome for themselves," he said from the bench.

WHEN ZARRAB FLIPPED a few months before Atilla's trial, it supercharged our wider investigation. The Southern District had his cooperation and a great deal of other evidence.

It also had the assistance of a Turkish police detective who made his way into the United States and gave us a deep trove of material. It was serious evidence—wiretaps, searches, electronic surveillance. He had pictures of the cash in shoeboxes and other things that pointed directly to high-ranking people at the bank and in the Turkish government.

You can't just cart this kind of material into court and put it in front of a jury. It has to be authenticated and described by someone who was involved in accumulating it, who can say, "Yes, we did these wiretaps. We set up a camera in this location," and so on.

And the cop did that. At Atilla's trial, he was able to establish the chain of custody and control of this evidence. He had participated in a previous investigation of the scheme in Turkey. It resulted in Zarrab's being jailed, briefly, before the case was dismissed under suspicious circumstances and he went right back to the same scheme.

When I came in, we started focusing on what's next—which meant looking very closely at the bank.

Its culpability was not speculation. We just had a trial where evidence was introduced, which is very rare in a bank case. We got a guilty verdict. We had the wiretaps and all the other documentary evidence. We had a cooperator who pleaded guilty to the conspiracy. We were two or three steps ahead of the normal process.

We did what we call a "pros memo"—a prosecution memo. It's a summary of all the evidence and a tool to help determine whether it is strong enough to go forward. It left little doubt that we had a powerful case against the bank.

At this point, we began a series of meetings with Halkbank's lawyers, who were from the Atlanta-based firm King & Spalding. The sessions were not fruitful.

Their position, from start to finish, was that we should not charge the bank because no crime was committed. It strained credulity. We would say, "But we have verdicts against individuals. Those cases clearly show that crimes were committed by people working on behalf of the bank. That makes the bank culpable."

But I think their hands were tied by what their client Erdoğan told them they could or could not commit to. They informed us that the most the bank would contemplate was some unspecified civil resolution in which it admitted to unintentional lapses by low-level employees. We made it abundantly clear that was not going to cut it.

Tensions between different parts of the US government are

common in cases that involve foreign financial institutions. The State Department has its interests. So does Treasury. The Department of Justice (you hope) is pushing for the rule of law.

But as prosecutors, you have to be respectful of these competing interests. Halkbank's lawyers suggested our actions could cause the bank to fold, with devastating consequences for the Turkish economy. We did not see that as a realistic possibility. (Nor, ultimately, did it happen.)

WE WENT BACK and forth through the summer of 2018. Halkbank tried to go over our heads by talking directly with DOJ officials in Washington. It was told, initially, it had to deal with us, but those side conversations never ended.

By early November, what we were getting from Halkbank was nothing. It was radio silence. I thought this was kind of extraordinary. It was instructed to deal with the Southern District, but it felt no urgency to reach out.

In mid-November, we took the initiative and contacted King & Spalding to set out the minimally acceptable terms for a DPA, or deferred prosecution agreement. It required the bank to accept responsibility for its readily provable criminal conduct, cooperate with our office, accept a monitorship for some length of time, and agree to an unspecified monetary penalty reflective of its conduct. Those were the minimum parameters.

On November 30, Halkbank's general manager and other officers of the bank arrived at our office in New York with their counsel. It was their opportunity to respond.

We could not use our main office because of security concerns with such a large delegation. We decided to have the meeting at our civil division offices on Chambers Street, about two blocks away, where there was a conference room right by the entrance.

There were at least twenty people in the room. Rob Khuzami and Audrey Strauss sat at either side of me. Ilan Graff and Michael Ferrara, the chiefs of the national security unit, Alexander Wilson and Andrew Adams, the chiefs of the money laundering unit, and the criminal division chief, Lisa Zornberg, were at the table—along with the team of Michael Lockard, Sid Kamaraju, and David Denton, who had, with their FBI partners, built and successfully tried the case against Atilla. I sat in the middle of the table.

I would say the session was more interesting than tense. I was just trying to read the situation. What are they after? What's their real motivation? How far are they really willing to press this?

I believed we had the upper hand. It was a little fascinating to see them act as if they did.

The Halkbank general manager read a statement that was nothing but platitudes: "We would like to resolve this," "We want to go forward in a positive direction," and so forth. He did not address any of the specific issues.

Their attorneys acknowledged that they had been given numerous opportunities to pursue a resolution. The bank, they said, was willing to acknowledge only that low-level employees had made inadvertent mistakes. That was it.

The elaborate scheme to help Iran evade sanctions—the gold bars, the bribes, the cash in shoeboxes, all that was off the table. Halkbank would not admit any intent to violate the sanctions. It would not even pledge to say it was sorry for anything.

What the bank wanted was a DPA constructed so that the day after it was announced, it could claim it was vindicated. Case closed! There was no chance that was going to happen. It was the same as any other negotiation we had with criminal suspects: no one got anything from the Southern District without first admitting to their conduct.

Absent any deal, the hammer we had—or believed we had—was the ability to bring an indictment against the bank. But because the case involved a sovereign nation and touched on national security, we needed to get approval from Main Justice before bringing charges.

I HAD FIRST RAISED the issue of Halkbank with Matthew Whitaker during our dinner at the New York steak house not long after he became acting attorney general in November 2018, following Jeff Sessions's resignation. And as I wrote previously, I got nowhere.

Stand down for the time being, he said.

But after the meeting in New York with Halkbank and its counsel, I really felt I needed the authority to indict. That was the leverage I hoped could lead to a resolution.

I worked with our Halkbank team to draft a memo to Rod Rosenstein, the deputy attorney general, that outlined Halkbank's conduct and its refusal to consent to a reasonable DPA. I told him that I wanted to alert the bank of an imminent charge and give it a final opportunity to alter its long-standing posture, but it needed to know I could pull the trigger.

I told Rosenstein, "Give me the authority. I won't use it until I go back to them and we try to get something done."

Rod was involved in what seemed like an endless string of controversial issues in his two years as the top deputy at DOJ. He was a hero to some people, a villain to others. Or maybe both, at various times, depending on the situation.

I have no idea how history will regard him, but with our office he was good. He let us do our job.

A few days before Christmas, I took the train down to DC to meet with him. We were supposed to meet with Whitaker, but before that could happen, Whitaker called Rosenstein into his office without me.

After meeting with Whitaker, Rosenstein came back to the conference room and told me that Whitaker doesn't want to meet on Halkbank, but he's not long for the position. Why don't we wait him out and see what happens with the next attorney general?

I thought that was a sound idea. I knew Whitaker didn't like us. I'm pretty sure he didn't like me.

In a book he would write after his short tenure, mercifully, came to a close, he wrote, "Arrogant disregard for the executive branch is already the hallmark of the Southern District of New York, or the 'Sovereign district,' as other U.S. attorneys refer to New York City's seat of federal judicial power, which dreamed up new ways to torment President Trump throughout my tenure at the Department of Justice."

MY FIRST MEETING with Bill Barr came about two weeks after he was appointed attorney general in February 2019. It was to brief him on a number of different cases, and the first one I raised was Halkbank.

Rosenstein said to wait for the next guy, so I figured here he is. Halkbank had been a top priority since the day I took the job, and I wanted to move forward.

I had already given Barr a memo about the case, similar to what I sent off to Rosenstein previously—an overview of Halkbank's conduct and a request for authorization to indict.

Barr listened as we spoke in his office that day but did not commit to anything. He said he would take it under advisement. I didn't sense any animosity.

But it soon became clear that Halkbank and its counsel were talking directly to Main Justice. It also looked like whatever pressure Whitaker had felt from Trump to go easy on Turkey was now being exerted on Barr.

Three months later, I met with Barr again. He raised new concerns; he said that a deferred prosecution agreement with Halkbank, particularly one that came with a monitorship, could violate Turkish law. I said, fine, but let's get it to admit to its wrongdoing first. Then we'll try to work out the rest of it.

Over the next couple months, a buzz of activity took place around the Halkbank case, but increasingly it did not involve the Southern District. There was a "small-group meeting" scheduled at the White House to include Barr, the secretary of state, the secretary of the Treasury, and the national security adviser. It got postponed, but Barr called to tell me he had positive and informal discussions with some who were to participate.

On June 10, after the rescheduled meeting took place, I got an email from John Demers, the assistant attorney general for national security. He said that there was a good meeting at the White House that day and that I would be hearing from the AG.

Barr called the next day to say that he had been designated the administration's "point person" on Halkbank, which I found odd. This is a criminal case being run out of New York, right? As attorney general, Barr had a role to play. But why as a White House–designated point person? That was problematic.

Barr said that we could proceed to negotiations with Halkbank knowing that the authority to charge will be there if we need it. In other words, he was dangling the authority but still withholding it.

The next day, Barr had a meeting with officials from the Turkish Ministry of Justice—without me or anyone from the Southern District. I learned about it only after the fact.

At this point, it was abundantly clear that my legs were being taken out from under me. Barr, like Whitaker, was blocking us; he was just slightly more clever about it.

HALKBANK FELT CONFIDENT enough about its support at Main Justice that it actually hardened its position. On June 14, its lead attorney informed us that the bank wanted a "global resolution"— essentially, a toothless DPA for the bank and blanket immunity for any bank or government official we had already charged, knew to be involved in the scheme, or might discover in the future to have participated.

The request was made to Audrey Strauss, who had become my top deputy. She told them there was no chance we would dismiss any charges or agree to end the investigation.

But Barr was pushing for the same thing. On June 17, one of his top advisers wrote to Graff to relay that the "AG thinks we need to give them [Halkbank] global resolution for the facts at issue." He added, "No need to cave immediately," but emphasized that we would have to "play ball."

No need to cave immediately.

So, in other words, we're caving.

The Trump administration killed the Iran nuclear deal and strengthened the sanctions. Ostensibly, stopping the Iran nuclear program was an issue near and dear to the president. The sanctions were the law of the land, which I was sworn to enforce.

Halkbank had schemed to illegally funnel billions of dollars to

Iran at a time when the United States wanted to exert maximum economic pressure. So, on what basis were we going to give the bank a sweetheart deal and grant immunity to all bank and government officials involved in the scheme?

BARR SUMMONED ME on short notice to meet with him on June 21, the morning after the annual Director's Awards ceremony. Just me. None of my team was invited.

When I entered Barr's office, he was there with four of his aides. Maybe I should have known I was about to be dressed down and these underlings were his audience. But I still thought at this point there was the possibility of a rational discussion.

I restated my opposition to a global resolution, which was a fancy way of saying immunity. No prosecutor worth his or her salt gives immunity for nothing, and that's what we would have been doing.

Also, there are long-standing DOJ rules that you can't condition an individual resolution to a corporate resolution, because otherwise companies would say, "Okay. Let us pay you. We'll pay you $500 million, but you'll let our CFO and our CEO off." It's inappropriate.

I was sitting in a chair—I later thought of it as the hot seat—and Barr was to my right. After I stated my position, he leaned in my direction.

This implicates foreign policy, he said. This has been discussed by the leaders of the administration.

He was speaking slowly, with his voice steadily rising.

"Who do you think you are to interfere with this resolution?"

Who do you think you are?

When I heard that, my thought was, who the fuck does he think he is?

I've seen bullies work before. In fact, he had used the same words with me a little more than a year before when he got angry because he believed I had announced the appointment of Audrey Strauss as deputy without first getting his approval. It's completely ineffective, or it is with me. I would describe Barr's posture that morning as thuggish. He wanted to bludgeon me into submission.

And it was interesting that he felt I was interfering with some resolution, as if it were a fait accompli. The Southern District, which along with the FBI had built the case at issue, had not signed on to anything, so I was not interfering with anything.

I didn't confront him directly. I didn't raise my voice, because I felt that that would raise the temperature in a way that wouldn't get me where I wanted to be. I wanted him to think he could still work with me, because I didn't want to get fired and be replaced by someone who was completely compliant.

My goal was to pursue the Halkbank case without fear or favor and, as always, to protect the integrity and independence of our office.

I said to him in a very calm voice, "This is not the way we do things in the Southern District."

He could not go through with this plan without my agreement, because it required court documents. It required filings. It required approvals from Judge Berman. We couldn't just come in there without a good explanation and wipe it all away.

Barr raised the possibility that rather than grant official immunity to individuals, we could give them a side letter, a non-prosecution agreement that would not have to be disclosed to the court.

It was less than a month before we would indict Epstein, despite the secret agreement he had reached in Florida. Now, on a different kind of matter, but one of vital importance, Barr was proposing an Epstein-like deal. He wanted SDNY to do something completely off the record—to draft an agreement with the bank as well as bank and government officials that would be invisible to the public and the court.

I replied that this would be a corruption of the process. It would be a "fraud on the court" to hide part of a resolution with the bank. I don't think he appreciated that comment very much.

Barr asked me for the names of some of the other individuals we were looking at in the Halkbank case. He was my boss, the attorney general, so I gave him some names.

The meeting lasted about thirty minutes. I shook Barr's hand when it was over, but probably not everyone's. A couple of people were far enough away that I just waved and said, "See ya," and got out of there. I think everyone was relieved the meeting was over.

MORE THAN ONE YEAR LATER, on October 29, 2020, *The New York Times* published a story headlined "Turkish Bank Case Showed Erdogan's Influence with Trump."

It was an impressive piece of investigative reporting, but nothing in it shocked me, exactly. What the article reported, in great detail, were the behind-the-curtain influences that kept stopping us from moving forward on Halkbank.

These were the forces I could not see. But I felt them every step of the way.

According to the story, Trump directly discussed Halkbank with Erdoğan on several occasions. His former national security adviser John Bolton was quoted as saying, Turkey and Halkbank now "had a direct channel in the Oval Office—they weren't going to negotiate in good faith. . . . Why should they?"

As Trump was talking directly to Erdoğan, others in his orbit were lobbying officials in his administration on behalf of Halkbank. They included Rudy Giuliani, his personal lawyer, and Michael Flynn, his first national security adviser, who later pleaded guilty to a felony for lying to the FBI (and then was pardoned by Trump).

The story identified a lesser-known figure involved in trying to win leniency for Halkbank, a person with a direct link to Trump's business interests in Turkey: "One of the appeals came from Mehmet Ali Yalcindag, a Trump family friend who had been closely involved in developing the Trump towers in Turkey and who now leads a Turkey-U.S. business trade group. On a trip to Washington that April, he pressed administration officials about the bank."

One of Trump's conversations with Erdoğan about Halkbank occurred in Buenos Aires in late 2018 during a gathering of world leaders known as the Group of 20. Erdoğan handed Trump a memo written by Halkbank's lawyers that made an argument that our prosecution was misguided because the transactions were based on trades of gold and did not involve US banks. This was not true.

Bolton talked to *The New York Times* about this episode and also referenced it in his own book. "Erdogan provided a memo by the law firm representing Halkbank, which Trump did nothing more than flip through before declaring he believed Halkbank was totally innocent of violating U.S. Iran sanctions," Bolton wrote.

(In the *Times* piece, Bolton quoted Trump as saying, "Well, it looks convincing to me.")

Trump and Erdoğan later spoke by phone in late 2018 about Halkbank, according to Bolton, with the American president assuring his counterpart that Halkbank was close to being resolved and he would "get it off his shoulders."

In an interview in Turkey, Erdoğan recounted his call with

Trump and said the American president had promised to "instruct the relevant ministers immediately" on how to shut down the Halkbank matter.

THE DEPARTMENT OF JUSTICE is not supposed to operate according to the president's impulses, personal relationships, and business interests.

Whatever factors were at play with Halkbank, they flowed from Trump through Whitaker and then Barr—through various high-placed DOJ officials—and then they came to me.

As attorney general, Barr should have stood in the way of this kind of interference. He should be the one who says, "No, that's not how justice works in America." Instead, every indication is that he was open to it. He was looking for clever, invisible ways to let Trump undermine our rule of law on behalf of a foreign head of state. Ever the inside player, he was trying to work it out.

I was the one who wouldn't play along. After the blowup with Barr, Halkbank was taken away from the Southern District for several months. I got a call from Brian Rabbitt, who told me that the National Security Division at Main Justice would take over discussions with King & Spalding, Halkbank's attorneys.

Barr probably thought, "Look, this has to get done and it ain't happening with Berman. He'll do everything he can to plant land mines in our way, so I'm cutting him out."

A couple days later, we were asked to provide a safe passage letter for Halkbank's managing director—meaning that we would not have him arrested when he came into the country to accompany his lawyers to a meeting at DOJ headquarters in Washington. I gave my assurance that our agents were not going to be outside Main Justice to arrest the guy, although that would have been quite a gutsy move. (SDNY did not write any safe passage letter; I said that would be more appropriately written by the National Security Division, which was handling the case.)

I was not as readily agreeable when Main Justice requested that I send the AUSAs on the case to DC for NSD's get-together with Halkbank in July 2019. I didn't know what was going to come out of these meetings, and I didn't want to be tarred, or our office to be tarred, with whatever abomination they came up with.

I thought it was much cleaner for us to be able to say, "Hey, listen, it's not our show, you guys go ahead without us." I told Graff, who received the request, to tell them nobody from the Southern District was attending.

A few minutes later I got a call from Rabbitt telling me that it was "a directive" from Barr that one of our AUSAs attend the meeting the next day. He asked if I was disobeying that directive.

Less than three months earlier I had disobeyed Barr's directive to put Donoghue from the Eastern District in charge of our Cohen-related investigations. That was worth getting fired over. Having an AUSA attend a meeting was not. I told Rabbitt that a member of our team would be there.

Two days later I got an urgent call from an ally inside Main Justice warning that if I kept opposing Barr on Halkbank, he would fire me and appoint Ed O'Callaghan as acting US attorney. He said, "You've defended the integrity of the office, the independence of the office, and this is not the hill to die on."

I relented at that point, figuring I would have opportunities down the road to challenge the non-prosecution agreements, should they come to pass, and make it known that we had nothing to do with the resolution. I thought I was better off staying in place and fighting for SDNY than getting fired and replaced by a Barr loyalist.

No agreement was reached at Halkbank's July 2019 meeting with Main Justice, and we didn't hear anything from DOJ on the case for months.

Then something unexpected, and, in light of all that occurred previously, bizarre, occurred on October 15. Barr called me and said the team should put the Halkbank case in the grand jury that day so we could be in a position to indict.

Apparently, Trump had fallen out with Erdoğan. It was over Syria. Erdoğan had sent troops across the border into northeastern Syria, an area controlled by our Kurdish allies, and the resulting skirmishes killed hundreds of civilians and displaced thousands. Trump was getting criticized for withdrawing our troops from the area prior to Erdoğan's invasion.

The outcome, as it related to Halkbank, was just. A six-count indictment against the bank included charges of fraud, money laundering, and sanctions violations. (As I write this, Halkbank is awaiting trial.)

"Halkbank's systemic participation in the illicit movement of billions of dollars' worth of Iranian oil revenue was designed and executed by senior bank officials," I said in announcing the charges that day. "The bank's audacious conduct was supported and protected by high-ranking Turkish government officials, some of whom received millions of dollars in bribes to promote and protect the scheme. Halkbank will now have to answer for its conduct in an American court."

A LAST NOTE ON HALKBANK: On the first day of trading after my firing, shares of Halkbank shot up on Turkey's stock exchange. Apparently, investors thought Main Justice would close the case down in my absence.

As one news story explained, "Investment Consultancy Manager at Gedik Investment Üzeyir Doğan said the resignation of Geoffrey Berman, the chief federal prosecutor in New York who was also leading a U.S. case against the Turkish state lender Halkbank[,] had an impact on the rally in the BIST 100 [index] on Monday. Shares [of] Halkbank closed the day Monday up 5.56%, after surging as much as 9% within the day."

I never imagined I would be a man who moved markets, but there you go.

Part Five

THE FINAL DAYS

22

On Coming Home

One of my earliest memories is from when I was probably six years old and out for dinner with my family. We went every Sunday night into the old Italian neighborhood of Trenton, called Chambersburg, an enclave of narrow streets and small row houses originally built for the families of workers at a nearby Roebling Steel factory. Our go-to was a place called DeLorenzo's, for tomato pies, a local pizza delicacy.

As we were leaving one night, an older woman sitting on a porch called out to my father in a heavy Italian accent, "Thank you, Mr. Berman!" Several other people shouted their thanks, and one woman came out to the sidewalk and handed him a container of food: rigatoni with sausage in a creamy red sauce, still hot.

When I asked him later why they were thanking him, he explained that he had represented them in front of Trenton City Council after a developer asked for a zoning change that would have altered the character of the neighborhood. He helped them defeat it.

It was at this moment that I got a sense not only of what a lawyer did but also that it was a job in which you could do some good. You could help people.

That's a big part of why I became a lawyer. (It's also true I was probably not suited for too many other things. My brother and I got a job one summer in the furniture department of a local Macy's, moving stuff around, and we were not great; we broke . . . a lot of stuff.)

Much of the beginning part of my career was in public service: clerking for Judge Leonard I. Garth, an early and important mentor, in the US Court of Appeals for the Third Circuit in New Jersey; my stint at the Iran-Contra Independent Counsel's Office; and the first tour of duty at the Southern District.

SDNY, in particular, was formative in the way that intense, demanding, exciting jobs always are when you're young. I worked long days, and often weekends, but it was a time when I also made life-long friends.

Over the years, I occasionally had meetings at SDNY about cases involving clients I represented. But a quarter century elapsed from the time when I last had a desk at 1 St. Andrew's and when I walked back in as the new US attorney.

I had to win the trust of more than two hundred people whose primary point of reference for me was that Donald Trump put me in the job. What they had no way of knowing is that I felt as if I had come home. I'm not sure I fully anticipated it myself—the immediate sense that I was rejoining my tribe. But it hit me on day one.

I loved being back among the young AUSAs. I was no longer of that generation, I was their boss, but their passion and energy—their appetite for hard work and burning need to prove themselves—were qualities I recognized and admired.

All the AUSAs had their own offices, though most were quite small. Occasionally, they had to double up. I liked to walk the hall and pop into offices and ask what they were working on. That's just my style. I'm not a top-down manager. I don't think the supervisors loved this at first—they were accustomed to a more formal chain of command—but they got used to it as they came to know me better.

The direction and priorities of the office were set at weekly meetings with the unit chiefs, which were held in the eighth-floor Egan Conference Room. The room was named for Patrick Egan, a gifted and beloved AUSA who tragically passed away during my tenure, leaving a wife and three young children.

I sat at the head of a long conference table, closest to my personal office, as everyone gave updates about ongoing cases and alerted the executive staff to new ones. Here, and elsewhere, I tried to model a collaborative style. I listened before I talked.

For all the high-pressure, high-stakes matters we dealt with every day, I tried to keep in mind that it was a workplace like any workplace. Without some occasional fun and humor, it would just be intolerable.

I entered an intra-office Ping-Pong tournament, losing in a close, first-round match that required a tie breaker. (Very unfair seeding—my opponent was Michael Neff, a former college athlete who played some semipro baseball in Europe.)

Each of the units had occasional happy hours, starting at around 6:30 because everyone worked at least that late, and I tried to attend as many as I could. The more established attorneys in the office drank bourbon or scotch. The younger ones in general crimes served beer and White Claw, a hard seltzer—terrible stuff, but I drank it to be a good sport.

The US attorney delivers a State of the Office address in the fall to review cases and give shout-outs to the AUSAs for all their hard work. After my speech in 2018, I gave them each a gift, which I paid for, of course—flannel pajama pants with "SDNY" emblazoned across the butt. I said it was a cheeky way to recognize that they were all thinking of the office when they went to bed and when they got up. (I offered a pair to Sweeney, but he said he already had SDNY up his ass.)

My last four months in the job coincided with the beginning of the COVID epidemic. We took all possible precautions, and while most worked from home, some, including me, continued to come into the office.

Because it was so critical to keep those working remotely connected to the office, I sent daily email messages updating everyone on the office's achievements and the most recent COVID guidance for government workers. Those emails, however, after several weeks, were starting to feel perfunctory. One day Ed Tyrrell, our office administrator, suggested I send a voice message and taught me how to do it.

I loved the idea: a voice message was far more personal, informal, and conversational, and I could have a little more freedom with it. That day's message began, "Hi, everyone, this is Geoff." As I was nearing the end of the message, I wanted to convey how much I missed everyone and how concerned I was about the personal hardships so many were experiencing. I ended in a way that felt natural and right (if a tad unprofessional). "Love you all," I said.

Away from the office, I knew that many of my friends and acquaintances were not happy that I had accepted a job offer from Trump. Most everyone had the grace not to say much about it. (After my acrimonious exit, several of those who had held their tongues treated me like some kind of hero.)

But I took the position despite the egregious aspects of the Trump presidency. No AUSAs in the office quit in protest of Trump.

They needed a leader, and the office needed a leader who would forcefully repel attacks on its independence.

IN THE NATION'S EARLY HISTORY, US attorneys had expansive authority, while the first attorney general wrote to President Washington to complain he didn't even have a file clerk. The president forwarded his message to Congress, which declined to provide the clerk.

I've thought about this a great deal. All those wisecracks and backhanded compliments about the "Sovereign District" of New York actually miss the mark. SDNY should be the model, not the outlier.

US attorneys are typically drawn from the communities they serve and operate at greater remove from the politics of the moment than their counterparts in DC. Although there are times when AUSAs' coordination with subject matter experts at Main Justice can and does enhance the pursuit of justice, my experience illustrates the ways in which efforts by DOJ leadership to control US attorneys' work contribute to the politicization of the justice system.

The power concentrated at Main Justice and exerted by the attorney general and his inner circle does not derive from anything in the Constitution. It has accumulated over the course of many decades, like a slow-motion power grab, through rules written at the Department of Justice and through what has come to be perceived as precedent.

There is nothing to prevent some of it from being reversed. Lawyers and academics have proposed a variety of reforms that would strengthen the rule of law in the department charged with protecting it. But they focus excessively on Main Justice in Washington. The most effective reform for many of the challenges facing the justice system would be to devolve more power to the nation's ninety-three US attorney's offices.

To give some examples:

An easy improvement is to limit defense attorneys' ability to appeal decisions to indict to Main Justice—even up to the attorney general. Such appeals have become increasingly common over the years. A decision to indict by a US attorney should be the final word. If there needs to be an appeal, the sole grounds should be that the prosecution would violate clearly established DOJ policy, not the sufficiency of the evidence in a particular case.

Another obvious (and easy) reform: an ironclad policy that decisions made in US attorney's offices not to indict should stay there. If this were in place, the embarrassment of the Greg Craig prosecution—declined by our office and then shopped by Main Justice to the DC District—would never have occurred. Barr could not have taken the ludicrous John Kerry case to Maryland.

Reporting to Main Justice should also be scaled back. Under DOJ policy, US attorney's offices are required to file "urgent reports" when an investigation is initiated that might, when made public, attract national news coverage. The report must include, among other things, the possible crimes being investigated and the potential subjects and targets.

These reports are an invitation for political involvement at the highest levels of DOJ. Providing Main Justice a heads-up before a public event in such a case—such as an overt witness approach, the execution of a search warrant, or the return of an indictment—makes more sense.

DOJ should eliminate or revise many of the dozens of permissions that US attorneys must seek from Main Justice: to subpoena attorneys; investigate many public corruption offenses; prosecute some money laundering crimes; and investigate virtually any of the many crimes that implicate national security.

These approvals—adopted as a matter of policy, not statute—are sometimes necessary to ensure the uniform application of the law or avoid prosecutors stirring diplomatic conflicts overseas. Just as often, they provide a mechanism for political appointees to meddle in the work of justice.

And while consultation or approval requirements are often implemented to ensure coordination with DC-based subject matter experts on new and novel areas of enforcement, they are rarely revisited over time as knowledge and experience becomes better distributed across US attorney's offices. They instead remain as vestigial bureaucratic hindrances and opportunities for DOJ's political leaders to interfere with career prosecutors' work.

The permissions are enumerated in the policy document called, since 2018, the Justice Manual. It should get its old name back: the US Attorneys' Manual.

The most powerful way to depoliticize DOJ would be for Congress to affirm that prosecutors can apply obstruction statutes to officials—up to the president—who try to corruptly interfere in charging decisions for political purposes.

This would be the equivalent of posting a sign that says "Back off."

Congress should also amend the way US attorneys can be appointed on an interim or acting basis. Rather than have the flexibility to fire a US attorney and temporarily replace him or her with anyone of the president's choosing, a president should be allowed to make interim appointments only at the very beginning of his or her term, and they should otherwise be eliminated. The only acting appointment possible should be of an already-serving deputy. This would make it impossible for a president or attorney general to foist an outsider on a district to stop a pending investigation or indictment.

Current law already supports a good deal of autonomy for US attorneys, giving each one the authority to prosecute, within their districts, "all offenses against the United States." Under that statute, the only responsibility a US attorney has to Main Justice is to "make such reports as the Attorney General may direct." It is that broad statutory power entrusted to US attorneys that has been whittled away.

Well before my time in office, the leaders of the Southern District were the most aggressive about preserving and reclaiming their proper authority. Instead of asking what makes SDNY unique, the question should be, how can we make other districts more like it?

23

THE LAST DAY

On June 18, 2020, I received a message from Main Justice instructing me to meet with Bill Barr the following day, at noon, in a suite he was occupying at the Pierre hotel on the Upper East Side. That's a swanky place where even standard rooms can cost a thousand bucks a night or more.

Barr had a grand vision of himself. He traveled internationally as attorney general, and perhaps in the back of his mind he wanted to be secretary of state in a second Trump administration.

On a previous trip to New York, he met with Rupert Murdoch before stopping into the Southern District. I don't know what business the AG had with the chairman of Fox News. Maybe they talked about the network's coverage of the president. Whatever it was, Barr's summit with the planet's most powerful media titan strikes me as a scene right out of HBO's *Succession*.

I was not told why Barr wanted to talk with me. But just the day before, I had refused a request from Main Justice to add my signature to a letter to Bill de Blasio, the New York mayor, criticizing him for enforcing social-distancing rules to block religious gatherings while at the same time permitting big Black Lives Matter demonstrations. I figured that maybe I was in trouble for that.

The point DOJ wanted to make about de Blasio might have been defensible, legally, but the letter was a political stunt so Barr could say he was standing up for religious freedom. (Orthodox Jews in Brooklyn had been prevented from having a large funeral for a revered rabbi.)

My position was that the US attorney post is not a letter-writing job. If they want to make a political point, let the people in Main Justice, who have the responsibility for creating priorities and policies, send it out. But I didn't want anything to do with it.

Joanne drove me uptown, and I walked into the Pierre lobby about fifteen minutes early. As I waited, Maria Bartiromo, the Fox News personality, walked through after finishing an interview with Barr upstairs.

A few minutes later, after a member of Barr's security detail escorted me into his suite, I saw that no one was wearing a mask. The attorney general was not wearing one. So I took mine off.

He's my boss, right? I don't want to unnecessarily antagonize him, because every time I do that, there's a cost to it. I wanted to protect my health, but if I kept my mask on, they might have interpreted it as a political statement that I didn't agree with how they were behaving. I know that may sound almost ridiculous now, but it was my thinking at the time.

Three chairs were set up. Barr was sitting next to Will Levi, who had replaced Rabbitt as his chief of staff. Barr motioned for me to sit across from him. On a table next to us were three deli sandwiches wrapped in white paper, which we never touched.

"I want to make a change in the Southern District," Barr said at just about the same moment I lowered myself onto the chair. That's how he started. There were no pleasantries.

He continued by saying that he wanted me to resign my position and take an open position at Main Justice—chief of the Civil Division. He said that would create an opening for Jay Clayton, who was chairman of the Securities and Exchange Commission, to be nominated for SDNY.

In my mind, he did not have to say another word. I knew exactly where this was headed because I had seen a version of it before.

In mid-December 2019, Jessie Liu, the US Attorney for DC, called me. We had met several times since our appointments and had established a cordial professional relationship. "Geoff," she said, "I would like to ask you for some advice."

She proceeded to tell me a shocking story. She had been called by Rabbitt, who told her that Barr needed her out of the position and wanted her to take a job at Treasury. She did not want to resign, but was advised that if she did not, she would be fired.

She was not sure who would replace her if she stepped down. She said she would push for her second-in-command, but there were no guarantees. My advice was for her to firmly but respectfully decline the job at Treasury.

It is not without cost for a president or attorney general to fire a sitting US attorney, particularly in a district like DC with many high-profile, politically charged cases. In 2006, when the then attorney general Alberto Gonzales oversaw the firing of seven US attorneys, it triggered a congressional investigation into whether those firings were politically motivated. Ultimately, Gonzales was forced to resign. Eight other senior DOJ officials involved in the firings also resigned.

In January 2020, Jessie Liu resigned as US Attorney for DC and took a job at Treasury. What followed can only be described as a hostile takeover of that office by Barr.

He immediately installed his trusted senior counsel, Timothy J. Shea, who had never been a prosecutor in DC, passing over Liu's deputy. Soon after Shea was appointed US Attorney for DC, there was a flurry of submissions in cases involving friends of President Trump's: Roger Stone and Michael Flynn.

Barr got what he seemed to want and what clearly would please the president: requests for lighter treatment of Trump's friends. Shea quickly sought to dismiss charges against Flynn, who had already pleaded guilty. And Barr intervened in the Stone case, recommending a lighter sentence than the career prosecutors on the case were seeking.

Those submissions, signed by Shea, caused three career prosecutors in the office to withdraw from the case and one to resign from DOJ.

I KNEW JAY CLAYTON and liked him. He lived in Tribeca, near me, and I had run into him a couple of times when we were each out for drinks with people from our offices. He is an extremely talented lawyer but had never been a prosecutor, which is—or should be—a prerequisite for leading SDNY.

But my meeting with Barr at the Pierre, and his request for my resignation, had little to do with Clayton. I could have stayed on as

US attorney until Clayton was nominated and confirmed. But he wanted me out.

The reason Barr wanted me to resign immediately was so he could replace me with an outsider he trusted—just as he had done a few months earlier in DC. I was determined to dig in and not let it happen.

I asked Barr if he was in any way dissatisfied with the work I've done in the office. I wanted to get his response on the record, because I knew this whole meeting was likely going to be part of a lawsuit I filed. He said that he was not at all dissatisfied.

It was my belief that I could not be fired by Barr because of how I was appointed—by the judges in the Southern District. Only they could remove me. I did not believe I could even be fired by the president.

I was prepared for this moment and had been ever since Barr shut us down on Cohen. I already had lawyers in place: William Treanor, dean of the Georgetown University Law Center and a dear friend since we worked together on the Iran-Contra investigation; and Gregory Joseph, one of the top litigators in New York.

A motion and brief existed in draft form. They just needed to be revised to plug in the latest facts and could be quickly filed.

This was all a piece of my modus operandi with Barr—to be always respectful but ever wary. I stayed prepared because he had given me many reasons to distrust him.

I told him I liked my current job—that I believed it was important to see the current cases through—and that I had absolutely no desire to step down. But he kept pushing.

"This is what I want you to do," he said. "This is what you *should* do," he repeated several times.

ONE ELEMENT OF BARR'S ATTEMPT to move me aside was especially tawdry. He said I should take the post in the Civil Division because I could leverage it to make more money after I left government.

"At some point, you're going to want to go into the private sector," he said. "You're going to be in a law firm, I assume, and you're going to want to have clients. And this will help you attract clients and build a book of business because you'll have experience as chief of the Civil Division in addition to being US attorney."

He asked me if I had civil litigation experience, which of course I did. I had been in private practice for many years and had done plenty of civil cases. But it was a truly amazing question—almost comical, if any of this were funny. He tries to maneuver me into a job leading the Civil Division of the US Department of Justice, and yet he doesn't know if I have any expertise in civil litigation?

And he thinks I'm going to walk out on SDNY—and on people I have absolutely treasured working with—in order to "build a book" of future clients? I told Barr that I had no interest in the position he was offering and that I intended to stay in the job.

He then, predictably, lifted the hammer. "If you do not resign from your position, you will be fired, and that will not be good for your résumé and future job prospects."

I thought to myself, what a gross and colossal bully this guy is to threaten my livelihood. I told Barr that I did not want to get fired, but that I would not resign.

Not getting the reaction he expected, he pivoted. He said he would try to think of other jobs in the administration that I might be interested in and call me later that day (Friday). I responded that I was always happy to talk to him, but I also wanted to set his expectations. "General, there is no job you can offer that would lead me to resign."

He asked for my cell phone number, and I wrote it on a piece of paper and handed it to him. "We'll continue the conversation," he said.

I tried to keep it a little light and made some kind of joke as I was leaving—that if I knew this was going to be the topic, I would have said I had other plans I couldn't break. I turned and walked out, not knowing exactly what was coming next.

JOANNE WAS STILL NEARBY, visiting with a friend, and as soon as I exited the hotel, I texted her and said when you're ready, you can pick me up. In the meantime, I started making calls as I paced the sidewalk on the side of the Pierre. My first calls were to Audrey, Laura Birger, and Ilan Graff. I called Bill Treanor and Greg Joseph to tell them that it was very likely that I would be fired in the next couple days and asked them to dust off our earlier drafts.

If I was fired, I wanted to immediately move to enjoin that on the ground that I was court appointed and could not be fired by Barr or the president. I'd file in the Southern District.

Throughout the afternoon and evening, I reached out to others, including Mary Jo White and Bob Fiske, to get their sense of things. I told them that Barr is trying to push me out and he's going to do it in a way that he wants my immediate resignation.

I talked to my lawyers multiple times, who told me that they might be able to get the papers ready over the weekend in time to file on Monday.

Barr called me later that same afternoon with a new idea: Would I want to be chairman of the Securities and Exchange Commission, the job Clayton would be vacating?

Maybe I was qualified for that, maybe not. I wasn't the most logical choice, and most important, I didn't want the job.

And there was another big stumbling block Barr was conveniently ignoring: It was not his to offer. He didn't have the power to appoint me or anyone else chairman of the SEC. The person holding down that position is nominated by the president and confirmed by the Senate.

Barr seemed as if he were just winging it—trying to think of the highest position I might be interested in and seeing if I would bite. It was utterly absurd. I mean, here's a guy who tries to give off this air of gravitas, who was lauded as an "institutionalist," and he's like, what about this job? What about that one?

I gave him the same answer to the SEC post as I did when he offered the Civil Division: no.

But just to stall him, I asked to have our final conversation on Monday, to give myself a couple days to strategize with my executive staff and huddle with my lawyers. I told him I needed to talk with my leadership team.

"Why do you need to talk to your staff?" he said. "You don't need to do that. This is about you." He said he would call the next day.

OUR THREE KIDS, two of college age and one a graduate, were at our home in Princeton that weekend. After Barr's call, and my own calls to the people I trusted for advice, I said to Joanne, look, nothing's going to happen tonight. Let's go see the kids.

We exited the New Jersey Turnpike and were about three minutes from home when our cell phones started going crazy with people texting us. I was driving, so unable to look at my phone. Joanne read to me the texts she was getting, which were in the vein of "OMG, so sorry to hear." "Is Geoff OK?" "Is he good with this?"

She quickly googled my name and saw the press release that Barr had just put out, stating that I was resigning. We couldn't believe it.

"I am pleased to announce that President Trump intends to nominate Jay Clayton, currently the chairman of the Securities and Exchange Commission, to serve as the next United States Attorney for the Southern District of New York," he wrote.

After extolling Clayton's qualifications, the press release stated that pending Clayton's confirmation, Barr was appointing as acting US Attorney for the Southern District not my deputy, Audrey Strauss, but an outsider, Craig Carpenito, the US Attorney for New Jersey. Carpenito would continue to serve in New Jersey and take over as acting head in SDNY—as if being US Attorney for the Southern District were a part-time job.

This was, of course, exactly Barr's playbook from DC: force the resignation of the sitting US attorney and replace him or her with someone from the outside.

The press release concluded, "Finally, I thank Geoffrey Berman, who is stepping down after two and a half years of service. . . . With tenacity and savvy, Geoff has done an excellent job leading one of our nation's most significant U.S. attorney's offices, achieving many successes on consequential civil and criminal matters. I appreciate his service to the Department of Justice and the nation, and wish him well in the future."

It was a lie, plain and simple. I clearly told him I was not stepping down.

Barr is the attorney general, the nation's top law enforcement officer. In addition to being honest, he should be smart. And this was really stupid on his part—a complete miscalculation about whom he was dealing with. He should have known at this point that I was not going to go quietly.

MONTHS LATER, a Freedom of Information Act request from a journalist unearthed a text of Barr's that seemed to indicate he tried to give me a heads-up, which I never received.

"Tried you just now," he wrote. "Your phone did not go to voicemail. I asked the WH to go forward with intent to nominate Jay. Please call me."

No mention of me "stepping down." No mention of Carpenito. Even in this final message he continued to conceal.

He sent out the press release twenty minutes later.

WHEN I CLERKED for Judge Garth four decades earlier, he gave me advice I never forgot: the only way to deal with a bully is to punch him in the nose. I never sought confrontation with Barr, and in fact tried hard to steer away from it.

But he tried to fire me by press release, so I fired back in a press release. Mine was short, to the point, and, unlike his, honest.

"I learned in a press release from the Attorney General tonight that I was 'stepping down' as United States Attorney," it said. "I have not resigned, and have no intention of resigning my position, to which I was appointed by the Judges of the United States District Court for the Southern District of New York. I will step down when a presidentially appointed nominee is confirmed by the Senate. Until then, our investigations will move forward without delay or interruption. I cherish every day that I work with the men and women of this Office to pursue justice without fear or favor—and intend to ensure that this Office's important cases continue unimpeded."

I chose the words carefully. While I did not reference the obstruction of justice statute, the words I chose—variants of "delay," "impede," "interrupt"—were often used when we charged obstruction. My statement was a shot across the bow of the attorney general, and it received massive media attention.

That night I received more than one hundred emails from AUSAs in the office thanking me for defending the integrity and independence of the office. I responded to each one and did not go to bed until after 3:00 a.m.

Early the next morning, Joanne and I drove into New York. When I arrived at the office, there were about a dozen reporters. I told them that I was "just here to do my job" and walked inside for what I knew might be the last time. I spent the morning on the phone with my executive staff and my attorneys.

Later that day, Barr publicly released a letter purportedly written to me. (I never actually got it; it was really a press release formulated as a letter.) The "letter" was even more nonsensical than his initial press release.

"Dear Mr. Berman," it began. "I was surprised and quite disappointed by the press statement you released last night. As we discussed, I wanted the opportunity to choose a distinguished New York lawyer, Jay Clayton, to nominate as United States Attorney and was hoping for your cooperation to facilitate a smooth transition. When the Department of Justice advised the public of the President's intent to nominate your successor, I had understood that we were in ongoing discussions concerning the possibility of your remaining in the Department or Administration in one of the other senior positions we discussed, including Assistant Attorney General for the Civil Division and Chairman of the Securities and Exchange Commission.

"While we advised the public that you would leave the U.S. attorney's office in two weeks, I still hoped that your departure could be amicable. Unfortunately, with your statement of last night, you have chosen public spectacle over public service. Because you have declared that you have no intention of resigning, I have asked the President to remove you as of today, and he has done so."

Buried within Barr's idiotic diatribe was a major concession: he was not appointing Craig Carpenito on an acting basis, as he said in his initial press release.

If he had tried that, I would have gone to court immediately in the Southern District to stop it, and I liked my chances. I would have been prepared to litigate it up to the Supreme Court. It would have all taken a while. There was a presidential campaign going on. Trump didn't need another ongoing controversy.

So, instead of Carpenito, Barr's letter stated, "by operation of law, the Deputy United States Attorney, Audrey Strauss, will become the Acting United States Attorney and I anticipate she will serve in that capacity until a permanent successor is in place."

That was a surrender on Barr's part. For the Southern District, it was a victory. In fact, every time he or the Trump Justice Department tried to steamroller us, we held the line. They never succeeded.

I would miss the job, but I stepped aside because I had full confidence that the work of the office—its ongoing investigations of anyone, whether they be friends or enemies of the White House— would continue unabated with Audrey in charge.

I sent my last email that afternoon to everyone at SDNY. "It has been the honor of a lifetime to serve as this District's U.S. attorney and a custodian of its proud legacy, but I could leave the District in no better hands than Audrey's," I wrote. Under her leadership, I continued, "this Office's unparalleled AUSAs, investigators, paralegals, and staff will continue to safeguard the Southern District's enduring tradition of integrity and independence."

I TALKED TO Trump just once after he appointed me, when I was three weeks into the job. My phone rang, and "Unknown Caller" flashed on the screen.

I was in downtown Manhattan, standing outside a store, while Joanne picked up a present for a friend's birthday dinner we were about to attend. I answered, and the caller said, "Hello, Geoff." I asked who it was, and he replied, "This is your favorite president."

Our conversation lasted only about four minutes. "You're getting good press coverage," the president said. "The reports are good."

I think he was referring to a story in which Joon Kim, who served as acting US attorney in the Southern District after Preet Bharara's departure, had said some gracious things about me to a newspaper. Trump spoke about his trip to the World Economic Forum in Davos, from which he had just returned.

He said that when I was in Washington, I should feel free to stop by the White House, adding that I could bring my family for pictures in the Oval Office. I thanked him but had no intention of accepting the invitation. It would have been improper.

I went through a lot of what-ifs with my leadership team after taking the job, and one of them was, "What if the president calls?" Everyone agreed that I should take it. He's the president.

If he asks something inappropriate, you tell him that on the phone. Trump did not ask me about any cases or raise anything else that was out of bounds, but I reported the call to the White House liaison in Jeff Sessions's office.

I never speculated about the specific reasons Barr wanted me out. As an attorney, I avoid allegations that I do not yet have the facts to support. But it was no secret to me that much of what we did at the

Southern District—and did not do—displeased Trump. And if it displeased the president, it would have displeased Barr. That's how it worked.

From the Greg Craig case through the non-prosecution of John Kerry and on up to the prosecutions and ongoing investigations of those in his inner circle, it was clear to Trump that he could not control SDNY. We were not loyal to him; our fealty was to the mission.

At the time I was fired in mid-June 2020, the presidential election was less than five months away. I'm sure that Barr was tired of the Southern District's independence. But it is also fair to assume there was a political component in his move to oust me.

Barr did the president's bidding, no matter how he may try to deny that now. He no doubt believed that by removing me he could eliminate a threat to Trump's reelection.

It was remarkable how many times Barr intervened in the Southern District, over the course of less than a year and a half, in ways that would benefit or please Trump. He shut down the Cohen investigation and tried to impose Donoghue in Brooklyn to take it out of our hands. He shopped the Kerry probe to Maryland. On Ukraine-related matters, he set up a system to keep information away from us and keep those matters from spiraling in new directions. In the *Trump v. Vance* case, he turned the DOJ into the president's personal lawyer. He sought inappropriate and unprecedented non-prosecution agreements in Halkbank.

Outside the Southern District, Barr forced out Jessie Liu; submitted filings to help Trump's friends Roger Stone and Michael Flynn; and misrepresented the Mueller report to the public. He appointed John Durham to conduct a criminal probe into alleged FBI misconduct in its Trump-Russia investigation. Barr later admitted that a purpose of the probe was to "get the story out." Finally, he disgraced his position and himself by standing shoulder to shoulder with Trump at the grotesque Lafayette Square stunt.

Barr wrote his own book and in March 2022 set off on a book and rehabilitation tour. When he was asked about me in an interview with NBC, he told yet another easily disproved lie. My firing, he said, had nothing to do with politics or the upcoming election.

"I didn't think there was any threat to the president," Barr said. "I hadn't really thought much of him. I wanted to make the change."

He hadn't thought much of me, and yet he offered me one of the top jobs at Main Justice, chief of the Civil Division? And, when I said I was not interested, offered an even bigger job— chairman of the Securities and Exchange Commission?

Why would you want to place someone whose abilities you did not value in jobs like those?

The truth was that Barr was desperate to get me out of the job I was in, and it was not to put a better US attorney in my place. The reasons were perfectly obvious. They were based in politics.

Barr scurried off the ship after Trump's election defeat, resigning in mid-December. But at the time he fired me, he was still seeking to be the MVP of Trump's cabinet, and that meant taking care of the problem in the Southern District of New York.

IN MY PRESS RELEASE, I referenced the need for the office's investigations to move forward "without delay or interruption" and for important cases to "continue unimpeded." But I did not specify which ones.

Journalists who closely followed the Department of Justice were under no such constraints.

"President Trump on Saturday fired a top federal prosecutor who has overseen sensitive investigations into the president's allies, taking aim at yet another government official who has exposed misdeeds or maladministration by Trump or his appointees and associates," the *Los Angeles Times* wrote.

The New York Times led its story this way: "President Trump on Saturday fired the federal prosecutor whose office put his former personal lawyer in prison and is investigating his current one, heightening criticism that the president was carrying out an extraordinary purge to rid his administration of officials whose independence could be a threat to his re-election campaign."

A *Washington Post* story headlined "Barr's Botched Effort to Remove a Prosecutor Who Probed Trump Allies" highlighted the shambolic way that Barr tried to maneuver me out: "Whatever one thinks of Attorney General William P. Barr, even his detractors have generally agreed on something: He's a shrewd, calculating political operator.

"The events of this weekend would sure seem to undermine that image.

"Barr's halting, problematic effort to remove the U.S. attorney for the Southern District of New York, Geoffrey Berman, appears to have reached its conclusion. Berman signaled Saturday that he will step aside after Barr notified him that President Trump had fired him. But getting to that point required a series of missteps—and the outcome is apparently far from what Barr desired."

The story pointed out that by offering me the position to lead the Civil Division, Barr seemed to be acknowledging that I had performed capably at SDNY. "If Berman wasn't pushed aside because of job performance issues, then what might this all have been about?

It becomes very difficult to completely separate this from the investigations he was pursuing."

Barr's attempt to push me out was so bungled that he and Trump couldn't even get their stories straight. Barr's press release said that he had asked the president to remove me, "and he has done so."

But when Trump was asked about it that Saturday as he boarded a helicopter, he said he had nothing to do with it. "That's [Barr's] department, not my department," he said. "That's really up to him. I'm not involved."

So he fired me, but he wasn't involved? Is that even possible? Did he *sign* something? I don't actually know.

AFTER MY DEPARTURE, I heard from hundreds of people in the legal profession, and their words were immensely gratifying.

Judge Colleen McMahon, the chief judge of the Southern District during my tenure, wrote, "You came to your august position in a most unorthodox way, and you held office in most unorthodox circumstances, at a most unorthodox time in the history of our Republic. Yet you succeeded, I believe, precisely because you followed the most orthodox of prosecutorial rules: look into questionable behavior whenever it comes to your attention; don't worry about who might be involved or what the implications could be; follow the facts; make a dispassionate decision whether or not to prosecute; and let the chips fall where they may."

This message, and so many others that I received, buoyed me. I left the Southern District proud of the work we had done: finally bringing Epstein to justice; the opioid convictions; combating violence; Halkbank; repatriating art stolen by the Nazis; and so much else.

And I took some pride in having resisted the worst of the attempted interference, whether from Main Justice or the White House. But I did not leave with a sense of triumph.

What I felt—and continue to feel—is worry. The Southern District stands for all that justice in America should be. Barr and others tried to take it down.

Without some of the reforms I've suggested—and whatever smart changes others might propose—it could easily be attempted again by some future administration. Or even by elements of this same gang.

THEY QUICKLY TURNED OFF the service on my DOJ-issued cell phone and revoked access to my email. Our chief of security apologized for doing it so abruptly, explaining, "I was told to get you out of the office immediately."

I sent my last message to everyone at SDNY on Graff's email. I was allowed to come into my old office the next weekend to box up my personal belongings and take them home.

I heard from just about everyone who worked for me at the office, as well as from hundreds of Southern District alums spread out all around the country. The young AUSAs in general crimes, the General Crimesters, as they are known, got in touch as a group.

It was a video email sent to my personal account, with twenty-two of them on gallery view. They were all dressed in blue, which was the color of suit I almost always wore to the office.

They made a toast to me, with each of them, on cue, raising their beverage of choice in the air—White Claw.

"A fun fact," one of them said as the call ended. "We love you."

I love them, too. I loved the job. I love SDNY.

My fervent hope is that this book will serve, in some way, to help protect it—and to preserve all that is great about the American system of justice.

EPILOGUE

In March 2020, I was asked if Bill Barr had interfered in our Lev and Igor prosecution. The question came to me during a press conference on an unrelated case, having to do with illicit doping of Thoroughbred horses.

"The Southern District of New York has a long history of integrity and pursuing cases and declining to pursue cases based only on the facts and the law and the equities, without regard to partisan political concerns," I replied. "My primary commitment is and has been to maintain those core values and that's how our office is operating."

This was my only public statement as US attorney about the office's political independence, and it was mild. But I did not answer that Barr never interfered for partisan reasons, because that would not have been true. That might have earned me another demerit. I was fired a few months later.

It did not hurt my future job prospects, as Barr had threatened. I am back in private practice as a partner at Fried Frank, a New York law firm.

Fried Frank is small for a prestigious firm, with about the same number of attorneys in its New York office as the Southern District. Its history dates back to the early twentieth century, when it was a landing spot for talented Jewish lawyers who could not become partners at the city's established white-shoe firms. Ilan Graff has joined me there, and Audrey Strauss, who was previously a partner at the firm, has returned. So it feels a little like getting the old gang back together.

I have also served as a visiting professor at Stanford Law School, my alma mater, teaching a course called "Prosecutorial Discretion and Ethical Duties in the Enforcement of Federal Criminal Law"—an area with which I am not unfamiliar.

It was an immense honor to be in attendance at the Harlem Armory on November 19, 2021, as Damian Williams was sworn in as US Attorney for the Southern District of New York, after having been appointed by President Biden. He followed Audrey, who served ably and admirably in the job for more than a year after I left.

The ceremony combined a sense of deep tradition with a welcome evolution. Almost all the living former heads of the Southern District were there, presenting a united front for all that the Southern District has stood for over its long history.

Damian had served for nearly a decade at SDNY. He is a graduate of Harvard College and Yale Law School and a former Supreme Court clerk. When he was sworn in, he became the first Black US attorney in the 232-year history of the Southern District.

He had something characteristically gracious to say about each of the former US attorneys in the audience. I was overwhelmed by what he said when he turned to me: "When the hour demanded true courage and independence and the demonstration of what it means to be a Southern District of New York prosecutor, he showed all of America what that meant."

The truth is, in the two and a half years that I was US attorney, I never felt I was displaying courage. I kept my head down and did the work and made sure everyone around me did the same.

I benefited from extraordinary support, including from Bill Sweeney and the FBI's New York field office and from the Southern District judiciary, which has its own sterling reputation. (It is widely known as the Mother Court.)

I look back with a sense of optimism but not comfort. We fought back and protected a cornerstone of American justice, but it is important to understand how fragile the system is and how vulnerable it can be when powerful people attempt to abuse it for political gain.

In SDNY, we did not let that happen. But it still could.

ACKNOWLEDGMENTS

When I set out on this book, I knew I would need guidance and representation from the wisest in the industry. Now is a good time for me to express my wholehearted thanks to them.

Luckily for me, Robert Barnett and Michael O'Connor at Williams & Connolly responded to my out-of-the-blue email and agreed to represent me. Given their roster of clients, it was a bit of a shock that they took a flier on me, but thank goodness they did. Their savvy advice throughout this process was critical, and I am very grateful for it.

I am also grateful for, and would like to acknowledge, the expert assistance of Michael Sokolove in the research and writing of this book. Michael and I spent many hours together. He is an accomplished and talented author and writer, and his contributions and insight helped immeasurably.

I also want to thank Scott Moyers, my editor at Penguin Press. Scott believed in this book from the very start and was patient, incisive, and encouraging during the drafting process. Through his thoughtful edits and suggestions, Scott always kept sight of the forest and the trees. Thank you to all the other professionals at Penguin who helped bring this book to publication: Mia Council, Ingrid Sterner, Michael Brown, and Amanda Dewey.

When I got fired in June 2020, I was, for the first time in my life, unemployed. I always told my kids, if you can avoid it, don't leave a job until you have another one lined up. I want to thank my alma mater, Stanford Law School, and my 1L professor, Robert Weisberg, for giving me that next job. I loved serving as the Edwin A. Heafey Jr. Visiting Professor of Law. I was grateful to get to know many of my students despite it being completely remote.

Ryan Nees, my excellent teaching assistant, helped me develop a syllabus and guided me through the arcana of law school administration. Not surprisingly, many of the themes of my course, on prosecutorial ethics and discretion, are highlighted in this book. I want to thank Professor Joseph Grundfest, co-director of Stanford's Rock Center for Corporate Governance, for allowing me to affiliate with that important organization.

I also want to thank my partners at Fried Frank and, in particular, firm chairman David Greenwald, for welcoming me so warmly and making me feel immediately like part of the family. It is a privilege to practice alongside such talented and public-minded people.

US attorneys in SDNY draft their personal assistants from the ranks of the paralegals in the office. I had four great ones during my tenure: Holly Meister, Alexander Beer, Luke Urbanczyk, and Madison Dunbar. Madison also helped with the research on the book.

A special thanks to legendary former US attorneys and mentors Bob Fiske and Mary Jo White. In the play *Hamilton*, there's a song with the lyrics: "It must be nice to have Washington on your side." That's how lucky I felt every day to have Bob and Mary Jo supporting me.

I would need another three hundred pages to thank all the present and former AUSAs who helped me before, during, and after my tenure. Let me start by acknowledging my executive staff, which was superb in every way: Rob Khuzami, Audrey Strauss, Craig Stewart, Ilan Graff, John McEnany, Ed Tyrrell, Neil Corwin, and Eric Blachman.

I had great chiefs of the criminal division, Lisa Zornberg and Laura Birger, and civil division, Jeff Oestericher. And a shout-out to the former AUSAs who graciously assisted me in reviewing parts of the book: Shawn Crowley, Ted Diskant, Sid Kamaraju, Ian McGinley, Max Nicholas, and Hadassa Waxman.

I want to thank Bill Treanor and Greg Joseph for all their work on the motions and briefs that we never had to file. I sincerely hope that no US attorney will ever need those drafts again.

To the judges of the Southern District, who had faith in and appointed me, I will be forever grateful. One of the great joys of the job was a front-row seat to the work of the most impressive bench in the country.

A shout-out and thank-you to some of my pals in general crimes, from back in the day in my first tour at SDNY, who have provided advice, guidance, and friendship over the years. Richard Appel was the funniest guy in the office and left for LA, where he wrote for *The Simpsons* and is now showrunner for *Family Guy*. Allen Applbaum and Lorin Reisner were not as funny and went on to impressive but more traditional legal careers.

I don't want to miss an opportunity to acknowledge our partners in law enforcement for all they do to keep us safe and build the type of prosecutions described in this book: the FBI, DEA, NYPD, HSI, IRS, ATF, the Manhattan and Bronx District Attorneys during my tenure, Cy Vance and Darcel Clark, and all the other state and federal agencies with which I and SDNY were lucky to work.

My mother and late father, Marie and Ronald Berman, instilled in me and my two brothers, Michael and Daniel, integrity, confidence, and a grounding that has served us well. My mother criticized me only once during my tenure: she couldn't understand why I didn't take a sandwich when I left Barr's suite at the Pierre.

Most of all, I want to thank my loving wife, Joanne, who has provided sage advice on the book and guided and inspired me through life, and our three beautiful children, Jeremy, Matthew, and Elisabeth. My family made many sacrifices during my tenure, and I will always, always be grateful.

INDEX

INDEX